PRINTHOUSE BOOKS PRESENTS

Hip-Hop History

The Incorporation of Hip Hop

Circa 1970-1989

Book I of III

ANTWAN 'ANT' BANK$

VIP INK Publishing Group, Inc.

Atlanta, GA.

All photos copyright held by photographer with original images on file.

Editor: A.L. Anderson

Cover designed by SK7

PrintHouse Books, Atlanta, GA.

Published 5-15-2018

www.PrintHouseBooks.com

VIP INK Publishing Group; Incorporated

All rights reserved. No parts of this book may be reproduced in any way, shape, or form or by any means without permission in writing from the publisher, or the author, except by a reviewer.

ISBN: 9781-5323-5436-6

Library of Congress Cataloging-in-Publication Data

#2017914506

Hip Hop History - Book 1

1. Rap 2. Music 3. Break Dancin

4. DJ 5. Antwan Bank$

Printed in the United States of America

Table of Contents

Foreword		*Page 4*
Know Your Business		*Page 6*
Circa 1970		*Page 7*
Circa 1971		*Page 34*
Circa 1972		*Page 65*
Circa 1973	*Hustlers Convention*	*Page 95*
Circa 1974		*Page 124*
Circa 1975		*Page 152*
Circa 1976		*Page 176*
Circa 1977		*Page 196*
Circa 1978		*Page 214*
Circa 1979	*Hip Hop Goes Main Stream*	*Page 233*
Circa 1980	*These are the Breaks*	*Page 251*
Circa 1981	*Reganomics*	*Page 271*
Circa 1982	*And You Don't Stop*	*Page 289*
Circa 1983	*Electro Funk*	*Page 310*
Circa 1984	*Sucker MC's*	*Page 326*
Circa 1985	*Def Jam*	*Page 344*
Circa 1986	*The Show*	*Page 364*
Circa 1987	*Iconic*	*Page 390*
Circa 1988	*Our Thing!*	*Page 424*
Circa 1989	*The Evolution*	*Page 472*
Most Influential		*Page 513*

Foreword

I consider myself lucky to have been born on the 29th of December in the year of 1970. On the other side of my mother's womb awaited afro's, bell bottoms, black power, and soul music. However, amidst the black love lay a dark cloud mixed with despair, poverty, racism, violent protest, and civil unrest. Soul music was the one constant that seemed to make it all go away, if only for a few minutes. I can remember my parents spinning the 12-inch vinyl's and 45's of Stevie Wonder, The Temptations, Teddy Pendergrass, Lou Rawls, James Brown, and so many more in our living room. There was a dark blue couch that looked like it was made of fur with two white leather straps across the arms. Crystal vases held fresh Crown, and Black Musk incents filled the air. Often my aunts, uncles, and their friends would gather at our place on the weekends to dance, play spades, drink, and party. That feeling of family, joy, and togetherness still warms my heart every time I hear one of the soul classics from back then.

It wasn't until I started elementary school that I realized how messed up the world really was. I wasn't in my little box anymore, protected by my parents, the music and family love. Racism was evident and still strong in the public schools back during the early 70's. I fought in school every day because of racial remarks toward me from white kids and sometimes even my own kind. As African Americans we were so confused in school that we even hated ourselves. All we had really was the lyrics of Marvin Gaye, Diana Ross, Stevie Wonder, Michael, and the like. Soul music thrived on making people feel good; it took our minds away from the negativity of the world. But it always knew when it had to focus on the bad just as well. As the decade moved along, the bad economy, racism, dirty politics, and poverty had begun to take their tolls, and the soul music couldn't mask our feelings anymore.

A new generation had found a way to speak out through music, but this time it would change the world and destroy anything or anyone in its path. Its content would be raw, bold, and transcending. One might compare the wrath of Hip Hop to a tsunami because nothing was going to stop this freight train. Fueled by desperation, police corruption, poverty, self-expression, crime, violence, and soul, this new genre of music would stand on the shoulders of giants while trailblazing its way to unthinkable heights. This is the history of Hip Hop, circa 1970-2010 in a three-book series; it is through this timeline that you will see how it became a multi-billion-dollar corporation and innovative industry. It is said, to actually see something for what it is, you need to step away from it and look at it from a distance to see all the moving parts.

I dedicate this book to the Original DJ's, the B-Boys, the Taggers, and the Original MC's who created Hip Hop to inform, inspire, empower, and entertain a nation when there was nothing or no one else to do the same. Your dreams, actions, and fortitude gave us an outlet from despair, poverty, welfare, hate, racism, and inferiority. The one thing that we cannot change is history! Hip Hop Nation, this is a chronological journey of the incorporation of our thing, and you may be surprised at what you'll find. This is *our* voice.

"Hip-Hop at its core is Authentic and Unapologetic,

without that you ain't Hip-Hop!"

-ANTWAN BANK$

Contact:

Banks4020@gmail.com

IG: Antwan_Ant_Banks

www.AntwanBanks.com

Know Your Business

In 1970, only 18 percent of Billboard's year-end *Hot 100* songs came from the urban music genre. This number will be important as we journey through the next 40 years of Urban Music charting Billboard's *Top 100*. Corporations then and now were responsible for getting this music to the masses via radio stations, clubs, concerts, street teams, and so on. Some even participated in what came to be known as *"payola" — When the DJ's were paid by execs to spin their artists' music, these executives worked for the corporations that we call Record Labels.* The structure of a label as a corporation is very unique. By incorporating, the labels become a separate entity that can sell shares of the companies to other corporations and individuals alike, while still maintaining control over the business.

The label's main purpose is to sign artists, promote them, and hold the majority ownership for the artists' music, in turn creating a catalogue. Ownership of these catalogues is what gives a record label its power. In the world of business, corporations sell shares of their companies all the time, be it to stockholders or other corporations. This practice will cause the ownership of a music catalogue to change hands several times from its inception throughout the life of the catalogue. Pay close attention to how some labels will merge, create subsidiaries, sell shares, or even go bankrupt, while the one constant remains — earning money for its catalogue in which the artist has no say and for which, more often than not, the artist receives no pay. In the end, it's the Record labels that always come out on top; just think about it for a second. Think of an artist who was once on top and is now sitting somewhere broke. *Why is that? Doesn't that artist own the rights to their music that once topped the charts and is still being played on some old school or classic radio station or for music still being sampled or remade? Aren't they getting royalties for those spins? Are they?*

Hip Hop hit the scene so raw and uncut that by the time the culture realized it had grown into a business it was too late to renegotiate some contracts. The major record labels had aligned themselves to reap most of the benefits, and boy did they get paid! Still are! So, clear your minds and pay close attention to the incorporation of Hip Hop and how the climate of the world influenced its pioneers as well as the music's content giving way to a consciousness that became a culture. If more of our pioneers were informed about incorporating themselves as an *Entity* instead of being signed as an *Artist*, then their stories would be very different today, maybe there would be more Gordy's, Russell's, Rick's, Sylvia's, Andre's, Diddy's, Dre's, Knight's, Eazy E's, Dupree's, Carter's, Dash's, Master P's, Slim's and Baby's running Hip Hop instead of the present-day hitmen. Even the majority of the afore-mentioned eventually fell victim to the bait and switch.

Circa 1970

On January 1st, Hip Hop Pioneer, **Grand Master Flash** turns 12 years old. *(Born 1-1-1958)*

January 8, 1970, *Marvin Gaye* releases his album *That's the Way Love Is* on Motown's subsidiary label *Tamla*. The album did well in the UK, but none of the songs charted in the U.S. The album consisted of remakes from other greats such as The Temptations, The Isley Brothers, The Beatles, and The Marvelettes. Although some of the songs were good this would not be one of Marvin's best bodies of work according to the music charts.

On January 11th, Hip Hop Pioneer, **Big Bank Hank** turns 14 years old. *(Born 1-11-1956)*

On January 15, 1970, *Atlantic Records* releases the 17th album, *This Girl's in Love with You*, for Aretha Franklin, aka *The Queen of Soul*. The album reached number 20 on Billboard's Top 100. To name just a few of the great writers who contributed to the chart-topping album, one could list legends such as, Paul McCartney, John Lennon, and Burt Bacharach. Aretha's music, like so many times before, came at a time when the nation needed it most.

On January 21st, Hip Hop Pioneer, **Jam Master Jay** turns 5 years old. *(Born 1-21-1965)*

1970 - Urban American
Grammy Award Recipients - 12th Annual

Awards, 1970: Bill Cosby wins Grammy Award for Best Comedy Album. *Sports (Bill Cosby Album)*

Awards, 1970: Quincy Jones wins Grammy Award for Best Instrumental Jazz performance. *(Walking in Space)*

Awards, 1970: The 5th Dimension, win a Grammy Award for Best Contemporary Vocal Performance by a Group. *(Aquarius/Let the Sunshine In)*

Awards, 1970: Aretha Franklin wins a Grammy Award for Best R&B Vocal Performance by a Female. *(Share Your Love with Me)*

Awards, 1970: Joe Simon wins a Grammy Award for Best R&B Vocal Performance by a Male. *(The Chokin Kind)*

Awards, 1970: The Isley Brothers win a Grammy Award for Best R&B Performance by a Duo or Group. *(It's Your Thing)*

Awards, 1970: King Curtis wins a Grammy Award for Best R&B Instrumental Performance. *(Games People Play)*

Awards, 1970: Richard Spencer (songwriter) wins a Grammy Award for Best R&B Song. *(Color Him Father)*

⇒ **Dance: The 70's** ushered in a new energetic dance style led by the Godfather of Soul, **James Brown**. It would be his hit *Get on the Good Foot,* and its associated dance called the *Good Foot* that would inspire New York teens of the 70's to bring his energetic dance style to the clubs, streets, and to later develop it into a competitive dance style that would become known as **Break Dancing**. This style would replace fights amongst street gangs in the South Bronx, New York; B-Boys (*dancers*) from each gang would battle each other for turf, bragging rights, and the like. As Breakin' became more popular, so did the emergence of dance crews and each came with its own style.

On February 24, 1970, *Funkadelic* releases its self-titled album, *Funkadelic* on **Westbound Records**. The funk band was known for heavy bass and big rhythm sections along with outlandish extraterrestrial characters. Funkadelic proved to be what the world craved in the time of war, post-civil rights, drugs, racism, and freedom of expression. Although the album didn't hit the charts, Funkadelic sold out shows and acquired millions of fans in the process. The album consisted of remakes from greats like: Diana Ross and The Supremes, and The Parliaments, an earlier band that features George Clinton.

⇒ **Drugs: In 1970**, heroin, cocaine, weed and LSD were the drugs of choice. At this time, the Government had yet to form the now DEA. It was believed that cocaine was not addictive, but studies have since proven that to be false.

On March 2nd, Hip Hop Pioneer, DJ Scott La Rock turns 8 years old. *(Born 3-2-1965)*

On March 6, 1970, *The Temptations* release *Psychedelic Shack* on *Motown Records.* The title track would go on to hit the Billboard Top 100 for the year. The album was out of the norm for The Mighty Temps and the Motown sound, written by Norman Whitfield and Barrett Strong, showed the Temps in a different light. Its energy gave life to the poverty-stricken days and miserable nights, the way only great music could.

On March 10th, Hip Hop Pioneer, Rick Rubin turns 7 years old. *(Born 3-10-1963)*

⇒ **News: March 1970, The United States Post Office** goes on strike for two weeks. President Nixon called on the Armed Forces and National Guard to deliver the mail. Before the strike, the postal workers had no collective bargaining rights and worked in poor job environments. The strike led to a more corporate working environment and gave rights to collective bargaining. *(But not the right to strike)*

On March 25, 1970, *Jimi Hendrix* releases *Band of Gypsys* on **Capitol Records.** The music is a live recording from the Fillmore East in New York earlier that year on January 1st. Hendrix was known for mixing funk with rhythm and blues as well as hard rock. This style of music would later come to be known as Funk Rock.

⇒ **News: In 1970, the U.S media** found it fitting to give reports on the number of deaths that occurred each week during the Vietnam War. This being broadcast only added to the stress Americans felt at home during protest to end the war and bring our soldiers home.

On April 6th, Hip Hop Pioneer, Sylvia Robinson turns 34 years old. *(Born 4-6-1936)*

On April 13, 1970, *Diana Ross and The Supremes* release *Farewell* on **Motown Records.** The album is a compilation of live recordings from the Las Vegas New Frontier Hotel and Casino. It would be the last time that Diana Ross performed with The Supremes. Diana would go on to chart Billboards Top 100 as a solo artist this year.

On April 16th, **Hip Hop Pioneer, DJ Kool Herc** turns 15 years old. (Born 4-16-1955)

On April 19th, **Hip Hop Pioneer, Afrika Bambaataa** turns 13 years old. (Born 4-19-1957)

On April 26, 1970, *Motown Records* releases *Right On* by **The Supremes**. This will be the first record released by the group without Diana Ross. The group consisted of Jean Terrell as lead singer along with Mary Wilson and Cindy Birdsong. The album pinned two Top 40 singles and reached number 25 on Billboard's Top 200 charts. Great writers and producers such as Smokey Robinson, Norman Whitfield, Frank Wilson, and Ivy Jo Hunter all contributed to its success proving that great team work always prevails.

On April 28, 1970, *Smokey Robinson and The Miracles* release *What Love has…. Joined Together* on *Motown Record's Tamla* label. The album charted 97 on Billboard's Top 200 album chart and number ten on Billboard's R&B chart. A long list of composers and writers contributed to the project such as Marvin Gaye, The Beatles, John Lennon and Paul McCarthy, Berry Gordy, and Stevie Wonder to name a few.

⇒ **News: On April 30, 1970: The United States Armed Forces** invades Cambodia. President Nixon announces the invasion on national television to the American people and states that it's our duty.

On April 30th, Hip Hop Pioneer, Wonder Mike turns 12 years old. *(Born 4-30-1958)*

In April of 1970, *Ike and Tina Turner* release *Come Together* on **Liberty Records.** It would be their first record released with Liberty and it went on to chart 25 on Billboard. The duo hadn't charted in the past eight years before this album. The project featured covers from Sly and the Family Stone as well as The Beatles.

◊ *Fashion 1970*: Shades with the huge lenses were in and complimented the fashion trends of the era.

In April of 1970, *Miles Davis* releases his double album *B****es Brew* on **Columbia Records**. The album was his first to go Gold and also went on to win a Grammy. Miles is considered to be a genius of jazz musicians.

In April of 1970, *Ray Charles* releases *My Kind of Jazz* on the **Tangerine Label**. The album was produced by his good friend, Quincy Jones. It didn't chart any hits like his other albums but remains a timeless classic.

In April of 1970, *The 5th Dimension* releases *Portrait* on **Bell Records**. This would be their first album on the Bell label. The album garners a hit single called *One Less Bell to Answer* which reached number two on the Billboard charts.

In April of 1970, *James Brown* releases *Soul on Top* on the **King Record label**. The album consists of classics like *Poppas Got a Brand New Bag* and *It's a Man's, Man's, Man's World*. The God Father of Soul as he's known compiled this album with Louie Bellson and his live 18-piece jazz orchestra. Maceo Parker and Oliver Nelson would also join James in completing this awesome project.

- ⇒ **News: Spring 1970, Black Panther Party**, The Oakland branch of BPP engage in another ambush of police officers.
- ⇒ **Politics: May 1970, Black Panther Leader, Huey Newton's** conviction is overturned but officials refuse to release him.
- ⇒ **Protest News: May 4, 1970, Kent State Massacre**: Students protesting the Cambodian Campaign announced by President Nixon, were shot by Ohio State National Guardsman while protesting on campus. Four students were killed and nine others injured. All of the students were unarmed and some weren't even on campus when fired upon.

On May 8, 1970, *The Jackson 5* release their 2nd album titled *ABC* on the *Motown* label. The album would garner a few number 1 hits and also chart as high as number four on the Billboard music charts. The J5 brought a hard work ethic and superb showmanship to the music industry that would become the blueprint for many future artists.

⇒ **News: On May 9, 1970, 100,000 Americans** march on D.C to protest the *Vietnam War*. This would be the biggest protest to date. With the recent deaths at the Kent State protest still lingering, tensions were high, but this would turn out to be a peaceful rally. President Nixon even found time to come out and mingle with the protestors.

⇒ **News, On May 15, 1970, The Jackson State Masacre occurred** on campus in Jackson, Mississippi where a group of students protesting the invasion of Cambodia during the Vietnam War were confronted by city and state police officers about their protest. Shortly after midnight the officers opened fire on the students killing 2 and injuring 12.

On May 31st, Hip Hop Pioneer, DMC turns 6 years old. *(Born 5-31-1964)*

◊ *Fashion 1970*: Turtle necks! Fashionable and in all sorts of colors and patterns.

On June 19th, 1970, *Diana Ross* releases her self-titled debut album on *Motown Records*. Song writers and producers Nickolas Ashford and Valerie Simpson joined Diana and her team to make a successful solo album that would go on to the top of the Billboard music charts. Her remake of Marvin Gaye and Tammi Terrell's, *Aint no Mountain High Enough* peaked at number 1 on the Hot 100. This would be the beginning of a great solo career for Diana.

◊ *Fashion 1970*: Black pride was strong in the African American community and the afro was one way of self-expression.

In June of 1970, *Jerry Butler* releases album, *You and Me*. He would go on to chart several songs that year. Butler, known for his spectacular writing and soul singing, was also the original lead singer of *The Impressions* which featured Curtis Mayfield as well.

⇒ **Radio News: On the 4th of July 1970**, the internationally syndicated radio show **American Top 40** debuts across radio land. It featured a countdown of music's 40 hottest singles. Casey Kasem hosted the show in addition to being one of its founders, who also included, Don Bustany, Tom Rounds, and Ron Jacobs. The program started off as a production of Watermark, Inc.

On July 7, 1970, *George Clinton and Parliament* release *Osmium* on *Invictus Records*. Funkadelic also played as musicians on this psychedelic album which was produced by Clinton and Ruth Copeland.

◊ *Fashion 1970*: The Platform shoe would make its mark on 70's new funky culture.

In July of 1970, *The Delfonics* release their self-titled album on *Philly Groove Records*. The album charted Billboard's Top 100 and also garnered 5 chart topping singles. Produced by Thom Bell, The Delfonics album remains a classic. One of the most popular tracks, *Didn't I (Blow Your Mind This Time)* is an all-time favorite.

In July of 1970, *Funkadelic* releases their second album of the year titled *Free Your Mind… and Your Ass Will Follow* on **Westbound Records**. George Clinton states that the inspiration behind this project was to see if they could cut an album while they were all tripping on acid. The album charted 11 on Billboard's Black Albums chart and 92 on its pop music charts.

⇒ **News: August 1970, Black Panther Party leader, Huey Newton** is released from incarceration. **On August 7, Incarcerated Panther and George Jackson's brother, Jonathan**, hijacks a Miran County Courtroom, frees prisoners, and takes *Judge Harold Haley* as prisoner demanding the release of the Soledad brothers (one being his brother George). Haley and two others were killed as they attempted to drive away from the courthouse.

On August 7, 1970, *Stevie Wonder* releases *Signed, Sealed & Delivered* on **Tamla Records**. Wonder, known as a musical genius, charted 25 on Billboard's Pop Album charts and number seven on the R&B charts further cementing his legacy.

On August 9th, Hip Hop Pioneer, Kurtis Blow turns 11 years old. *(Born 8-9-1959)*

On August 12, 1970, *The Great Roberta Flack* releases her 2nd album titled *Chapter Two* on *Atlantic Records*. On this project Flack worked with greats such as Donny Hathaway, Bob Dylan, Curtis Mayfield, and Buffy Sainte-Marie to name a few.

On August 20th, Hip Hop Pioneer, KRS-One turns 5 years old. *(Born 8-20-1965)*

On August 24, 1970, *Aretha Franklin* releases her 2nd album titled *Spirit in the Dark* earning her second album of the year on *Atlantic Records*. This would be the Queen of Soul's 18th album to date. The album had singles to peak at 11 on the Hot 100 and number 1 on the R&B charts. The title track would go on to chart number three on the R&B charts and 23 on Hot 100.

⇒ **Film News: Cotton Comes to Harlem** is released. Directed by *Ossie Davis*

In August of 1970, *Little Richard* releases *The Rill Thing* on **Reprise Records**. Two of the album singles would go on to chart the billboards breaking the Top 50.

⇒ **Film News**: **Watermelon Man** is released. Directed by *Melvin Van Peebles*

In August of 1970, *James Brown* releases *Sex Machine* on **King Records**. The album is a live recording featuring the title track as well as Bootsy and Catfish Collins playing with the JB's. This album would add to the already prolific catalogue of the Godfather of Soul.

⇒ **Film News: King: A Filmed Record from Montgomery to Memphis**, a documentary of events with Dr. Martin Luther King starting with the Montgomery Bus Boycott of 1955. Directed by *Joseph L. Mankiewicz* and *Sidney Lumet*.

On September 8, 1970, *The Jackson 5* release their 2nd album of the year titled *Third Album* on *Motown Records*. This was J5's bestselling album to date selling over six million copies worldwide. It was their 4th consecutive number one single with the album charting at four on the Billboard Album charts and number one on the R&B charts. With only their 3rd album to date, the world was truly in love with the Jackson 5!

On September 18, 1970, *famed guitarist Jimi Hendrix*, 27 years old, is found dead of a drug overdose in his London Hotel room. He had just performed on stage with Eric Burdon & War the night before.

On September 26th, Hip Hop Pioneer, Andre Harrell turns 10 years old. *(Born 9-26-60)*

On September 30th, Hip Hop Pioneer, Dj Marley Marl turns 8 years old. *(Born 9-30-1962)*

On September 30, 1970, *The Miracles* release their 2nd album of the year *A Pocket full of Miracles* on **Tamla Records**. The album would go on to chart 56 on Billboard's Pop Album charts and peak 10 on its R&B charts.

⇒ **TV News—Talk Show: The Ed Sullivan Show** is nearing its last year. Many musicians performed live on the show in front of millions as they watched from home. The *CBS* production launched in 1948 and ran every Sunday night.

In September of 1970, *Curtis Mayfield* releases *Curtis* on his own label, **Curtom Records**. Curtis charted at number one on Billboard's Black Albums for a total of five weeks and 19 on Billboard's Pop Music charts. Mayfield would go on to receive rave reviews from all the music critics.

⇒ **TV's Musical Entertainment News: American Band Stand** featured Top 40 music that was introduced by host *Dick Clark* as teenagers danced on set. This was also another platform for musicians to perform and be seen by millions watching from home.

In September of 1970, *Motown Records* releases a collaborative album combining The Supremes (post Diana Ross) and The Four Tops. The album titled *The Magnificent 7* featured covered songs from Ike & Tina Turner and former Supremes lead singer Diana Ross. The cover of Ike & Tina's *River Deep-Mountain High* would go on to chart 14 on Billboard's Singles chart.

On October 4th, Hip Hop Pioneer, Russell Simmons turns 13 years old. *(Born 10-4-1957)*

On October 15, 1970, *Motown Records* releases *The Jackson 5 Christmas Album*. This would be the third album released this year by the famed group. Tracks *Santa Claus is Coming to Town* and *I Saw Mommy Kissing Santa Claus* are still Holiday favorites. The album charted at number one for four consecutive weeks on Billboard's Holiday Album charts.

◊ *Fashion 1970:* Bell-bottoms and butterfly collars were the way to go for both women and men alike.

On October 22, 1970, *Miles Davis* releases his live performance album *Miles Davis at Fillmore* on **Columbia Records**. This would be his 2nd album released this year. The double LP featured musicians, Keith Jarrett, Chick Corea, and Fender Rhodes.

⇒ **News: In 1970,** various members of the **Black Panther Party** were being indicted in New Haven, Connecticut for the 1969 murder of 19-year-old Alex Rackley. Rackley was a fellow Panther who was thought to be a snitch.

In October of 1970, *B.B King* releases his 18th album, *Indianola Mississippi Seeds* on **MCA Records**. The album is one of King's highly regarded bodies of work. Produced by Bill Szymczyk the album peaked at 26 on the pop charts, seven on Billboard's Jazz Album charts and number eight on the Black Album charts.

⇒ **1970** 's **News** came to report the year as the culmination for several preceding events. The *Chicago 7* were found not guilty of a conspiracy but charged for intent to incite a riot, which took place in Chicago during the 1968 Democratic National Convention. Among the protestors was *Bobby Seale* of the Black Panther Party, who was actually considered to be the 8th man before the judge, severed his trial during the proceedings for contempt of court. *The Nigerian Civil War* ended earlier this year; it originally started on the 6th of July in 1967. The campaign was over the *Republic of Biafra,* a new state in Nigeria that was fighting for its independence. The State was in existence from July 6, 1967 to January 25, 1970.

In October of 1970, *The Supremes* release *New Ways but Love Stays* on the *Motown* label. The environment in the mid 70's caused the super group to change the album's title from its original name, *Stoned Love* because the title was said to reference drugs. The group however, kept the former title as a single, and it went on to peak at number seven on the Hot 100 and number one on the Billboard R&B Singles chart. During this era, the nation was experiencing the Black Power movement and Motown provided part of the soundtrack for this critical part of history with this 3rd album of the year from the newly led Supremes.

On November 14th, Hip Hop Pioneer, RUN of RUN DMC turns 6 years old. *(Born 11-4-1964)*

On November 27th, Hip Hop Pioneer, Dj Red Alert turns 14 years old. *(Born 11-27-1956)*

On November 21, 1970, *Epic Records* releases *Sly and The Family Stone Greatest Hits Album*. The album is a compilation of chart topping singles from the albums *Dance to the Music, Life* and *Stand*. It also includes 1969 hit singles *Hot Fun in the Summertime, Thank you (Falettinme Be Mice Elf Agin)* and *Everybody Is a Star*. The album went on to sell 5 million copies in the U.S.A making it certified quintuple platinum.

In November of 1970, *Minnie Riperton* releases her debut album *Come to My Garden* on *GRT Records*. Produced by Charles Stepney, the album didn't claim much commercial success but is considered to be a master piece among musicians. It would go on to peak at 160 on the Billboard's Top 200. Riperton would go on to be known for her high octave voice and the album still brings chills to anyone who hears it today.

In November of 1970, *Stax Records* *(Enterprise)* releases **Isaac Hayes'** third album, *The Isaac Hayes Movement*. The album consists of four extended cover tracks which include: The Beatles *Something*, Jerry Butler's *I Stand Accused*, David Bacharach *I Just Don't Know What to Do with Myself,* and Chalmers and Rhodes *One Big Unhappy Family*. The album spent seven straight weeks as number one on Billboard's Soul Album charts, peaked at number one on the Jazz Album charts and number eight on Billboard's Top 200.

In November of 1970, *Stax Records* releases *Isaac Hayes'* 4th album. *"..To be Continued"*. The album, like the ones before it, would garner chart topping success. It peaked at number one on Billboard's Black Albums and Jazz Albums charts, as well as 11 on Billboard's Top 200.

On December 19th, Hip Hop Pioneer, Angie Stone turns 9 years old. *(Born 12-19-1961)*

In December of 1970, *Brunswick Records* releases *The Chi-Lites'* 2nd album, *I Like Your Lovin' (Do You Like Mine?)*. Although the success was moderate, the album produced by Eugene Record, did not break Billboard's Top 100. The group would go on to be one of the staples of the R&B culture with chart topping singles.

This year in music 1970, *Nina Simone* releases her album titled *Black Gold* on *RCA, Victor Records*. The album features a song that would become the civil rights anthem, *To Be Young, Gifted and Black* and would go on to be a Top 10 hit. Simone's voice is forever penetrated into our souls as an iconic black woman who loved us all through the words in her music.

In the year 1970, *Quincy Jones* releases *Gula Matari* on **A&M Records**. The most notable track on the Jazz album was Art Garfunkel and Paul Simon's, *Bridge Over Troubled Water*. Jones, a legend in his own right, would continue to pave the way for many as a musician and producer.

In the year of 1970, *Wilson Pickett* releases *Right On* on **Atlantic Records**. The album garnered some success as singles reached number four on R&B and number 68 on the Pop charts. Most notable tracks were the cover of The Supremes *You Keep Me Hangin' On*, *Sugar, Sugar* by the Archies, and the original track, *She Said Yes*.

1970 – Billboards Year End – Hot 100 Singles

1970	Urban Music is 18% of Billboard's year-end Hot 100	18%
5	**Edwin Starr** – *War*	Gordy
6	**Diana Ross** – *Aint No Mountain High Enough*	Motown
7	**Jackson 5** – *I'll Be There*	Motown
15	**Jackson 5** – *ABC*	Motown
16	**Jackson 5** – *The Love You Save*	Motown
19	**Sly & The Family Stone** – *Thank You (Falettinme Be Mice Elf Agin)*	Epic
24	**The Temptations** – *Ball of Confusion*	Gordy
28	**Jackson 5** – *I Want You Back*	Motown
31	**Stevie Wonder** – *Signed, Sealed, Delivered I'm Yours*	Tamla
35	**Clarence Carter** – *Patches*	Atlantic
58	**The Four Tops** – *Still Water (Love)*	Motown
71	**The Delfonics** – *Didn't I (Blow Your Mind This Time)*	Philly Groove
76	**The Spinners** – *It's A Shame*	V.I.P
79	**Ike & Tina Turner** – *I Want to Take You Higher*	Liberty
88	**The Supremes** – *Up the Ladder to the Roof*	Motown
91	**The Temptations** – *Psychedelic Shack*	Gordy
95	**Dionne Warwick** – *I'll Never Fall in Love Again*	Scepter
98	**BB King** – *The Thrill Is Gone*	Bluesway
100	**Aretha Franklin** – *Call Me*	Atlantic

1970 – Record Labels in Urban Music

Motown Records: Originally founded in Detroit Michigan by **Berry Gordy, Jr.** on January 12, 1959 as *Tamla Records,* then later incorporated into *Motown Record Corporation*. Motown cashed in this year with chart topping albums and singles from *Diana Ross, The Temptations, Jackson 5, Stevie Wonder, Smokey Robinson and The Miracles, The Spinners, The Supremes,* and *The Four Tops*. The re-release of *War* by *Edwin Starr* also charted as high as number one this year (The track was originally recorded in 1969 by *The Temptations*). Motown's Rock Subsidiary Label **Rare Earth** also charted with the band of the same name.

Atlantic Records: Known for R&B, Rock & Roll, and Jazz, Atlantic charted three artists in the Hot 100 this year, *Aretha Franklin, Roberta Flack* and *Wilson Pickett*. The label was also responsible for distributing the catalogue of **Stax Records**, a partnership the corporations put in place. Three years earlier *Atlantic* was 100% acquired by **Warner Brothers Seven Arts**.

Westbound Records: This being its inaugural year, the Detroit-based label distributed by *Janus Records* found immediate success with *Funkadelic* charting on the Hot 100. (*Founded by Armen Boladian*)

Capitol Records: The first official West Coast based label was originally established in 1962. Although a veteran in the game, *Capitol* had only managed to have one artist of the Urban Music genre chart this year. (*Jimi Hendrix*)

Liberty Records: The label charted this year with the release of *Ike & Tina Turner's* album. Liberty's better years however were in the early 60's.

Columbia Records: Founded in 1888, *Columbia* is the Flagship of the Record business. Although stable and precise, *Columbia* only charted one artist of the Urban Music genre on the Hot 100 this year. (*Miles Davis*)

Tangerine Records: *Tangerine* was owned by *Ray Charles* and was distributed and promoted by ABC – Paramount. Ray charted on the Hot 100 this year as an artist and label owner.

Bell Records: A New York label founded in 1952 by *Arthur Shimkin* would chart this year with The 5th Dimension. (The label would be reorganized a few years later giving birth to Arista Records.)

King Records: Originally founded in 1942 by *Syd Nathan* the Ohio based label was responsible for the racial integration of American Music. *King* charted this year with *James Brown*.

Invictus Records: The Detroit-based label formed in 1969 by former *Motown* producers, Brian Holland, Lamont Dozier, and Edward Holland, Jr. was distributed by *Capitol Records* and charted with *George Clinton and Parliament* first album.

Philly Grove Records: The Philly based label founded by Stan Watson and Sam Bell in 1967 was distributed by *Bell Records* and contributed to the Philly Sound. The label charted this year with *The Delfonics*.

Reprise Records: Founded in 1960 by Old Blue Eye's aka *Frank Sinatra* but sold to *Warner Brothers* in 1963 because of low sales. The label was originally launched to allow artist creative freedom and by signing *Little Richard* as one of his acts, the label now under Warner Bros. still held true to form as it charted this year with *Little Richard's* release.

Curtom Records: Founded by *Curtis Mayfield* and *Eddie Thomas*, the name a combination of Curtis and Thomas, was launched in 1968. Curtis Mayfield, member and Thomas, associate of the famous *Impressions*, are known to be one of the 1st African-American Artist collective to own a record label. *Curtom* would chart this year with Curtis's self-titled album. Through its history the label would be distributed by *Buddah Records, Warner Bros, RSO Records* and *Arista*.

MCA Records: Initially a Talent Agency and TV production company, *MCA* acquired New York based *Decca Records* in 1962 which was established in 1934 and also included labels *Brunswick* and *Coral Records*. The catalogue of the three labels would be combined into *MCA Records*. Because of the power they would hold as a label due to the merger, MCA was forced out of the Talent Agency. *Decca* also owned *Universal Pictures* which would now fall under the **MCA Corporation**. The label would chart the Hot 100 this year with *BB King*.

Epic Records: Originally launched in 1953 by *Columbia Records* to market Jazz, Pop, and Classical music that did not fit with the catalogue of *Columbia*. The label also distributed *Philadelphia International Records* and charted the Hot 100 this year with *Sly & The Family Stone*.

GRT Records: *General Recorded Tape* was a manufacturer of reel-to-reel, 8-tracks, and cassette tapes. The company grew and its heads became owners of *Chess Records, Janus Records*, and also released artists under *GRT Records*. With a new artist catalogue to add to its established tape production business, *GRT* charted a hit this year with **Minnie Ripperton**. In 1969, GRT acquired **Chess Records** from *Leonard* and *Phil Chess* for $6.5 Million and also gave them 200,000 shares of the GRT stock for 100% of **Chess Records**. GRT was founded by *Alan J. Bayley* in 1965.

Stax Records: The Memphis-based label was originally founded by *Jim Stewart* and *Estelle Axton* as *Satellite Records* in 1957 then changed its name to *Stax* in 1961. The label was known for Southern Soul; distributed by *CBS Records*, it rivaled *Motown Records* in the Urban Music Genre. *Stax* charted the 100 twice this year with hits from *Isaac Hayes*.

Brunswick Records: Originally founded in 1916 and now owned by *Decca Records*, *Brunswick* would chart quite a few hits this year with R&B group, *The Chi-Lites*.

RCA Victor Records: Founded in 1901, *RCA* is the 2nd oldest label in U.S History. It has three divisions, **RCA** for Pop, Rock, Country music and R&B; **RCA Victor** for Blues, World music, Religious music, Jazz, and musicals; **RCA Red-Seal** for Classical music. RCA manufactured its own records, and all music was distributed by *Decca Records*. The *RCA Victor label* charted this year with the release from *Nina Simone*.

A&M Records: Formed in 1962 by *Herb Alpert* and *Jerry Moss* distributed by Ode Records. *A&M* charted this year with *Quincy Jones*.

Circa 1971

On January 15, 1971, *John Lee Hooker and Canned Heat* release *Hooker n' Heat* on *Liberty Records*. This would be Hooker's first album to chart and it reached 78 on the Billboard.

On January 14, Hip Hop Pioneer, Slick Rick turn 6 years old. *(Born 1-14-1965)*

On January 22, Hip Hop Pioneer, DJ Jazzy Jeff of Jazzy Jeff and The Fresh Prince, turns 6 years old. *(Born 1-22-1965)*

In January of 1971, *Booker T. and The M.G.s* release *Melting Pot* on *Stax Records*. Originally members of the Stax records house band and credited for the Memphis Southern Soul sound, the group charted success as they hit 45 on the Hot 100.

In January of 1971, *Freddie Hubbard* releases *Straight Life* on **CTI Records**. The album would be received as one of the Trumpeter's best bodies of work.

On February 1, 1971, *The 5th Dimension* releases *Love's Lines, Angles and Rhymes* on **Bell Records**. The title track was written by Dorothea Joyce and sung originally by Diana Ross in 1970. The 5th Dimension, however, charted 19 on the Hot 100, six on the contemporary charts, 19 in Canada and 28 on the R&B charts.

⇒ **Politics—Civil Rights**: **On February 2, 1971, 15 African-American members of Congress** formed the Congressional Black Caucus to present a united African-American voice in Congress.

In February of 1971, *Earth, Wind and Fire* release their self-titled album on *Warner Brothers Records*. The album would receive mixed reviews and chart at 24 on the Black Albums chart.

⇒ **Finance News**: **On February 8, 1971**: A new stock market index known as **Nasdaq** is born.

In February of 1971, *Miles Davis* releases *Jack Johnson* on *Columbia Records*. Released as a film score for the documentary about boxer, Jack Johnson, the album only charted 159 on the Billboard 200. The album is still considered one of *Miles Davis'* best bodies of work.

In February of 1971, *Kool and The Gang* release their first ever live album called *Live at The Sex Machine* on **De-Lite Records**. The album reached number six on the R&B charts and remained there for 33 straight weeks.

On February 18, Hip Hop Pioneer, Dr. Dre turn 6 years old. *(Born 2-18-1965)*

On February 20, Hip Hop Pioneer, Daddy-O of Stetsasonic turns 10 years old. *(Born 2-20-1961)*

On March 16, Hip Hop Pioneer, Flavor Flav of Public Enemy turns 12 years old. *(Born 3-16-1959)*

On March 16, 1971, The Grammy Awards are aired live on television for the first time showing the *13th Annual Grammy Awards*.

1971 – Urban American

Grammy Award Recipients - 13th Annual

Awards, 1971: Flip Wilson wins Best Comedy Recording. *(The Devil Made Me Buy This Dress)*

Awards, 1971: T-Bone Walker wins Best Ethnic or Traditional Recording including Traditional Blues. *(Good Feelin')*

Awards, 1971: Miles Davis wins Best Jazz Performance – Large Group or Soloist with Large Group. *(B****s Brew)*

Awards, 1971: Dionne Warwick wins Best Contemporary Vocal Performance, Female. *(I'll Never Fall in Love Again)*

Awards, 1971: Aretha Franklin wins Best R&B Vocal Performance, Female. *(Don't Play That Song)*

Awards, 1971: B.B. King wins Best R&B Vocal Performance, Male. *(The Thrill Is Gone)*

Awards, 1971: The Delfonics win Best R&B Performance by a Duo or Group, Vocal or Instrumental. *(Didn't I, Blow Your Mind This Time)*

Awards, 1971: Martin Luther King, Jr. wins Best Spoken Word Recording. *(Why I Oppose the War in Vietnam)*

In March of 1971, *Track Records* release a *Jimi Hendrix* album titled *The Cry of Love* which featured tracks he had been working on for an album before his death. The album charted at number two in the U.K, three on Billboard 200, and six on Top R&B Albums.

- ⇒ **Sports News: On March 8, 1971**: **Smoking Joe Frazier** defends his Heavyweight title against **Muhammad Ali** at the Madison Square Garden in New York City, winning by unanimous decision after 15 rounds.
- ⇒ **Politics—Civil Rights & Integration: In April 1971,** *(4-20-1971)* **The Supreme Court in** *Swann v. Charlotte-Mecklenburg Board of Education,* upholds busing as a legitimate means for achieving integration of public schools. This would continue in major cities across the United States until the late *1990's*.
- ⇒ **TV News: On March 23, 1971,** *Julia,* one of the first weekly sitcom's starring an African-American, featured on *NBC* and starring **Diahann Carroll**, would air for the last time.
- ⇒ **Film News: On March 24, 1971, Columbia Pictures** release *"Brother John"* starring *Sidney Poitier*. The film was directed by James Goldstone, written by Ernest Kinoy, produced by Joel Glickman, and scored by *Quincy Jones*.

On April 2, 1971, *Donny Hathaway* releases his self-titled album on *Atco Records*. This was the 2nd album Hathaway released, but this one, however, was compiled mostly of cover music. The most popular being Leon Russell's *A Song for You*.

On April 8, Hip Hop Pioneer, Biz Markie turn 7 years old. *(Born 4-8-1964)*

On April 8, 1971; *The Isley Brothers* release *Givin' it Back* on **T-Neck Records**. The album was a cover of music from white artists such as Neil Young, James Taylor, and Bob Dylan to name a few. The Isley Brothers found it fitting to cover this music after their songs *Shout* and *Twist and Shout* were covered so many times by white artists. The album would chart with the covers of *Lay Lady Lay, Love the One You're With,* and *Spill the Win.*

On April 12, 1971, *The Jackson 5* release their 5th album *Maybe Tomorrow* on **Motown Records**. Most notable tracks were *Never Can Say Goodbye* and the title track, *Maybe Tomorrow*. The album went on to chart number one on the Soul album charts for six weeks.

On April 12, 1971, *Stevie Wonder* releases *Where I'm Coming From* on **Motown Records**. The album would chart at number 10 on the R&B charts and 62 on the Pop charts.

On April 20, 1971: **The U.S Supreme Court** rules that busing students to achieve racial desegregation may be ordered.

On April 22, 1971, *The Temptations* release *Sky's the Limit* on **Gordy Records**. The album charted a number one hit with *Just My Imagination (Running Away with Me)*, which is still an all-time favorite.

On May 19, 1971, *Aretha Franklin* releases her 2nd live album *Aretha Live at Fillmore West* on **Atlantic Records**.

On May 21, 1971, *Marvin Gaye* releases *What's Going On* on **Tamla Records**. Produced by Marvin himself, the concept album was written from the point of view of a Vietnam Veteran who came home from war and saw nothing but hatred, injustice, and poverty. The album is a classic and considered to be one of the 500 greatest albums of all time.

In May of 1971, legendary musician **Bo Diddley** releases *Another Dimension*. Known as the originator, Bo has influenced many of the greats with his style of play and abilities to transform across genres of music.

In May of 1971, *Freda Payne* releases *Contact* on **Invictus Records**. The album didn't do as well as her prior gold and platinum chart topping albums. Freda is also the older sister of Supreme singer, *Scherrie Payne*.

In May of 1971, *Curtis Mayfield* releases his 1st live album *Curtis/Live* on **Curtom Records**. The album would reach number nine on the Jazz Album charts, three on Black Albums, and 21 on the Pop Album charts.

In May of 1971, *Bill Withers* releases *Just As I Am* on **Sussex Records**. Most noted for *Aint No Sunshine,* still a favorite today, the track ranked 280 on Rolling Stone magazine's 500 greatest songs of all time.

In May of 1971, *Shirley Bassey* releases *Something Else* on **United Artist Records**. The album charted number 7 in the UK; Bassey is also the voice singing the theme songs to the James Bond movies: *"Goldfinger," "Diamonds are Forever,"* and *"Moonraker".*

⇒ **Drugs**: **In June of 1971, President Nixon** declared a *"War on Drugs"*. In doing so he increased the size and presence of Federal drug control agencies. This came with no-knock warrants and strong mandatory sentences. He also placed marijuana in the most restrictive category of schedule 1 temporarily pending a Government review. It is now estimated that the U.S spends $51 Billion annually on the *"War on Drugs."*

⇒ **News: In June of 1971, The Black Panther Party** split into two warring factions. The party had been under attack by the FBI, who set out to divide and conquer. Out of this came violent protest, murder within, and party disagreements. In the end, the FBI succeeded.

In June of 1971, *Ike and Tina Turner* release *Live at Carnegie Hall/What You Hear is What You Get* on **Liberty Records**. The album sold half a million copies and gave the group their first gold album. Ike and Tina would later sign a 5-year deal with **United Artist Records** a subsidiary label of **Liberty Records**.

In June of 1971, *Chuck Berry* releases *San Francisco Dues* on **Chess Records**. Known as one of the true Pioneers of Rock and Roll music, Berry's long catalogue of work includes many chart topping hits.

In June of 1971, *Melvin Van Peebles* releases *Sweet Sweetback's Baadasssss Song* on **Stax Records**. The album was the sound track to his movie of the same name; the songs were written by Peebles and recorded by a newly formed band called *Earth, Wind and Fire*.

In June of 1971, *The Supremes* release *Touch* on **Motown Records**. The album charted number four on the Billboard R&B charts.

⇒ **Film News: In July of 1971, K-Calb Productions** release *"The Bus is Coming"* starring Mike B. Sims, directed by Wendell Franklin.
⇒ **Film News: On July 2, 1971, MGM** releases *"Shaft"* starring Richard Roundtree, directed by Gordon Parks and scored by *Isaac Hayes*.

On July 6, 1971, *Diana Ross* releases *Surrender* on **Motown Records**. This would be Diana's third solo album since she left The Supremes. The album reached number 10 on the R&B charts.

On July 12, 1971, *Funkadelic* releases *Maggot Brain* on **Westbound Records**. The album would reach 14 on the Black Albums chart and 108 on the pop albums chart. Rolling Stone Magazine also listed it as number 479 of its Top 500 Greatest Albums of All time.

In July of 1971, *The Chi-Lites* release *(For God's Sake) Give More Power to the People* on **Brunswick Records**. Most noted track *Have You Seen Her* reached number one on the R&B charts and three on the Hot 100.

In July of 1971, *Isaac Hayes* releases his double album *Shaft,* the soundtrack for the *MGM* movie of the same name on *Stax Records (Enterprise)*. This would go on to be Hayes' best known work and the hottest album ever released on the Stax label.

On August 1, Hip Hop Pioneer, Chuck D of Public Enemy turns 11 years old. *(Born 8-1-1960)*

On August 1, Hip Hop Pioneer, Professor Griff of Public Enemy turns 11 years old. *(Born 8-1-1960)*

On August 8, Hip Hop Pioneer, Kool Moe Dee turns 9 years old. *(Born 8-8-1962)*

On August 14, 1971, *Al Green* releases *Al Green Gets Next to You* on **Hi Records**. Most noted single, *Tired of Being Alone* reached number eleven on Hot 100 and seven on Hot Soul singles.

⇒ **Economy: On August 15, 1971, President Richard Nixon** announces that the U.S would no longer convert dollars to *gold* at a fixed value.

On August 20, Hip Hop Pioneer, Wise of Stetsasonic turns 6 years old. *(Born 8-20-1965)*

On August 25, Hip Hop Pioneer, Shock G of Digital Underground turns 8 years old. *(Born 8-25-1963)*

On August 27, 1971, *Smokey Robinson and The Miracles* release *One Dozen Roses* on **Tamla Records**. The album would chart in the Top 20 of the Hot 100 while reaching number one in England.

In August of 1971, *Shuggie Otis* releases *Freedom Fight* on **Epic Records**. The album included the original version of *Strawberry Letter 23* which was later re-recorded by The Brother's Johnson with chart topping success.

In August of 1971; *Howlin' Wolf* releases *The London Howlin' Wolf Session"* on **Chess Records**. The Blues musician, *Wolf* would chart 79 on the Billboard 200.

On September 7, Hip Hop Pioneer, Eazy E of NWA turn 8 years old. *(Born 9-7-1963)*

On September 8, 1971, formally known as Patti Labelle and the Bluebelles, **Labelle** releases their self-titled album on **Warner Brothers Records**. This coming after group member Cindy Birdsong left to join The Supremes. The group's founding member *Patti Labelle* would go on to become a musical legend in her own right.

On September 9, 1971, *Aretha Franklin* releases her 2nd compilation album *Aretha's Greatest Hits* on **Atlantic Records**. The album also featured three new singles and charted in Billboard's Top 20.

⇒ **Animated TV News: On September 11, 1971, The Jackson 5** Saturday Morning Cartoon series based on the **Motown Records** group premiers on *ABC*.

On September 29, 1971, *The Jackson 5* releases *Goin' Back to Indiana* on **Motown Records**. The album was a live recorded soundtrack from the *Goin' Back to Indiana ABC* TV special on September 16th, 1971.

In September of 1971, Latin Rock band *Santana* releases their self-titled album on *Columbia Records*. Lead guitarist and founder *Carlos Santana* and band would go on to be musical legends. The album would chart at number 12 in the U.S.

⇒ **TV News—Soul Train: On October 2, 1971**, the first episode of **Soul Train** aired in syndication. The show would feature urban dancers with the newest moves, the hottest music of the era, and live performances from Urban Music's favorite artists. Founded by *Don Cornelius*, who was the definition of soul from the Afro to the fist to the fashionable bell bottoms, Soul Train would transcend generations and become legendary for its famous Soul Train line as well as its long list of guest artists.

On October 4, 1971, *Atlantic Records* releases *Twins,* a compilation album consisting of outtakes from recording sessions from Saxophonist and Composer **Ornette Coleman**. Known as the inventor of *Free Jazz, Coleman* would have no input on assembling this album for release.

In October of 1971, *Little Richard* releases *The King of Rock and Roll* on **Reprise Records**. The album charted at number 193 on Billboard Pop Albums.

In October of 1971, *Kool and The Gang* releases *Live at PJ's* on **De-Lite Records**. This is the 3rd album of many to come from the legendary band.

In October of 1971, **Reprise Records** releases the 2nd posthumous *Jimi Hendrix* album titled *Rainbow Bridge*. The album is compiled of recordings by Hendrix after the breakup of the *Jimi Hendrix Experience*.

In October of 1971, **Curtis Mayfield** releases *Roots* on **Curtom Records**. The album charted six on the Top R&B charts, another success for Mayfield and his Record Label.

⇒ **TV News — Education: On October 25, 1971, The Electric Company** aired on *PBS*. The show was an educational children's TV series that starred *Morgan Freeman*, whose main focus was to help elementary kids develop their reading and grammar skills.

On November 6, 1971, *The Stylistics* release their self-titled album on *Avco Records*. The album reached number three on the R&B charts and 23 on the Billboard 200 with several singles also charting the Top 10 of Billboard's Hot 100.

On November 8, Hip Hop Pioneer, Eric B of Eric B & Rakim turns 6 years old. *(Born 11-8-1965)*

On November 8, 1971, *Billy Preston* releases *I Wrote a Simple Song* on *A&M Records*. The album would reach number nine on the R&B charts; its most noted single *Outta-Space* reached number one on the Singles chart and would go on to win a Grammy.

On November 17, 1971, *Miles Davis* releases *Live-Evil* on ***Columbia Records***. The album included live performances of Miles and received great reviews.

On November 20, 1971, *Sly and The Family Stone* release *There's a Riot Goin' On* on ***Epic Records***. The album reached number one on the Pop and Soul Album charts upon its release.

⇒ **Dance: 1971, Don "Campbellock" Campbell & Toni Basil** founded the Los Angeles dance crew, *The Lockers*. The crew consisted of members: Don "Campbellock" Campbell, Toni "Mickey" Basil, Fred "Mr. Penguin" Berry aka Re-Run, Greg "Campbelloc, Jr." Pope, Adolfo "Shabba-Doo" Quinones, Bill "Slim the Robot" Williams, and Leo "Fluky Luke" Williamson; their style became known as *Pop Locking*.

In November of 1971, *War* releases *All Day Music* on **United Artist Records**. The album stayed on Billboard's Hot 100 for 22 weeks; its most noted single, *"Slippin into Darkness,"* is still a favorite.

In November of 1971, *Isaac Hayes* releases *Black Moses* on **Enterprise Records**. This would be Hayes' second double album, the most noted single a remake of The Jackson 5's *Never Can Say Goodbye* reached 22 on the Hot 100.

In November of 1971, *Earth, Wind and Fire* release *The Need of Love* on **Warner Brothers Records**. This would be the 2nd album released by the elements of the earth; it reached 35 on the Black Albums chart and 89 on Pop Albums.

In November of 1971, *Ike and Tina Turner* releases *Nuff Said* their 1st album for **United Artist Records** under their new 10-album contract.

In November of 1971, *Roberta Flack* releases *Quiet Fire* on **Atlantic Records**. The album reached 18 on Billboard's Top LP's and is the 3rd album released by Flack.

⇒ **Film News**: **On November 26, 1971,** The Interracial movie *"Honky"* starring *Brenda Sykes* was released. It was directed by William A. Graham and scored by *Quincy Jones*.
⇒ **Film News**: **In 1971,** *"Man and Boy"* starring **Bill Cosby** was released. It was directed by E.W. Swackhamer and scored by Jazz trombonist, *J.J. Johnson*.
⇒ **Civil Rights**: **On December 18, 1971, Rev. Jesse Jackson** forms **PUSH** (People United to Serve Humanity), an influential movement designed to emphasize African-American Economic Advancement and Education.

On December 27, 1971, *The Jackson 5* release their 1st *Greatest Hits Album* on **Motown Records**. The album sold over 5.6 Million copies and also included a new track *Sugar Daddy* which charted as a Top 10 Single.

In December of 1971, *Wilson Picket* scored another number one hit with the release of *Don't Knock My Love* on **Atlantic Records**. This would be the last album Pickett released while on Atlantic before signing with **RCA Records**.

In December of 1971, *The Supremes* and *The Four Tops* release *Dynamite!* on **Motown Records**. This would be the 3rd and final collaborative album by the two groups and would reach 21 on the R&B charts.

Dubbed **Hitsville USA, Motown Records** had built its brand to be a force in the industry.

1971 – Billboards Year End – Hot 100 Singles

1971	Urban Music 23% of Billboard's year-end Hot 100	23%
9	The Temptations – *Just My Imagination*	Gordy
12	Al Green – *Tired of Being Alone*	Decca
13	Honey Cone – *Want Ads*	Hot Wax
14	The Undisputed Truth – *Smiling Faces Sometimes*	Motown
15	Cornelius Brothers & Sister Rose – *Treat her like a Lady*	United Artist
17	Jean Knight – *Mr. Big Stuff*	Stax
21	Marvin Gaye – *What's Going On*	Tamla
23	Bill Withers – *Ain't No Sunshine*	Sussex
40	Jackson 5 – *Never Can Say Goodbye*	Motown
46	The Dramatics – *Whatcha See is Whatcha Get*	Volt
48	Stevie Wonder – *If You Really Love me*	Tamla
49	Aretha Franklin – *Spanish Harlem*	Atco
52	Aretha Franklin – *Bridge over Troubled Water*	Atco
55	Ike & Tina Turner – *Proud Mary*	United Artist
62	Marvin Gaye – *Mercy Mercy Me (Ecology)*	Tamla
64	8th Day – *She's Not Just Another Woman*	Invictus
66	Rare Earth – *I Just Want to Celebrate*	Rare Earth
70	Honey Cone – *Stick Up*	Hot Wax
86	Jackson 5 – *Mama's Pearl*	Motown
89	Isaac Hayes – *Theme from Shaft*	Stax
90	Gladys Knight & The Pips – *If I Were Your Woman*	Motown
93	Wilson Pickett – *Don't Knock My Love*	Atlantic
98	The 5th Dimension – *One Less Bell to Answer*	Bell

1971 – Record Labels in Urban Music

Gordy Records: The label is a subsidiary of *Berry Gordy, Jr.'s* **Motown Records Corporation** which started as *Tamla Records* then went on to be the label Gordy used to release music outside of the U.S., yet still under the Motown Umbrella. The combination of labels charted several hits from several of its artists on Billboard's Hot 100 this year. The heavy hitters included *The Temptations, The Undisputed Truth, Marvin Gaye, The Jackson 5, Gladys Knight and The Pips,* and *Stevie Wonder*. Both J5 and Marvin charted with more than one single this year. Another Motown subsidiary label, *Rare Earth* the Rock label also charted with the band of the same name *Rare Earth*, and their hit single *I Just Want to Celebrate*.

Decca Records: Although Decca shut down its Classical department this year, the historic label scored big with the *Al Green* hit single *Tired of Being Alone*.

Hot Wax Records: The label formed by prior Motown producers, *Edward Holland Jr., Lamont Dozier,* and *Brian Holland* aka **Holland-Dozier-Holland** scored two hit singles on Billboards year-end Hot 100 with their female group *Honey Cone*, proving that they still had the magic. Its sister label *Invictus* also made the charts with a hot single from *8th Day* titled *She's Not Just Another Woman*. The former Motown producers took the Gordy blueprint and churned out hit after hit.

United Artist Records: After its 1969 merger with *Liberty* and *Imperial Records*, United found itself with two Hot 100 year-end hits from *Ike and Tina Turner* and *Cornelius Brothers and Sister Rose*. Ike and Tina's *Proud Mary* brought the heat as did *Treat Her Like a Lady* by *Cornelius Brothers and Sister Rose*.

Stax Records: Now under the direction of Al Bell, Stax managed to produce some chart-topping hits from *Jean Knight* and *Isaac Hayes*. Knight's *Mr. Big Stuff* kept the dance floors packed, while Hayes' *Theme from Shaft* became immortal and charted as *Stax Records* bestselling album ever. *The Dramatics* also added to the label's success with the Hot 100 Single, *Whatcha See is Whatcha Get*.

Sussex Records: The Los Angeles based label founded by *Clarence Avant* in 1969 was distributed by *Buddah Records*. It was the second brainchild of Avant after the setup of another black music label, *Venture Records*, which he launched for *MGM*. Sussex charted the year-end Hot 100 with *Bill Withers, Aint No Sunshine*.

Atco Records: A subsidiary of *Atlantic Records*, Atco charted two singles from The Queen of Soul, Aretha Franklin this year, *Spanish Harlem* and *Bridge Over Troubled Water*. **Atlantic** also charted with Wilson Picket's Hot 100 single, *Don't Knock My Love*.

Bell Records: The New York based label, founded in 1952 by *Arthur Shimkin* managed to get another hit on the Hot 100 this year with a hit single from The 5th Dimension. The group was no stranger to charting hits and pinned another classic with *One Less Bell to Answer*.

Circa 1972

⇒ **TV News — Comedy: On January 14, 1972, Sanford and Son** debuts on *NBC*.

On January 24, 1972, *Michael Jackson* releases his first solo album *Got to Be There* on *Motown Records*. The single of the same name went on to sell over 3.2 Million records world-wide as the album went certified gold.

On January 24, 1972, *Aretha Franklin* releases *Young, Gifted and Black* on *Atlantic Records*. Aretha won a Grammy Award for this album, and it charted Top 10 as Gold-Certified.

⇒ **News: On January 25, 1972, The first African American Congresswoman, Shirley Chisholm** announces her run for President of the United States.

On January 31, 1972, *Al Green* releases *Let's Stay Together* on **Hi Records**. Al reached number eight on the Pop Album charts and held the number one spot for six weeks on the Soul Album charts.

In January of 1972, *Polydor Records* released a posthumous live and in concert album of *Jimi Hendrix* from several of his performances. The album was also released again in February by **Reprise Records**. Simply titled *Hendrix in the West,* the album reached #7 in the UK and #12 on the Billboard 200.

⇒ **News: On February 5, 1972, Founder of the *New York Renaissance* Black Basketball Team, Bob Douglas** becomes first African American to be elected to the Basketball Hall of Fame.

⇒ **News: On February 15, 1972, The United States** gives Federal Copyright protection to sound recordings. Records were only protected at State level in some States prior to this

In February of 1972, *Quincy Jones* releases compilation album *Ndeda* on *Mercury Records*. The album reached #70 on Billboard 200 and #12 on Jazz album charts.

⇒ **Judicial News: On February 18, 1972, The California Supreme Court** voids the state's Death Penalty, changing all death sentences to life in prison.
⇒ **TV News: On February 1972: Singer, Actor, Sammy Davis Jr.** makes an appearance on the controversial bigot-driven TV Show, *All in the Family*.
⇒ **Politics: On February 23, 1972, American Political Activist, Angela Davis** is released from jail. Rodger McAfee Caruthers, a California farmer, helped Davis make bail.

In February of 1972, after an earlier split up four years prior, some of the original *Ohio Players* decided to take another chance at it and signed with *Westbound Records* to release a new single called *Pain*. This would only be the 2nd studio album released by The Ohio Players. The single reached #21 on Billboard's Top Soul LPs and #177 in Top LPs. Not to be forgotten are the suggestive photos of women that dawned their covers, which became an Ohio Player's trademark.

On March 3, 1972, *Martha Reeves and the Vandellas* released *Black Magic* on *Gordy Records*. This would be the last studio album the group released with the label, even though several of the album tracks charted. *Bless You* featuring the Jackson 5 reached #53 on the Pop charts, #29 in R&B, #33 on the UK Pop charts and #16 in Canada. Singles *In and Out of My Life* and *Tear it Down* reached Billboards Top 40 R&B charts.

On March 3, 1972, at 21 years old, *Stevie Wonder* releases *Music of My Mind* on *Tamla Records*. Now considered a classic, the album charted #6 on the R&B charts, #21 on the Pop charts, and two of the album singles also made the charts. *Keep on Running* charted #36 on Black Singles and #90 on Pop. *Superwoman (Where Were You When I Needed You)* charted #13 on Black Singles and #33 on Pop.

⇒ **News: On March 3, 1972,** Sculptured figures of Stonewall Jackson, Robert E. Lee, and Jefferson Davis are completed at **Stone Mountain, GA**.
⇒ **Politics: On March 10, 1972, The First National Black Political Convention** meets in Gary, Indiana; the city had a black Mayor at the time.
⇒ **Film News—Blaxploitation Western: On March 17, 1972, Paramount Pictures** releases "*The Legend of N***** Charley*" directed by Martin Goldman starring **Fred Williamson**.
⇒ **News: On March 21, 1972, President Nixon** signs *The Drug Abuse Office and Treatment Act* into law.

⇒ **Politics: On March 22, 1972, The 92nd Congress of the U.S.** votes to send the proposed Equal Rights Amendment to the states for ratification.
⇒ **News: On March 22, 1972, The National Commission on Marijuana and Drug Abuse** recommends legalizing possession and sales of small amounts of cannabis sativa. But President Richard Nixon and Congress ignore the idea.
⇒ **Film News — Crime Saga:** On March 15, 1972 in N.Y.C, and March 24 in the U.S.A: *Paramount Pictures* releases "*The Godfather*" directed by *Francis Ford Coppola* starring **Marlon Brando, Al Pacino, James Caan,** and **Robert Duvall**.
⇒ **News: On March 24, 1972, Congress** passes *Equal Employment Opportunity Act*. The act granted the EEO Commission the power to file class-action law suits and extended its jurisdiction to cover state and local governments as well as educational institutions.

1972 – Urban American
Grammy Award Recipients -14th Annual

Awards, 1972: Bill Cosby wins Best Recording for Children. *(Bill Cosby Talks to Kids about Drugs)*

Awards, 1972: Isaac Hayes wins Best Original Score written for a Motion Picture or Television Special *(Shaft)*

Awards, 1972: Isaac Hayes & Johnny Allen win Best Instrumental Arrangement *(Theme from Shaft)*

Awards, 1972: Muddy Waters wins Best Ethnic or Traditional Recording *(They Call Me Muddy Waters)*

Awards, 1972: Charley Pride wins Best Gospel Performance (other than soul gospel) *(Let Me Live)*

Awards, 1972: Shirley Caesar wins Best Gospel Performance *(Put Your Hand in the Hand of the Man from Galilee)*

Awards, 1972: Charley Pride wins Best Sacred Performance *(Did You think to Pray)*

Awards, 1972: Duke Ellington wins Best Jazz Performance by a Big Band *(New Orleans Suite)*

Awards, 1972: Quincy Jones wins Best Pop Instrumental Performance *(Smackwater Jack)*

Awards, 1972: Aretha Franklin wins Best R&B Vocal Performance, Female *(Bridge Over Troubled Water)*

Awards, 1972: Lou Rawls wins Best R&B Vocal Performance, Male *(A Natural man)*

Awards, 1972: Ike and Tina Turner win Best R&B Vocal Performance by a Group *(Proud Mary)*

Awards, 1972: Bill Withers wins Best Rhythm and Blues Song *(Aint No Sunshine)*

On April 2, Hip Hop Pioneer, *Prince Paul* **of** *Stetsasonic* turns 5. *(Born 4-2-1967)*

In April of 1972, *Arthur Alexander* releases his self-titled album on **Warner Records**. Alexander, a country soul singer, received mediocre reviews on the album, but one of the songs he featured, *Burning Love* would be recorded by Elvis Presley and would go on to be one of Presley's biggest hits.

⇒ **Film News — Western: On April 28, 1972, Columbia Pictures** release *"Buck and the Preacher"* directed by *Sidney Poitier* starring **Sidney Poitier, Harry Belafonte,** and **Ruby Dee**.

In April of 1972, *The Chi-Lites* released their 4th album, *A Lonely Man,* on **Brunswick Records**. The album would reach #5 on the Pop charts while its most popular single, *Oh Girl* charted on the Pop and R&B charts at #14.

On May 2, 1972, *The Isley Brothers* release *Brother, Brother, Brother* on **T-Neck Records**. The album garnered rave reviews and also spawned a Top 40 hit single with *Pop that Thang*. This however would be the last album that *The Isley Brothers* released on the **T-Neck label** that was distributed by **Buddah Records**.

On May 6, 1972, *Roberta Flack* and *Donny Hathaway* release their self-titled album on **Atlantic Records**. The album is a composition of duets from the two Howard University Alumni. The first single to hit the charts, *You've Got a Friend* reached #29 on the Hot 100 and #8 on the R&B Top 10. The follow up single, *You've Lost that Lovin' Feelin'*, reached #30 on the R&B charts, but both of those got trumped by their smash hit, *Where is the Love*.

On May 8, 1972, *Billy Preston* becomes the first Rock and Roll performer to headline New York's *Radio City*.

On May 22, 1972, *Funkadelic* releases double album *America Eats Its Young* on **Westbound Records**. The album charted at #22 on the R&B charts and #123 on Pop,; its hit single *A Joyful Process* reached #38 on the R&B Singles chart.

⇒ **News: On May 23, 1972,** In Berkley California, six members of the **Black Panther Party** announce their candidacy for the Berkley Community Development Council. (Board members of the council are responsible for funneling government funds into meaningful programs in the low and no income neighborhoods.) Black Panther Member's: Ericka Huggins, Herman Smith, Henry Smith, Norma Armour, William Roberts, and Audrea Jones ran for office. Four out of the six won seats, while Norma Armour and Henry Smith both lost to Chicanos, who also received support from the party. Also during this time, Bobby Seale was campaigning for Mayor of Oakland, and Elaine Brown for City Councilwoman.

On May 23, 1972, *The Jackson 5* releases *Lookin' Through the Windows* on **Motown Records**. As expected, the album would do great and sell over 3.5 million copies worldwide.

⇒ **News: In May of 1972, The Detroit Chapter of the Black Panther Party** implemented a *Survival Day*, giving away over 1000 free bags of groceries to residents of the *Jefferies Projects*.

On May 30, 1972, Bobby Womack releases *Understanding* on **United Artist Records**. The album charted #7 on the R&B charts and #43 on Billboard Pop Album charts.

In May of 1972, *The Supremes* release *Floy Joy* on **Motown Records**. The title song, along with another single, *Automatically Sunshine*, both charted in the U.S and U.K. *Floy Joy* broke the Top 20, while *Automatically Sunshine* broke the Top 40. Both singles broke the U.K Top 10.

In May of 1972, *Bill Withers* releases *Still Bill* on **Sussex Records**. The album's hottest singles, *Lean on Me* and *Use Me* charted at number #1 and #2 on Billboard's Pop and R&B charts. *Lean on Me* has been listed as #205 on *Rolling Stone's* 500 greatest songs of all time.

In May of 1972, *The Delfonics* release *Tell Me this is a Dream* on **Philly Groove Records**. The album received mediocre reviews, although three singles did reach some success. *Tell Me this is a Dream* reached #15 on the R&B charts and #86 on Pop. *Walk Right Up to the Sun* reached #13 on the R&B charts and #81 on Pop. *Hey Love* reached #17 on the R&B charts and #52 on Pop.

⇒ **Film News—Blaxploitation: On May 31, 1972, New World Pictures** release *"The Final Comedown"* directed by *Oscar Williams* starring **Billy Dee Williams**.

On June 1, 1972, *Aretha Franklin* releases *Amazing Grace* on **Atlantic Records**. The album sold over 2 million copies and went double platinum.

On June 4, 1972, U.C.L.A Professor, Angela Davis was acquitted of all false charges brought on by the state. Davis had been rejected as a Professor at the University because of her political beliefs. She did not agree with the racism, fascism, and greed of America and wasn't afraid to make it known.

⇒ **Film News — Crime Drama**: **On June 8, 1972, MGM** release *"Shaft's Big Score"* directed by *Gordon Parks* starring **Richard Roundtree**.

On June 9, 1972, *James Brown* releases *There It Is* on **Polydor Records**. The album reached #10 on the R&B charts and #60 on the Billboard 200.

On June 10, Hip Hop Pioneer Buff Love of *The Fat Boys* turns 5. *(Born 6-10-1967)*

- ⇒ **Film News—Adult: On June 12, 1972, Bryanston Pictures** release *"Deep Throat"* directed by *Jerry Gerard* starring **Linda Lovelace, Doll Sharp** and **Carol Connors**.
- ⇒ **News: On June 17, 1972,** *Five White House Operatives* are arrested for burglarizing the office of the Democratic National Committee. The break in would come to be known as *Watergate*.

In June of 1972, *Syreeta Wright,* the ex-wife of *Stevie Wonder* releases her debut self-titled album on *MoWest Records*. Although produced by Wonder, the album didn't garner much success.

- ⇒ **News: On June 23, 1972, The Watergate Scandal:** U.S. President **Richard Nixon** and White House Chief of Staff **H.R. Haldeman** are unknowingly taped while discussing how to use the *C.I.A.* to obstruct the *F.B.I's* investigation into the *Watergate* break-ins.
- ⇒ **Civil Rights: On June 23, 1972, Congress** passed *Title IX*, a portion of the United States Education Amendments of 1972, which prevents a person from being excluded from federal financial assistance due to gender.
- ⇒ **Judicial News: On June 29, 1972, The Supreme Court of the United States** rules that the death penalty is unconstitutional. *(Furman v. Georgia)*
- ⇒ **Government News**: **On July 1, 1972,** *ATF,* the Bureau of Alcohol, Tobacco and Firearms becomes independent from the *IRS*.
- ⇒ **Film News—Drama: On July 19, 1972,** *Paramount Pictures* release *"The Man"* directed by Joseph Sargent starring James Earl Jones. *(Drama)*
- ⇒ **Film News—Blaxploitation: On July 21, 1972, Warner Brothers** release *"Super Fly"* directed by *Gordon Parks, Jr.* starring **Ron Oneal**.

⇒ **News: On July 25, 1972, The Tuskegee Study** is revealed when U.S. Health Officials admit that African-Americans were used as guinea pigs in the study of untreated syphilis in the Negro male.

On July 27, 1972; *The Temptations* releases *All Directions* on **Gordy Records**. Several singles from the album reached the charts and also garnered Grammies, most noted, *Papa was a Rollin' Stone*.

On July 27, 1972, *Smokey Robinson and The Miracles* release *Flying High Together* on **Tamla Records**. The album reached #46 on the Billboard Pop charts while singles, *We've Come Too Far to End It Now* reached #9 on the R&B Singles chart, and *I Can't Stand to See You Cry* reached #21 on the R&B charts as well as #45 on Pop.

⇒ **Film News — Blaxploitation: In July of 1972, New World Pictures** release "*The Big Bird Cage*" directed by *Jack Hill* starring **Pamela Grier**.

In July of 1972, *Curtis Mayfield* releases the *Super Fly Soundtrack* on **Curtom Records**. The album was another huge success for Mayfield's Curtom Records, selling over 2 million records. Hit singles: *Freddies Dead* reached #2 on the R&B charts and #4 on Pop, while *Super Fly* reached #5 on R&B and #8 on Pop. The soundtrack goes down as one of the only albums to outsell the movie that it scored.

⇒ **Film News—Horror: In July of 1972, New World Pictures** releases *"Bone"* directed by *Larry Cohen* starring **Yaphet Kotto**.

On August 2, 1972, *Ella Fitzgerald* releases *Jazz at Santa Monica '72* on **Pablo Records**. The album included work from Count Basie Orchestra, Jazz at The Philharmonic Allstars, Oscar Peterson, Tommy Flanagan, Ed Thigpen, and Frank DeLaRosa.

On August 4, 1972, *Michael Jackson* releases his 2nd Solo album *Ben* on **Motown Records**. The album reached the Top 10 of the Billboard 200. *Ben* was *Michael's* first #1 hit as a solo artist, even though he released this album while still with the *Jackson 5*.

On August 28, Hip Hop Pioneer Too Short turns 6. (Born 8-28-1966)

In August of 1972, *The O'Jays* release *Back Stabbers* on **Philadelphia International Records**. Back Stabbers broke Billboard's Top 10 and went certified Gold as singles *Love Train* and *Back Stabbers* both reached #1 on the Pop Singles chart.

⇒ **Film News — Blacula: On August 25, 1972,** American International Pictures releases "*Blacula*" directed by *William Crain* starring **William Marshall**.

In August of 1972, *Harold Melvin and The Blue Notes* release their self-titled debut album on *Philadelphia International Records*. The album reached #4 on the Soul LPs charts and #53 on Billboard Top LPs. Hit singles: *I Miss You (Part 1)* reached #7 on the R&B charts, and *If You Don't Know Me by Now* reached #1 in the U.S. and #9 in the U.K.

In August of 1972, *Gil Scott-Heron* releases *Free Will* on *Flying Dutchman Records*. Scott, an activist for Black Pride, let his feelings and beliefs be known through his music.

⇒ **Animated TV News: On September 9, 1972, Fat Albert and The Cosby Kids** debuts on CBS.

On September 17, Hip Hop Pioneer, Doug E Fresh turns 6. *(Born 9-17-1966)*

⇒ **Film News—Drama Action: On September 20, 1972, United Artist** releases *"Hammer"* directed by *Bruce Clark* starring **Fred Williamson**.
⇒ **Film News—Crime: On September 20, 1972, United Artist** releases *"Hickey & Boggs"* directed by *Robert Culp* starring **Bill Cosby** and **Robert Culp**.
⇒ **Film News—Drama:** On September 24, 1972, **20th Century Fox** release *"Sounder"* directed by *Martin Ritt* starring **Cicely Tyson** and **Paul Winfield**.

On October 1, 1972, *Polydor Records* release the 3rd *Jimi Hendrix* posthumous album *War Heroes*. The album reached #48 on Billboard 200 and #23 in the U.K.

On October 8, 1972, *Billy Preston* releases *Music is My Life* on *A&M Records*. The album garnered his 1st #1 single *Will it Go Round in Circles*.

On October 11, 1972, *Santana* releases *Caravanserai* on **Columbia Records**. The album went gold in France and Canada, while going platinum in the U.S. reaching #6 on the R&B charts and #8 on Billboard 200.

On October 11, 1972, *Miles Davis* releases *On the Corner* on **Columbia Records**. The album received sub-par reviews because of its cutting-edge style at the time, but would gain more appreciation as time passed.

⇒ **Film News—Crime Drama: This year 1972,** American International Pictures releases "*Slaughter*" directed by *Jack Starrett* starring **Jim Brown**.

In October of 1972, *Diana Ross* releases the soundtrack to *"Lady Sings the Blues"* on *Motown Records,* a biopic on the life of *Billie Holiday.* Ross also played Holiday in the successful movie. The album reached #1 and sold over 2 million copies in the U.S., reached #2 on the R&B charts and #50 on the U.K. Album charts where it also went gold and sold over 100,000 copies.

⇒ **Film News — Biopic: On October 12, 1972, Paramount Pictures** release *"Lady Sings the Blues"* directed by Sidney J. Furie starring **Diana Ross, Billie Dee Williams** and **Richard Pryor**.

⇒ **Film News — Drama: This year 1972, First American Films** releases *"Black Rage"* directed by *Chris Robinson* starring **Anthony Scott** and **Chris Robinson**.

On October 23, 1972, *Al Green* releases *I'm Still in Love with You* on **Hi Records**. The album reached #1 on Top R&B Albums and #4 on Billboard 200. Most noted singles, *Love and Happiness, I'm Still in Love with You,* and *Look What You Done for Me,* all broke Top 5 on the Pop charts. *Love and Happiness* would place at #98 on *Rolling Stones* 500 Greatest Songs of all time.

On October 28, 1972, *Stevie Wonder* releases *Talking Book* on **Tamla Records**. Wonder won his first Grammy for this album as well as charting #1 with singles *You are the Sunshine in My Life* and *Superstition* on Billboard's Hot 100.

In October of 1972, *Chuck Berry* releases *The London Chuck Berry Sessions* on **Chess Records**. The live shortened recorded edition of *My Ding-A-Ling* would become the Rock and Roll legend's first #1 hit.

In October of 1972, *The Stylistics* release Round 2 on **Avco Records**. The album reached #3 on the R&B charts and #32 on Billboard 200. Most noted singles, Break up to Make Up, I'm Stone in Love with You, and You'll Never Get to Heaven (If you Break my Heart), all reached Top 10 on the R&B singles charts.

⇒ **Film News—Crime Drama: On November 1, 1972, 20th Century Fox** releases *"Trouble Man"* directed by *Ivan Dixon* starring **Robert Hooks** and **Paul Winfield**.

On November 1, Hip Hop Pioneer Willie D of the *Geto Boys* turns 6. *(Born 11-1-1966)*

On November 4, Hip Hop Pioneer Kool Rock Ski of *The Fat Boys* turns 6. *(Born 11-4-1966)*

⇒ **Politics: On November 7, 1972, African-American Politicians, Andrew Young and Barbara Jordan,** are elected to the House of Representatives. Young from Georgia and Jordan from Texas.

⇒ **TV News: On November 8, 1972, Home Box Office (HBO)** is launched, in Wilkes-Barre, Pennsylvania.

On November 20, 1972, *James Brown* releases *Get on the Good Foot* on **Polydor Records**. The classic album garnered several hot singles including the title track. Most noted are: *Cold Sweat, I Got a Bag of My Own, Lost Someone, My Part/Make it Funky,* and *Please, Please, Please.*

In November of 1972, *Motown Records* releases *The Supremes Produced and Arranged by Jimmy Webb*. This last album to feature lead singer *Jean Terrell* sold over 100,000 copies in the U.S.

In November of 1972, *War* releases *The World is a Ghetto* on **United Artist Records**. The album went on to reach Billboards #1 spot and also holds spot #444 on *Rolling Stones* Magazine 500 Greatest Songs of All Time.

On December 8, 1972, *Marvin Gaye* releases soundtrack *Trouble Man* to the film of the same name on **Tamla Records**. The album reached #12 on Billboards 200.

⇒ **Magazine News: On December 8, 1972,** *Diana Ross* lands the cover of *Life*.

On December 8, Hip Hop Pioneer Bushwick Bill of the *Geto Boys* turns 6. *(Born 12-8-1966)*

On December 11, Hip Hop Pioneer, Dj Yella of *NWA* turns 5. *(Born 12-11-1967)*

On December 16, 1972, *Bobby Womack and J.J Johnson* release soundtrack *Across 110th Street* to the movie of the same name on ***United Artist Records***. The title track would go on to reach #19 on Billboard's Black Hot Singles chart.

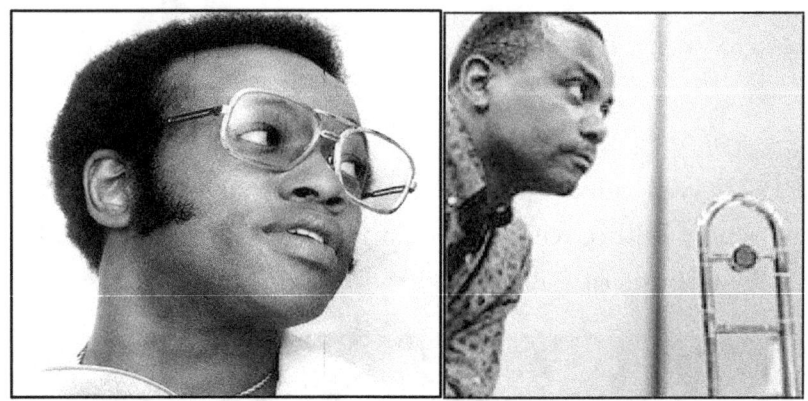

⇒ **Film News — Crime Drama: On December 19, 1972, United Artist** releases "*Across 110th Street*" directed by *Barry Shear* starring **Yaphet Kotto, Anthony Quinn**, and **Anthony Franciosa**.

In December of 1972, *The Ohio Players* release *Pleasure* on ***Westbound Records***. Most noted single, *Funky Worm* went on to reach #1 on the Billboard R&B charts.

This year, 1972, *The Staple Singers* release *Be Attitude: Respect Yourself* on **Stax Records**. The album reached #3 on the Top Soul Albums charts and #19 on Pop. Most noted singles: *Respect Yourself,* reached #12 on the Pop charts, and #2 on Soul charts, while *I'll Take You There* reached #1 on Pop and Soul.

This year, 1972, Jazz Pianist *Herbie Hancock* releases *Crossings* on **Warner Brothers Records**. This album was the 2nd of his to feature electronic sounds as well as the talent of *Patrick Gleeson* on synthesizer.

This year, 1972, The Four Tops release *Keeper of the Castle* on **Dunhill Records**. The album's most noted single, *Aint No Woman (Like the One I've Got)* went on to be a hit.

⇒ **Fashion**: **In 1972**, women wore shirtwaist dresses, cashmere pullovers, and cardigans as well as wrapped jackets and pants. Men wore sports jackets, fitted pants, and jeans. Plaid, hounds tooth checks, and Donegal tweeds were the most popular print designs.

⇒ **Magazine News**: **This year 1972,** *Jermaine Jackson* lands the cover of *Right On*.

1972 – Billboard's Year End – Hot 100 Singles

1972	Urban Music 33% of Billboard's Year-End Hot 100	33%
1	Roberta Flack – *The First Time Ever I Saw Your Face*	Atlantic
5	Sammy Davis, Jr. – *The Candy Man*	MGM
6	Joe Tex – *I Gotcha*	Dial
7	Bill Withers – *Lean On Me*	Sussex
11	Al Green – *Let's Stay Together*	Hi
13	The Chi-Lites – *Oh Girl*	Brunswick
15	Chuck Berry – *My Ding-A-Ling*	Chess
16	Luther Ingram – *(If Loving You is Wrong) I Don't Want to be Right*	KoKo
18	The Stylistics – *Betcha by Golly Wow*	Avco
19	The Staple Singers – *I'll Take You There*	Stax
20	Michael Jackson – *Ben*	Motown
22	Billy Preston – *OutaSpace*	A&M
23	War – *Slippin into Darkness*	United Artist
29	The Main Ingredient – *Everybody Plays the Fool*	RCA
31	The 5th Dimension – *(Last Night) I Didn't Get to Sleep at All*	Bell
34	Cornelius Brothers & Sister Rose – *Too Late to Turn Back Now*	United Artist
35	The O'Jays – *Back Stabbers*	Philadelphia International
41	Michael Jackson – *Rockin Robin*	Motown
49	Betty Wright – *Clean Up Woman*	Alston
53	The Dramatics – *In the Rain*	Volt
54	Al Green – *Look What You Done for Me*	Hi
58	Roberta Flack & Donny Hathaway – *Where is the Love*	Atlantic
59	Al Green – *I'm Still in Love with You*	Hi
61	Aretha Franklin – *Day Dreaming*	Atlantic
74	Charley Pride – *Kiss an Angel Good Morning*	RCA
78	Bill Withers – *Use Me*	Sussex
79	Sly & The Family Stone – *Family Affair*	Epic
82	Curtis Mayfield – *Freddie's Dead*	Curtom/Buddah
84	Jerry Butler & Brenda Lee Eager – *Ain't Understanding Mellow*	Mercury
95	The Detroit Emeralds – *Baby Let Me Take You (In My Arms)*	Westbound
98	Love Unlimited – *Walkin in the Rain with the One I Love*	UNI
99	James Brown – *Get on the Good Foot*	Polydor
100	The Isley Brothers – *Pop that thang*	T-Neck

1972 – Record Labels in Urban Music

Atlantic Records: The label charted at #1 with Roberta Flacks' *The First Time Ever I Saw Your Face,* #58 with Donny Hathaway & Roberta Flacks' *Where is the Love.* They also charted again at #61 with Aretha Franklin's *Day Dreaming.* The company is a subsidiary of Warner Bros. – Seven Arts.

MGM Records: The label reached number #5 with *The Candy Man,* a classic by Sammy Davis, Jr. MGM, however, would be later purchased this year by Polygram Records and would be eventually phased out.

Dial Records: The Nashville based label pinned one of its first hits with Joe Tex hot track titled *"I Gotcha"* when it reached #6 on Billboard.

Sussex Records: The LA based label pinned two hits this year thanks to Bill Withers' #7 classic, *Lean On Me* and his #78 hit, *Use Me.*

Hi Records: With three hits on the Billboard 100, the label had a record-breaking year. Al Green, however, would be the man that made it happened with his #11 chart topper, *Let's Stay Together,* #54 ballad, *Look What You Done to Me,* and #59 hit, *I'm Still in Love with You.*

Brunswick Records: The MCA run label managed to pin another hit with The Chi-Lites', *Oh Girl* charting at #13, but it was clear that their imprint was not as robust as it once was.

Chess Records: Originally founded in 1950, the Chicago based label, after several R&B and Pop hits from years past, would for the 1st time hit the top of the Billboard Hot 100, and it was Chuck Berry's *My Ding-A-Ling* that charted at end of the year at #15 on the year-end Hot 100 Singles list.

KoKo Records: The label proved that you can be small and still pin a hit when they charted #16 this year with Luther Ingram's classic *(If Loving You is Wrong) I Don't Want to be Right.* The small label was owned by manager and record producer Johnny Baylor.

Avco Records: Originally started in 1968 by producers and composers Hugo Peretti, Luigi Creator, and Joseph E. Levine as Avco Embassy Records, the label charted #18 with *Betcha by Golly Wow* by The Stylistics.

Stax Records: Still on a roll the label charted #19 this year with The Staple Singer's *I'll Take You There.*

Motown Records: With the rise of new kid sensation Michael Jackson, the label pinned two hits by the young star, #20 *Ben,* and #41 *Rockin' Robin*. These only a couple from a long list of previous and future hits to come.

A&M Records: The label pinned a #22 hit on the Hot 100 this year with Billy Preston's *Outta Space.*

United Artist: The label ended the year with the classic *Slippin into Darkness* by WAR at #23 and *Too late to Turn Back Now* by Cornelius Brothers and Sister Rose at #34.

RCA Records: The label charted #29 with a classic by The Main Ingredient called *Everybody Plays the Fool* and #74 with *Kiss an Angel Good Morning* by Charley Pride.

Bell Records: The label charted another hit from their bestselling group, The 5th Dimension called *(Last Night) I didn't Go to Sleep at All* which placed at #31.

Philadelphia International Records: Originally founded in 1971 by writers and producers, Kenneth Gamble and Leon Huff whose goal was to showcase Philly Soul, this year would be the one to pin a classic by one of its most prolific groups, The O'Jays who charted the year end Hot 100 with *Back Stabbers.*

Alston Records: Originally founded in 1964 by Steve Alaimo and Henry Stone, Alston charted at #49 with Betty Wright's classic *Clean Up Woman.*

Volt Records: The Stax, Atlantic, Atco subsidiary made the year end Hot 100 with a classic by The Dramatics called *In the Rain.*

Epic Records: With the classic by Sly and The Family Stone called *Family Affair* charting year end at #79, the label would continue its prolific catalogue of hits.

Curtom Records: Cashing in yet again on his own talents, Curtis Mayfield ended the year on the Hot 100 with *Freddie's Dead*, a track from the Super Fly movie soundtrack, charting at #82.

Mercury Records: Originally formed in 1945 in the city of Chicago by Irving Green, Berle Adams, Arthur Talmadge, and Ray Greenberg. In the early years the label made most of their bones in jazz, blues, classical, country, and rock & roll. This year, however, they managed to end the year at #84 with Jerry Butler & Brenda Lee Eager's *Aint Understanding Mellow.*

Westbound Records: The label ended the year at #95 with *Baby Let Me Take You (In My Arms)* by The Detroit Emeralds.

UNI Records: aka Universal City Records was originally established in 1966 by MCA, Inc. executive Ned Tanen and developed by Russ Regan. In early 1971 Uni was merged with Kapp and Decca to form MCA Records and Uni label would be used to release new music until later this year. In the midst of the merger, the label did manage to chart the year end at #98 with *Walkin in the Rain with the One I Love* by Love Unlimited.

Polydor Records: Originally an independent branch of a label based in Germany which was first used in 1924, it didn't become a popular music label until 1946 and made it's real claim to fame in the early 1960's when it signed the now legendary group The Beatles. It then opened a USA branch in 1969 and didn't really become a presence in America until it purchased the contract and back catalog of ***James Brown*** in 1971. Its parent company Polygram would also go on to absorb the MGM Records label. Needless to say, it ended this year on the year end Hot 100 at #99 with James Brown's classic *Get On the Good Foot*.

T-Neck Records: Originally founded by The Isley Brothers in 1964, they would hit the year end Hot 100 at #100 with their hit *Pop That Thing*. This would be one of the few songs that the group released on their own label. It should also be noted that the label would be one of the first to nationally distribute recordings of their guitarist Jimi Hendrix.

Circa 1973

- ⇒ **Sports**: On January 1, 1973, *CBS* **(Columbia Broadcasting System)** sells the New York Yankees to George Steinbrenner and 11 other partners for $10 Million. CBS profited $3.2 Million from the deal.
- ⇒ **Drugs**: On January 3, 1973, New York Governor Nelson Rockefeller called for a mandatory 15-year to life long sentence for drug dealers and addicts. It included even those caught with small amounts. This was the beginning of overpopulated prisons and all that comes with that.

On January 14, 1973, Hip Hop pioneer, LL Cool J turns 5. *(Born 1-14-1968)*

- ⇒ **Politics**: On January 15, 1973; President Richard Nixon announces the suspension of attacks in North Vietnam. On the 27th, Nixon would sign the Paris Peace Accords to end U.S involvement in Vietnam.
- ⇒ **Film News—Blaxploitation**: On January 19, 1973; American International releases *"Black Mama White Mama"* starring **Pam Grier** and **Margaret Markov** the film was directed by *Eddie Romero*.
- ⇒ **TV News—Soul Train**: On January 6, 13 & 27, 1973 Curtis Mayfield, The Main Ingredient, Hank Ballard – Stevie Wonder, The Moments, Fully Guaranteed - Johnny Nash, Billy Butler & Infinity and Brighter Side of Darkness were guests.

On January 28, 1973, Hip Hop legend Rakim of Eric B & Rakim turns 5. *(Born 1-28-1968)*

- ⇒ **TV News—Music**: February 2, 1973, **NBC** premieres its music based late night TV show called *The Midnight Special*. The show featured guest appearances from recording artists and comedians alike; it was the first of its kind that showcased live performances.
- ⇒ **Film—Blaxploitation**: On February 7, 1973, American International Pictures releases *"Black Caesar"* starring **Fred Wiiliamson, Julius Harris** and **Gloria Hendry**. **James Brown** was responsible for the soundtrack.

On February 21, 1973, *The Temptations* release *Masterpiece* on **Gordy Records**. This album received mediocre reviews from fans and critics alike, but spite all the negative criticism, it became a #1 hit on the R&B Singles charts and #7 on the Hot 100. Norman Whitfield, yet again, proved that he was a hit maker as other tracks from the album like *Papa was a Rolling Stone* hit #40 on the Hot 100 and *Hey Girl (I Like Your Style)* also became a hit.

TV News—Soul Train: On February 3, 10, 17 & 24, 1973, The Dramatics, Syl Johnson, The Smith Connection – James Brown, Lin Collins – The Four Tops, Otis Clay, James Brown & Teddy Brown – The Spinners & Sister Love all were featured guests. *The Soul Train Dance Contest Semifinals* was also so held on the 17th.

In February 1973, *James Brown* releases *Black Caesar* soundtrack for the movie of the same name on **Polydor Records**. The album received mixed reviews and only one single from the album made the charts. *Down and Out in New York City* charted #13 on the R&B charts and #50 on the Pop charts. The track was written by Bodie Chandler and Barry De Vorzon.

⇒ **Film News—Blaxploitation:** On March 28, 1973, **Russ Meyer** releases *"Blacksnake"* starring **Anouska Hempel, Percy Herbert** and **David Warbeck**.

⇒ **TV News—Soul Train: On March 3, 10 & 31, 1973, Al Green, Mel & Tim – Friends of Distinction, Timmy Thomas, The Independents, Richard Pryor – The Chi-Lites, The Honey Cone, G.C. Cameron & Pam Grier** blessed the Soul Train stage.

On March 27, 1973, *Barry White* releases *I've Got So Much to Give* on **20th Century Records**. The album reached #16 on Billboard 200 and topped the R&B charts. Singles *I'm Gonna Love You Just a Little More Baby* and *I've Got So Much to Give* reached the R&B Top 10. Also garnering top positions on the Hot 100 and UK singles charts, this album was indeed a hit.

On March 29, 1973, *The Jackson 5* release their 8th studio album *Skywriter* on **Motown Records**. This would go down as one of the lowest selling albums ever by J5. At this point, Michael was maturing and the content that the group took on wasn't a good fit. The fans nor the group seemed to agree with its new direction.

On March 30, 1973, *Herbie Hancock* releases *Sextant* on *Columbia Records*. This would be the 1st album Hancock recorded with Columbia, but because of his direction, the album would receive poor sales which would alter his next project for the better.

In March of 1973, *The Chi-Lites* release *A Letter to Myself* on *Brunswick Records*. Several singles went on to chart, with most noted being *We Need Order* which charted #13 on the R&B charts. This would be their third consecutive album to make the R&B Top 5. The album was produced mostly by Eugene Record.

In March of 1973, Gladys Knight and & the Pips release *Neither One of Us* on **Soul Records,** a Motown label. This would be the last album released on the label while signed to Motown. The group scored #2 on the Pop charts and #1 on the R&B charts with its titled track. They would later go on to sign with **Buddah Records**.

Hip-Hop (Poetry, Social, Conscious): In the year of 1973, poet Jala Mansur Nuriddin aka Lightning Rod of *The Last Poets* released his street classic album *Hustlers Convention* and introduced the masses to the underground lifestyle of the hustler. Jala is the original emcee, the first to put reality rap on wax and his work will never be forgotten.

Jala Mansur Nuriddin the Godfather of Rap

City: *Brooklyn, New York*

1973 – Urban American Grammy Award Recipients – 15th Annual

Awards, 1973: Roberta Flack & producer, Joel Dorn win Record of the Year *(The First Time Ever I Saw Your Face)*.

Awards, 1973: Ewan MacColl, songwriter, wins Song of the Year *(The First Time Ever I Saw Your Face)*.

Awards, 1973: Aretha Franklin wins Best Soul Gospel performance *(Amazing Grace)*.

Awards, 1973: Freddie Hubbard wins Best Jazz Performance by a Group *(First Light)*.

Awards, 1973: Duke Ellington wins Best Jazz Performance by a Big Band *(Togo Brava Suite)*.

Awards, 1973: Donny Hathaway & Roberta Flack win Best Pop Vocal Performance by a Duo *(Where is the Love)*.

Awards, 1973: Billy Preston wins Best Pop Instrumental Performance by an Instrumental Performer *(Outta Space)*.

Awards, 1973: Isaac Hayes wins Best Pop Instrumental Performance with Vocal Coloring *(Black Moses)*.

Awards, 1973: Aretha Franklin wins Best R&B Vocal Performance by a Female *(Young, Gifted and Black)*.

Awards, 1973: Billy Paul wins Best R&B Vocal Performance by a male *(Me and Mrs. Jones)*.

Awards, 1973: The Temptations win Best R&B Vocal Performance by a Duo, Group or Chorus *(Papa Was a Rollin' Stone)*.

Awards, 1973: Norman Whitfield & Paul Riser win Best R&B Instrumental *(Papa Was a Rollin' Stone)*.

Awards, 1973: Songwriters, Norman Whitfield & Barrett Strong win Best R&B *(Papa Was a Rollin' Stone)*.

- ⇒ **News—Invention: On April 3, 1973, Martin Cooper** makes the first handheld cellular phone call in New York City.
- ⇒ **New York News: On April 4, 1973, The World Trade Center** opens in New York.
- ⇒ **Film News—Blaxploitation: On April 11, 1973, AVCO Embassy Pictures** releases *"Book of Numbers"* starring **Raymond St. Jacques, Philip Michael Thomas** and **Freda Payne**. The film was directed by *Raymond St. Jacques*.

On April 13, 1973, *Bob Marley & The Wailers* release *Catch a Fire* on **Island Records**. This would be the 1st album the group released on Island, but its 5th album over all. *Catch a Fire* reached #51 on the Billboard 200 and was also listed as #126 on Rolling Stone Magazine's list of 500 Greatest Albums of All Times. Marley wrote all of the tracks, with the exception of two that were written by Peter Tosh.

On April 13, 1973, Michael Jackson releases *Music & Me* on **Motown Records;** although this was his 3rd solo album, Michael wasn't happy with the project for several reasons, and this would eventually lead to the Jackson 5 leaving Motown. The title track reached #14 on the R&B charts while another single, *Happy* reached #31 in Australia and #52 in the UK.

On April 18, 1973, The Miracles release *Renaissance* on **Tamla Records**. This would be the first album not to feature lead singer Smokey Robinson but Billy Griffin instead. The single *Don't Let It End* reached #26 on the R&B charts, but the album itself only reached #174 on the Pop charts, nothing like their prior success with Smokey at the lead.

In April of 1973, Al Green releases *Call Me* on **Hi Records**. This album came to be an instant classic. It reached #1 on the Soul Album charts and reached Billboard's Top 10 Pop charts. Three singles from the album reached the Top 10: *Call Me*, *You Ought to Be with Me*, and *Here I am (Come and Take Me)*.

⇒ **TV News — Soul Train: On April 7, 14, 21 & 28, 1973, The Impressions, Tyrone Davis, Billy Preston, Diana Ross, Brenda Sykes – Aretha Franklin & Cecil Franklin – The O'Jays, David Ruffin, Sylvia – The Sylvers, Ronnie Dyson, Archie Bell, The Drells & Rosie Grier** all appeared.

In April of 1973, *The Spinners* release *Spinners* on **Atlantic Records**. The album pinned a #1 hit with *I'll be Around* along with chart toppers, *How Could I Let You Get Away, Could It Be I'm Falling in Love,* and *One of a Kind (Love Affair).* The album would reach #14 on the Top 20 and much credit went to producer Thom Bell. This was an awesome start for The Spinners being that they just left *Motown* and signed with *Atlantic*; not too bad for their first album with a new label.

⇒ **Film News—Blaxploitation:** On April 4, 1973, Cinerama Releasing Corporation releases *"The Mack"* starring **Max Julien** and **Richard Pryor**. The film was directed by *Michael Campus.*

⇒ **Film News—Blaxploitation:** On April 18, 1973, David Paradine Productions releases *"Charley One-Eye"* starring **Richard Roundtree** and **John Cameron**.

⇒ **Film News—Blaxploitation:** In 1973, Warner Bros. releases *"Cleopatra Jones"* starring **Tamara Dobson**. The film was directed by *Jack Starrett.*

⇒ **Film News—Blaxploitation:** On April 20, 1973, **Chiz Schultz** produced *"Ganja & Hess"* starring **Marlene Clark** and **Duane Jones**. The film was written and directed by *Bill Gunn.*

⇒ **Film News—Blaxploitation:** On May 16, 1973, **Paramount Pictures** releases *"The Soul of N***** Charley"* starring **Fred Williamson**. The film was directed by *Larry Spangler.*

In May of 1973, Earth, Wind & Fire release *Head to the Sky* on **Columbia Records**. The album pinned two hot singles, *Evil* and *Keep Your Head To The Sky*, which are still favorites to this day. *Head to the Sky* reached #2 on the Black Albums charts and went on to be certified platinum.

⇒ **TV News—Soul Train: On May 5, 12, 19 & 26, 1973, The Manhattans, Lyn Collins, Lee Auston, James Brown – The Supremes, Lloyd Price – Bobby Womack, The Whispers, Thelma Houston – Little Anthony & The Imperials, Edwin Starr & The Valentinos** were guests.

On May 13, 1973, Hip Hop legend Parrish Smith aka PMD of *EPMD*, turns 5. *(Born 5-13-1968)*

In May of 1973, Pointer Sisters releases *The Pointer Sisters* on **Blue Thumb Records**. The album charted at #13 on Billboards 200 and #3 on the R&B charts. It's most noted singles, *Yes We Can Can* and *Wang Dang Doodle* helped them go certified gold.

⇒ **Film News—Blaxploitation:** In May of 1973, **New World Pictures** releases *"Savage"* starring **James Inglehart** and **Lada Edmund, Jr.** Directed by *Cirio H. Santiago*.

In May of 1973, *Tower of Power* release their self-titled album *Tower of Power* on **Warner Bros. Records**. The album went gold and reached #15 on Billboard's Top LPs, while it's most noted single, *So Very Hard to Go*, reached #17 on the Hot 100.

⇒ **Film News—Blaxploitation: On May 25, 1973, MGM** releases "*Sweet Jesus, Preacherman*" starring **Roger Mosley** and **William Smith**. The film was directed by *Henning Schellerup*.

⇒ **Politics**: **On May 29, 1973, Tom Bradley** becomes the first black Mayor elected in the city of Los Angeles

⇒ **News: In May of 1973, Black Panther and Activist, Assata Shakur** is accused of killing a New Jersey State Trooper on the turnpike after being shot twice herself. Shakur has been charged with several crimes and had several of them dismissed or acquitted. As a former member of the Black Liberation Army, she maintains her innocence and has since left the country.

⇒ **Film News—Blaxploitation: In May of 1973, Wrigthwood Entertainment** releases "*Brother on the Run*" starring **Terry Carter** and **Gwenn Mitchell**. The film was directed by *Edward J. Lakso* and *Herbert L. Strock*.

⇒ **Film News—Blaxploitation: On June 13, 1973, American International Pictures** releases "*Coffy*" starring **Pam Grier**. The film was directed by *Jack Hill*.

⇒ **Film News—Blaxploitation: On June 14, 1973, Metro-Goldwyn-Mayer** releases "*Shaft in Africa*" starring **Richard Roundtree**. Directed by *John Guillermin*.

⇒ **Film News—Blaxploitation: On June 15, 1973, Paramount Pictures** releases "*Super Fly T.N.T*" starring **Ron O'Neal**. The film was also directed by *Ron O'Neal*.

⇒ **TV News—Soul Train: On June 16, 23 & 30, 1973, Bill Wilthers, Steve Manning – The Miracles, Chuck Jackson, The Jackson Sisters, Smokey Robinson – Chairman of the Board, Charles Mann, Sylvia and Jeffrey Bowen** were guests.

On June 19, 1973, *Smokey Robinson* releases *Smokey* on **Tamla Records**. This would be Smokey's first solo album, and it pinned a #7 hit with *Baby Come Close*, which received great reviews.

On June 22, 1973, Diana Ross releases *Touch Me in the Morning* on **Motown Records**. The album reached #1 on the R&B charts and pinned a #1 hit with the title track. That same track gave Diana her 2nd #1 hit, while the album also charted #5 on Billboard 200.

⇒ **Film News — Blaxploitation:** In 1973, **General Film Corporation** releases "*Detroit 9000*" starring **Hari Rhodes** and **Alex Rocco**. The film was directed by *Arthur Marks*.

On June 25, 1973, Aretha Franklin releases *Hey Now Hey (The Other Side of the Sky)* on *Atlantic Records*. The album reached #30 on the charts, but received mixed reviews from critics. Her single, *Angel* charted #1 on the R&B charts and reached #20 on the Pop charts.

⇒ **Film News: On June 27, 1973, United Artist** releases "*Live and Let Die*" starring **Roger Moore, Yaphet Kotto** and **Gloria Hendry**. The film was directed by *Guy Hamilton*.

⇒ **Film News—Blaxploitation: On June 27, 1973, American International Pictures** releases "*Scream Blacula Scream*" starring **William H. Marshall**. The film was directed by *Bob Kelljan*.

⇒ **TV News—Music: In 1973, Dick Clark**, founder of *American Bandstand*, releases *Soul Unlimited* on the *ABC* network to compete with *Soul Train*. The show was canceled, however, due to protest from *Soul Train's* founder *Don Cornelius* and activist, *Jesse Jackson*. They stated that Clark's *Soul Unlimited* was trying to undermine TV's only Black-owned show.

On June 30, 1973, Sly & the Family Stone release *Fresh* on *Epic Records*. The album pinned a #3 R&B hit with *If You Want Me to Stay*, and the single also charted #12 on the Pop charts.

⇒ **Drugs: On July 1, 1973, The *DEA* (Drug Enforcement Administration)** is founded.
⇒ **TV News—Soul Train: On July 7, 1973, Chuck Berry, Maxayan, Willie Hutch and Max Julien** blessed the Soul Train stage.

On July 9, 1973, Funkadelic releases *Cosmic Slop* on ***Westbound Records***. The album received mixed reviews and reached #21 on the R&B charts, but pinned no hit singles.

In July of 1973, *Rufus* releases their self-titled album *Rufus* on ***ABC Records***. Lead by Chaka Khan and Ron Stockert, the album reached #44 on the R&B charts. It pinned two notable singles, *Feel Good* and *Whoever's Thrilling You (Is Killing Me)*.

On August 1, 1973, *Roberta Flack* releases *Killing Me Softly* on **Atlantic Records**. The album reached #2 on the Soul charts and #3 on Billboard Top LPs. It also went certified gold 26 days after its release.

On August 3, 1973, *Stevie Wonder* releases *Innervisions* on **Tamla Records**. The album reached #4 on the album charts and featured three hit singles, *Higher Ground, Living for the City,* and *Don't You Worry 'Bout a Thing*. It also reached the Top 10 in the UK.

⇒ **South Carolina News: On August 6, 1973,** just 3 days after the release of *Innervisions*, Stevie Wonder gets into a fatal accident while leaving a performance in Greenville, South Carolina. While asleep in the passenger seat on the road driving through Durham, North Carolina, Wonder's friend John Harris was driving behind a log truck, when it stopped abruptly causing logs to slip off the rig. Unfortunately, one came through the front window hitting Stevie in the forehead. The accident placed him in critical condition, while swelling his head to an irregular size causing Wonder to fall into a coma for 4 days with a severe brain contusion.

On August 7, 1973, *The Isley Brothers* releases *3+3* on **T-Neck Records**. The album would be their first platinum album and featured several hits, *It's Your Thing, That Lady, "Summer Breeze,* and *What It Comes Down To.*

⇒ **Film News—Blaxploitation:** On August 8, 1973, **American International Pictures** releases *"Heavy Traffic"* starring *Joseph Kaufmann, Beverly Hope Atkinson* and *Frank Devoka*. The film was directed by *Ralph Bakshi.*

⇒ **Film News—Blaxploitation:** On August 9, 1973, **20th Century Fox** releases *"Gordon's of War"* starring *Paul Winfield*. The film was directed by *Ossie Davis.*

⇒ **Film News—Blaxploitation:** In 1973, **Exclusive International** releases horror movie *"Blackenstein"* starring *John Hart* and *Andrea King*. The film was directed by *William A. Levey.*

On August 7, 1973, *Labelle* releases *Pressure Cookin'* on **RCA**. Patti LaBelle and band mates pinned a few notable tracks, but the album didn't do well overall. To make matters worse, group member Cindy Birdsong left the group to join The Supremes prior to this album's release.

⇒ **Hip-Hop — Back to School Jam: August 11, 1973, DJ Kool Herc** throws his back to school jam at *1520 Sedgweck Ave.*, Rec Room in The Bronx, New York. This would go down as the 1st official Hip-Hop party that would display the Merry-Go-Round-Style of the Hip Hop DJ, originated by Kool Herc.

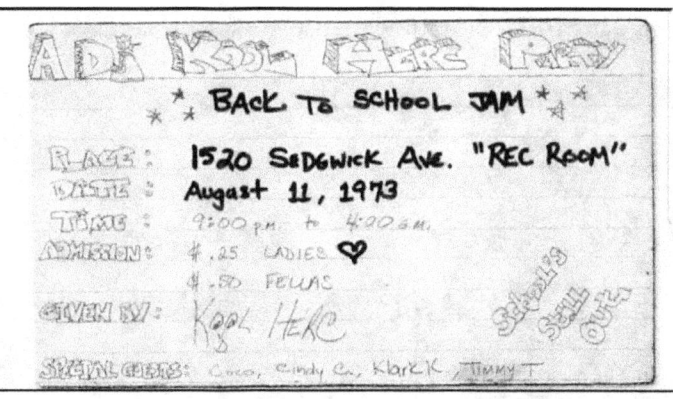

On August 28, 1973, *Marvin Gaye* releases *Let's Get It On* on *Tamla Records*. The album charted three singles, *Let's Get It On*, *Come Get to This*, and *You Sure Love to Ball*; needless to say, the album went on to be a classic.

In August on 1973, *Chuck Berry* releases *Bio* on *Chess Records*.

⇒ **Drugs & Government**: To help combat the trafficking of cocaine, heroin, and marijuana into the United States, the DEA opened foreign offices in Islamabad, Pakistan / Mazatlan, Mexico and Ottawa, Canada.

In August of 1973, *War* releases *Deliver the Word* on **United Artist Records**. The album charted several singles, and the title track pinned #8 in the US.

⇒ **TV News—Soul Train: On August 11 & 25, 1973, The Best of Soul Trains** airs featuring **James Brown, The Jackson 5, Chuck Berry, The O'Jays, The Temptations, Al Green, Curtis Mayfield, The Supremes, Teddy Brown, The Four Tops & Stevie Wonder – The Intruders, Foster Sylvers, Edmund and Ricky Sylvers** appear on the 1st episode of the 3rd season.
⇒ **Film News—Blaxploitation: On August 31, 1973, American International Pictures** releases *"Slaughters Big Rip Off"* starring *Jim Brown*. The film was directed by *Gordon Douglas*.
⇒ **TV News—American Bandstand: On September 8, 1973,** featured guest was **Curtis Mayfield**.

TV News—Soul Train: On September 1, 8, 15, 22 & 29, 1973, featured guests were, **The Whispers, Mandrill – Fred Wesley & the JB's, Lyn Collins & The Sly, the Slick and the Wicked – The Sylvers – The Isley Brothers, Betty Wright, Jr., Walker & The All-Stars – Eddie Kendricks, The Dramatics & Rufus.**

On September 8, 1973, Hip Hop legend Big Daddy Kane turns 5. *(Born 9-5-1968)*

On September 12, 1973, The Jackson 5 releases *G.I.T.: Get It Together* on *Motown Records*. Although J5 was not happy at the label, the album went on to sell over two million copies without any tracks charting in the top 10.

⇒ **Film News—Blaxploitation:** On September 18, 1973, Paramount Pictures releases *"Hit!"* starring **Billy Dee Williams** and **Richard Pryor**. The film was directed by *Sidney J. Furie*.

On September 21, 1973, *Billy Preston* releases *Everybody Likes Some Kind of Music* on ***A&M Records***. The album charted at #3 on the R&B charts and pinned two hit singles, *Space Race*, which hit #1 on the R&B Singles charts, and *You're So Unique* at #11.

In September of 1973, Kool & the Gang release *Wild and Peaceful* on **De-Lite Records**. The album produced three hit singles, *Funky Stuff, Jungle Boogie,* and *Hollywood Swinging*; all three tracks broke the Top 10 while the album itself reached #6 on the R&B charts.

⇒ **Film News—Blaxploitation:** In September of 1973, **United Artist** releases *"I Escaped from Devils Island"* starring **Jim Brown** and **Christopher George**. The film was directed by *William Witney*.

⇒ **Film News—Blaxploitation:** On September 21, 1973, **United Artist** releases *"The Spook Who Sat by the Door"* starring **Lawrence Cook** and **Paula Kelly**. The film was directed by *Ivan Dixon*.

⇒ **Film News—Blaxploitation:** On September 26, 1973, **MGM** releases *"The Slams"* starring **Jim Brown** and **Judy Pace**. The film was directed by *Jonathan Kaplan*.

⇒ **TV News—Soul Train:** On October 6, 13 & 27, 1973, **B.B King, The Moments – The Four Tops, Bloodstone, Lee Charles – Barry White, Love Unlimited, The Temprees & Lola Falana** were all featured guests.

⇒ **TV News—American Bandstand:** On October 13, 1973, **Johnny Taylor** was the featured guest.

On October 2, 1973, *Barry White* releases *Stone Gon'* on **20th *Century Records***. The album charted two hit singles, *Never, Never Gonna Give Ya Up,* and *Honey Please, Can't Ya See,* while the album topped the R&B charts as well as the UK charts.

⇒ **Atlanta News: On October 16, 1973, Maynard Jackson** becomes the 1st Black mayor of Atlanta, GA, and also the first of a major southern city.

On October 19, 1973, *Bob Marley and The Wailers* release *Burnin'* on **Island Records**. The album reached #41 on the Billboard 200 and also includes the classic hits. *Get Up, Stand Up,* and *I Shot the Sheriff*.

On October 26, 1973, *Diana Ross and Marvin Gaye* release *Diana & Marvin* on **Motown Records**. The duet album reached #7 on the R&B charts in the U.S and #6 in the UK.

⇒ **Film News — Blaxploitation:** **On October 25, 1973, United Artist** releases *"Five on the Black Hand Side"* starring **Clarice Taylor, Leonard Jackson** and **Virginia Capers**. The film was directed by *Oscar Williams*.

On October 26, 1973, Herbie Hancock releases *Head Hunters* on **Columbia Records**. Two notable tracks, *Chameleon* and *Watermelon Man,* would go on to push the album to classic status and earn a spot on Rolling Stones Greatest Albums of All Times Top 500 list.

In October of 1973, *Gladys Knight & the Pips* release *Imagination* on **Buddah Records**. Two of the album singles charted at #1 on the R&B Singles charts, *Best Thing That Ever Happened to Me* and *I've Got to Use My Imagination*, while *Midnight Train to Georgia* reached #1 on Billboard Hot 100.

In October of 1973, *Quincy Jones* releases *You've Got It Bad Girl* on **A&M Records**. The album was compiled with several covers of music from artists such as Stevie Wonder and Aretha Franklin, and the album reached #1 on the Jazz charts.

On November 10, 1973, *The O' Jays* release *Ship Ahoy* on **Philadelphia International Records**. The album spawned a hit single and soul classic, *For the Love of Money*, while the album itself reached #1 on the Black Albums chart.

On November 16, 1973, The DEA 1st Special Agent class of 40 graduated from Basic Training making Nixon's War on Drugs official.

On November 11, 1973, Hip Hop legend Eric Sermon of *EPMD* turns 5. *(Born 11-25-1968)*

On December 6, 1973, *Diana Ross* releases *Last Time I Saw Him* on **Motown Records**. The album reached #12 on the R&B charts, as the title track reached #1 on Adult Contemporary and #35 in the UK.

⇒ **TV News — Soul Train: On November 3, 10, 17 & 24, 1973, The Jackson 5 – Curtis Mayfield, Millie Jackson, Natural Four – Tower of Power, The Pointer Sisters, Tavares – Smokey Robinson, First Choice and Al Wilson** were featured guests.

On December 6, 1973, *Al Green* releases *Livin' for You* on **Hi Records**. Like many times before, Al would hit #1 on the Soul Album charts and pen a few hit singles in the process. *Unchained Melody* and the title track would go on to be classics.

On December 7, 1973, *The Temptations* release *1990* on **Gordy Records**. The album produced only one hit, *Let Your Hair Down*; this was mostly in part due to the direction of the group and the socially conscious songs written by Norman Whitfield that the group didn't agree with.

- ⇒ **Music News**: **On December 15, 1973, Jermaine Jackson** marries Hazel Gordy, the daughter of **Motown** founder Berry Gordy.
- ⇒ **Film News—Blaxploitation:** On December 16, 1973, **American International Pictures** releases "Hell Up in Harlem" starring **Fred Williamson** and **Margaret Avery**. The film was directed by *Larry Cohen*.
- ⇒ **Film News—Blaxploitation:** In December of 1973, **Universal Pictures** releases "That Man Bolt" starring **Fred Williamson**. The film was directed by *David Lowell Rich* and *Henry Levin*.

In December of 1973, *James Brown* releases *The Payback* on **Polydor Records**. The album reached #1 on the Soul Album charts, and the title track peaked at #1 on the R&B Singles chart.

- ⇒ **TV News — Soul Train: On December 1, 8, 15 & 22, 1973, The Temptations, G.C. Cameron – Bobby Bland, Ashford & Simpson, Barbara Jean English – Johnnie Taylor, Ann Peebles, Maceo & The Macks – Eddie Kendricks, The Persuaders & Eddie Floyd** blessed the Soul Train stage.
- ⇒ **TV News — American Bandstand: On December 15, 1973, Billy Preston** appeared on American Bandstand.
- ⇒ **TV News — American Bandstand: On December 29, 1973, Eddie Kendricks** appeared on American Bandstand.

1973 – Billboards Year End – Hot 100 Singles

1973	Urban Music 32% of Billboards Year-End Hot 100	32%
3	**Roberta Flack** – *Killing Me Softly with His Song*	Atlantic
4	**Marvin Gaye** – *Let's Get It On*	Tamla
8	**Billy Preston** – *Will It Go 'Round in Circles*	A&M
10	**Diana Ross** – *Touch Me in the Morning*	Motown
15	**Billy Paul** – *Me and Mrs. Jones*	Phila Intnl.
17	**Dobie Gray** – *Drift Away*	Decca
19	**Stevie Wonder** – *You Are the Sunshine of My Life*	Tamla
21	**The Isley Brothers** – *That Lady*	United Artist
22	**Sylvia** – *Pillow Talk*	Vibration
26	**Stevie Wonder** – *Superstition*	Tamla
32	**The O'Jays** – *Love Train*	Phila Intnl.
33	**Barry White** – *I'm Gonna Love You Just a Little More Baby*	20th Century
37	**Eddie Kendricks** – *Keep on Truckin*	Tamla
39	**Bloodstone** – *Natural High*	London
43	**Sly & the Family Stone** – *If You Want Me to Stay*	Epic
44	**Jermaine Jackson** – *Daddy's Home*	Motown
45	**Gladys Knight & the Pips** – *Neither One of Us (Wants to Be the First to Say Goodbye)*	Motown
55	**WAR** – *The Cisco Kid*	United Artist
58	**Johnnie Taylor** – *I Believe in You (You Believe in Me)*	Stax
60	**The Four Tops** – *Ain't No Woman (Like the One I've Got)*	ABC/Dunhill
62	**Stevie Wonder** – *Higher Ground*	Tamla
63	**Al Green** – *Here I Am (Come And Take Me)*	Hi
65	**Curtis Mayfield** – *Superfly*	Curtom/Buddah
76	**Tower of Power** – *So Very Hard to Go*	Warner Bros.
80	**The Temptations** – *Masterpiece*	Motown
82	**The Spinners** – *One of A Kind (Love Affair)*	Atlantic
84	**Ohio Players** – *Funky Worm*	Westbound
88	**The Stylistics** – *Break Up to Make Up*	Avco
93	**WAR** – *Gypsy Man*	United Artist
94	**WAR** – *The World is a Ghetto*	United Artist
95	**The Pointer Sisters** – *Yes We Can Can*	Blue Thumb
100	**The Temptations** – *Papa Was a Rollin' Stone*	Gordy

1973 – Record Labels in Urban Music

Motown Records: Ten of the Hot 100 Singles belong to Barry Gordy and his incorporation of Motown labels such as *Gordy & Tamla*. With a roster of talent to include Stevie Wonder, Diana Ross, Marvin Gaye, Eddie Kendricks, Gladys Knight & the Pips, The Temptations, and Jermaine Jackson all topping the charts. Hitsville USA had again proved perfect.

Atlantic Records: With chart-topping classics from The Spinners and Roberta Flack, Atlantic added more hits to its diverse catalog.

A&M Records: Although its roster of urban artists wasn't as deep as some of its competition, the label managed to hit the charts with one of Billy Preston's best singles ever.

Philadelphia International Records: Not to be out done by their peers, the Phila sound continued to make noise with hits from The O'Jays and Billy Paul.

20th Century Records: As a subsidiary of 20th Century Film studios, the movie production company had gotten a big pay off with Barry White's single charting the Hot 100. Prior to 20th Century Records, the studio had two earlier labels that were now defunct, but had similar names *20th Century Fox Records* and *20th Fox Records*.

London Records: The UK label that was set up to market to the U.S, Latin America, and Canada after the split of *Decca Records* had managed to hit the charts with Bloodstone.

Epic Records: With the continued success of Sly and the Family Stone, the label would again benefit from another one of the band's hits.

United Artist Records: Originally founded to release movie soundtracks for its film production company, the label, over time, built a full-fledged record company with a profitable catalog of artists. It hit pay dirt this year when WAR charted three singles on the Hot 100.

Vibration Records: One of several subsidiaries of Sylvia and Joe Robinson's *All Platinum Records*, Sylvia the singer, writer, and producer had released a hit herself this year that finally charted the Billboard Hot 100.

Decca Records: Although some changes were made in the corporate structure of the label it did still release a Hot 100 hit by Dobie Gray.

ABC/Dunhill Records: Following a purchase of Dunhill Records in 1967, the ABC Dunhill label was formed and would purchase Duke Records, Peacock Records, Back Beat Records, and Song Bird Records in May of this year. This acquisition expanded *ABC's* catalog, originally formed under American Broadcasting – Paramount Theaters, now known as ABC. The label pinned a hit this year with The Four Tops charting a Hot 100 Single.

Hi Records: Once again the label found itself back on the Hot 100 with another Al Green hit. It seems Al had the golden touch.

Curtom Records: Curtis Mayfield scored big yet again, but this time with the soundtrack title song *Superfly* charting the Hot 100.

Stax Records: Even though their rival in Detroit pinned several hits on the Hot 100, Stax did manage to chart at least one with Johnnie Taylor.

Warner Brothers: Originally founded in 1958 as the recorded division of Warner Brothers Pictures, by this time Warner was still a small player in the music industry. It did, however, pin a Hot 100 hit this year with the R&B band Tower of Power.

Avco Records: Thanks to The Stylistics, the label again found a place on the Hot 100.

Blue Thumb Records: Originally founded in 1968 by Bob Krasnow, and former *A&M* executives, Tommy LiPuma and Don Graham. It was later purchased by *Gulf and Western's Famous Music Group* in the previous year. This year however, they hit the Hot 100 with a hit from The Pointer Sisters.

Circa 1974

⇒ **Magazine News**: January 1974, 1st African American supermodel, **Beverly Johnson** lands the cover of *Glamour*.

On January 9, 1974, *Blue Magic* release their self-titled album *Blue Magic* on **Atco Records**. The most noted single and classic, *Sideshow*, topped the R&B charts and also reached #8 on the Hot 100.

On January 11, 1974, *Bobby Womack* releases *Lookin' for Love Again* on **United Artist**. The title track reached #1 on the R&B charts while the album pinned #5 on the Pop charts. Womack's single also reached #10 on the Hot 100.

⇒ **TV News — Soul Train**: On January 5, 12 & 26, 1974, Billy Preston, Creative Source, Eric Mercury – Johnny Nash, Kool & the Gang, The Originals – The 5th Dimension & Willie Hutch were all featured guests.

⇒ **Film News — Blaxploitation**: On January 23, 1974, Universal Pictures released "*Willie Dynamite*" starring **Roscoe Orman** directed by *Gilbert Moses*.

⇒ **TV News**: On January 31, 1974, *The Autobiography of Miss Jane Pittman*, a former slave who lived to be 110 years old and lived through the Civil War up to the Civil Rights Movement, aired on **CBS**. Actress **Cicely Tyson** had the honor of playing the role.

In January of 1974, *The Love Unlimited Orchestra* released *Rhapsody in White* on **20th Century Records**. Lead by Barry White, their hottest track, *Love's Theme*, reached #1 on the Hot 100.

- ⇒ **Film News—Blaxploitation:** In January of 1974, **American International Pictures** released *"Bamboo Gods & Iron Men"*. *Cesar Gallardo* directed the film and *James Iglehart* played lead.
- ⇒ **Film News—Horror Blaxploitation:** On February 7, 1974, **American International Pictures** released *"Sugar Hill"* starring *Marki Bey*.
- ⇒ **TV News: On February 8, 1974, Good Times** aired on **CBS**. The popular sitcom based in Chicago's then Cabrini-Green Projects was created by *Michael Evans* and *Eric Monte*. (Michael Evans also played Lionel on The Jefferson's.)
- ⇒ **American Music Awards: On February 19, 1974** the very 1st AMA's are broadcasted on **ABC** just 2 weeks before the *Grammys*.

On February 25, 1974, *Aretha Franklin* releases *Let Me in Your Life* on **Atlantic Records**. The album was another #1 hit for the Queen of Soul topping the R&B charts. Her most noted singles were *Aint Nothing like the Real Thing, Until You Come Back to Me,* and *I'm in Love*.

On February 26, 1974, *Donna Summer* releases *Lady of the Night* on **Groovy Records**. Although the album was only released in The Netherlands, it did pin a hit with its single *The Hostage* in The Netherlands. This would be the first glimpse of the disco diva.

- ⇒ **Film News – Blaxploitation: In 1974 Warner Bros.** released "*Black Belt Jones*" with *Jim Kelly* playing lead. *Robert Clouse* directed the martial arts saga.

In February of 1974, *the Pointer Sisters* release *That's a Plenty* on **Blue Thumb Records**. This became their 2nd certified gold album and also spawned them to be the 1st African-American group to perform at the Grand Ole Opry.

- ⇒ **Magazine News: 1974, Michael Jackson** lands Number 5 cover of UK Magazine *Look-In*.
- ⇒ **TV News – Soul Train: On February 9, 16 & 23, 1974, Johnny Mathis, The Dells – Marvin Gaye, The Whispers – Harold Melvin & the Blue Notes, Billy Paul & Maxine Weldon**, were all featured guests.

1974 – Urban American
Grammy Award Recipients – 16th Annual

Awards, 1974: Producer Joel Dorn and Roberta Flack won Record of the Year *(Killing Me Softly With His Song)*.

Awards, 1974: Stevie Wonder won Album of the Year *(Innervisions)*.

Awards, 1974: Cheech and Chong won Best Comedy Recording *(Los Cochinos)*.

Awards, 1974: Quincy Jones won Best Instrumental Arrangement *(Summer in the City)*.

Awards, 1974: Roberta Flack won Best Pop Vocal Performance, Female *(Killing Me Softly with His Song)*.

Awards, 1974: Stevie Wonder won Best Pop Vocal Performance, Male *(You Are the Sunshine of My Life)*.

Awards, 1974: Gladys Knight & the Pips won Best Pop Vocal Performance by a Duo, Group or Chorus *(Wants to Be the First to Say Goodbye)*.

Awards, 1974: Aretha Franklin won Best R&B Vocal Performance, Female *(Master of Eyes)*.

Awards, 1974: Stevie Wonder won Best R&B Vocal Performance, Male *(Superstition)*.

Awards, 1974: Gladys Knight & the Pips won Best R&B Vocal Performance by a Duo, Group or Chorus *(Midnight Train to Georgia)*.

Awards, 1974: Ramsey Lewis won Best R&B Instrumental Performance *(Hang On Sloopy)*.

Awards, 1974: Stevie Wonder won as a songwriter for Best Rhythm & Blues Song *(Superstition)*.

⇒ **Film News — Blaxploitation: On March 13, 1974, Cinemation Industries** released "*The Black Six*" directed by *Matt Cimber* and starring **Gene Washington**.

On March 15, 1974, *Smokey Robinson* releases *Pure Smokey* on **Tamla Records**. This would be Smokey's 2nd solo album since departing from the Miracles. His most noted single, *Virgin Man*, was the album's only hit.

⇒ **Film News — Blaxploitation: In 1974, Paramount Pictures** released "*Three Tough Guys*" starring **Lino Ventura**, and directed by *Duccio Tessari* with music by *Isaac Hayes*.
⇒ **TV News — Soul Train: On March 2 & 30th, 1974, Jerry Butler, The Delfonics, Cecil Shaw – Curtis Mayfield, The Main Ingredient & Bloodstone** were featured guests.

On March 25, 1974, Earth, Wind & Fire release *Open Your Eyes* on **Columbia Records**. The album went to #1 on the R&B charts and spawned several classics, such as: *Devotion* and *Mighty Mighty*, which also reached the top of the R&B singles charts.

In March of 1974, The Delfonics release *Alive & Kicking* on **Philly Groove Records**. The album would be the group's last and did not do well as their previous released classics.

In March of 1974, *The Spinners* released a classic, *Mighty Love,* on **Atlantic Records**. The album shot to the top of the R&B charts as did the title track on the R&B Singles charts. The title track and *I'm Coming Home* both broke Billboard's Top 20.

On April 3, 1974, *Billy Preston* releases *Live European Tour* on *A&M Records*. Preston recorded his live performances while on tour with The Rolling Stones.

⇒ **Film News—Blaxploitation: On April 5, 1974, American International Pictures** released *"Foxy Brown"* starring **Pam Grier** and directed by *Jack Hill*.

On April 19, 1974, *Miles Davis* releases *Big Fun* on **Columbia Records**. Even though released as a double album, Davis didn't do so well on the initial release.

On April 29, 1974, Funkadelic releases *Standing on the Verge of Getting It On* on **Westbound Records**. The album pinned a #13 spot on the R&B Albums charts and went on to become a fan favorite.

⇒ **Film News—Blaxploitation: On April 19, 1974, American International Pictures** released *"Truck Turner"* starring **Isaac Hayes** directed by *Jonathan Kaplan*.

In April of 1974, *The Four Tops* release *Meeting of the Minds* on **ABC Records**. Unlike most of their prior releases, this one only charted #118 in the U.S.

⇒ **Magazine News: In April 1974, Billy D. Williams** lands cover of *Ebony*.

In April of 1974, The Ohio Players release *Skin Tight* on **Mercury Records**. Skintight went to #1 on the Black Albums chart and #11 on Pop.

⇒ **TV News — Soul Train: On April 6, 13, 20 & 27th, 1974, Al Green, The Impressions – The Stylisitics, Bobby Womack, The Undisputed Truth – The Four Tops, Blue Magic, Barbara Mason – Eddie Kendricks, The Dramatics & Martha Reeves** were featured guest.

On May 5, 1974, *Billy Preston* releases *The Kids & Me* on **A&M Records**. The album pinned two hit singles, *Nothing from Nothing,* and *You are So Beautiful*.

In May of 1974, *Tower of Power* releases *Back to Oakland* on **Warner Bros Records**. Its most noted tracks, *Time Will Tell* was #27 on the Dance charts, and *Don't Change Horses (In The Middle of a Stream)*, #22 on the R&B charts, helped the album reach #13 on Billboard Top Soul charts.

⇒ **Film News—Blaxploitation:** On May 17, 1974, *Warner Bros. Pictures* released "*Black Eye*" starring **Fred Williamson** directed by *Jack Arnold*.

In May of 1974, *Quincy Jones* releases *Body Heat* on **A&M Records**. The album reached #1 on the R&B charts as well as #1 on Jazz charts.

In May of 1974, *Diana Ross* releases *Live at Caesars Palace* on **Motown Records**. The album of her live performances in Las Vegas reached #15 on the R&B charts.

⇒ **Politics: On May 9, 1974, The U.S House of Representatives** opens impeachment hearings against *President Richard Nixon* for his role in the Watergate scandal.

TV News — Soul Train: On May 4, 11, 18 & 25th, 1974, Gladys Knight & the Pips, Lamont Dozier – Sylvia Robinson, The Moments, Ecstasy, Passion &Pain – The Spinners, The Independents, Leroy Hutson – Bill Wilthers, The Soul Children & Melvin Van Peebles were featured guests.

In May of 1974, *Rufus* releases *Rags to Rufus* on **ABC Records**. Lead by Chaka Khan, the album pinned the #4 spot on the Black Albums charts. Their most noted singles, *Tell Me Something Good* charted at #3 on both the Pop and R&B charts, while *You Got the Love* charted at #1 on R&B.

In May of 1974, Curtis Mayfield releases *Sweet Exorcist* on **Curtom Records**. The album, unlike his others, didn't pin any hits.

⇒ **Magazine News: In May of 1974, Esther Rolle** and **John Amos** land cover of *JET*.

In May of 1974, *Gil Scott-Heron* releases *Winter in America* on **Strata-East Records**. The album charted #6 on Billboard's Top Jazz Albums.

⇒ **Music News**: **On June 5, 1974, Sly of the Family Stone** married model-actress, Kathy Silva during a sold-out crowd in NYC at Madison Square Garden.

⇒ **Film News—Blaxploitation:** On June 26, 1974 **Allied Artists Pictures Corporation** released *"Three the Hard Way"* starring *Jim Brown, Fred Williamson* and *Jim Kelly*.

On June 28, 1974, *James Brown* releases *Hell* on **Polydor Records**. The album included three chart topping singles, *My Thang, Papa Don't Take No Mess,* and *Coldblooded*.

In June of 1974, *Ashford & Simpson* release *I Wanna Be Selfish* on **Warner Bros. Records**. The album reached #21 on the R&B charts.

In June of 1974, *The Chi-Lites* release *Toby* on **Brunswick Records**. Toby reached #12 on the R&B charts.

⇒ **Atlanta News: On June 30, 1974,** *Alberta Christine Williams King,* the Mother of the late *Martin Luther King, Jr.*, was shot and killed during church service at *Ebenezer Baptist Church* in *Atlanta, GA.* by Ohio native, Marcus Wayne Chenault while sitting at the organ.

⇒ **Magazine News**: **In June of 1974, Cicely Tyson** lands cover of *People*.

◊ **Fashion**: The recession of 1974 had forced many clothing shops into closure during this year. This was also the era were T-shirts went from being known as underwear to regular everyday apparel. The plain T-shirt went from plain to bearing slogans, sports teams, images, etc.

⇒ **TV News – Soul Train: On June 1, 8, 15 & 22nd, 1974, Tyrone Davis, Hugh Masekela, Black Ivory – The Staple Singers, Bunny Sigler – Kool & the Gang, Al Wilson, Natural Four – The O'Jays, Ramsey Lewis – Sly & the Family Stone & The Tramps** were featured guests.

On July 3, 1974, Parliament releases *Up for the Down Stroke* on **Casablanca Records**. The title track was the group's first hit.

⇒ **Magazine News**: **On July 4, 1974, James Earl Jones** and Diahann Carroll land cover of *JET*.

⇒ **News: On July 15, 1974, WXLT-TV (Sarasota Florida),** American News Reporter, *Christine Chubbuck* pulls out a revolver and shoots herself in the head during a live broadcast.

⇒ **Film News – Blaxploitation: On July 17, 1974, Paramount Pictures** released *"The Education of Sonny Carson"* starring **Rony Clanton** and **Don Gordon,** directed by *Michael Campus*.

On July 22, 1974, Stevie Wonder releases *Fulfillingness' First Finale* on **Tamla Records**. This was album number 19 for Stevie, and it topped the R&B and Pop charts and went on to win 3 Grammy Awards.

On July 22, 1974, *The Commodores* release *Machine Gun* on **Motown Records**. The debut album pinned two singles, *Machine Gun* at #7 on the R&B charts, and *I Feel Sanctified*, #12 on the R&B charts, while the album reached #22 on the R&B charts.

⇒ **Film News—Comedy Blaxploitation:** On July 26, 1974, **Warner Bros.** released *"Uptown Saturday Night"* starring **Bill Cosby, Sidney Poitier** and **Harry Belafontè** directed by *Sidney Poitier*.

In July of 1974, *Sly & the Family Stone* release *Small Talk* on **Epic Records**. Unlike their prior projects, this album didn't do as well.

⇒ **Film News—Blaxploitation:** In August of 1974; *Warner Bros.* released *"Black Samson"* starring **Rockne Tarkington**, directed by *Charles Bail*.

On August 6, 1974, Barry White releases *Can't Get Enough* on **20th Century Records**. Barry would again top the charts both in the U.S and U.K. His most noted singles, *Can't Get Enough of Your Love, Babe*, and *You're the First, the Last, My Everything*, helped earn the album the #281 spot on *Rolling Stone* magazine's list of 500 Greatest Albums of All Times.

⇒ **Politics**: **On August 8, 1974, President *Richard Nixon*** becomes the first President to *resign* from office. This coming shortly after learning that he could not escape *impeachment*.

On August 9, 1974, Minnie Riperton releases *Perfect Angel* on **Epic Records**. Her most noted single, *Lovin You"* topped the Pop charts and would go on to be a classic.

In August of 1974, Average White Band releases AWB on *Atlantic Records*. AWB came out of the gate charting at #1 with its hit single *Pick Up the Pieces* on the Pop and Black Album charts.

⇒ **Magazine News**: **In August of 1974, Cicely Tyson** lands cover of *Ms*.

In August of 1974, *Tina Turner* releases *Tina Turns the Country On!* on **United Artist Records**. This was Tina's first solo album as she tried to find her way, unfortunately the album did not chart.

⇒ **Film News—Blaxploitation:** On August 30, 1974, United Artist released "*Amazing Grace*". The film was directed by *Stan Lathan* and **Moms Mabley** played lead.

⇒ **Film News—Blaxploitation:** In August of 1974, 20th Century Fox released "*Together Brothers*" directed by *William A. Graham* starring **Ahmad Nurradin** with music by *Barry White*.

⇒ **Magazine News: August 1974, Beverly Johnson** lands cover of *VOGUE*.

⇒ **Film News—Blaxploitation:** On September 3, 1974, Cinemation Industries released "*The Black Godfather*" directed by *John Evans,* starring **Rod Perry**.

⇒ **TV News: On September 4, 1974,** *That's My Mama* aired on **ABC**. The African American sitcom took place in a neighborhood barber shop in Washington D.C.; Actor **Clifton Davis** played the lead character.

⇒ **TV News—Soul Train:** On September 7, 14, 21 & 28th, 1974, *Billy Preston, Rufus, George McCrae – James Brown and the First Family of Soul, Fred Wesley & the JB's, Lyn Collins, Sweet Charles – Johnnie Taylor, The Joneses, Syreeta Wright – The Miracles, Herbie Hancock & Yvonne Fair* were featured guests.

On September 5, 1974, The Jackson 5 releases *Dancing Machine* on **Motown Records**. J5 reached platinum status with this album, and the title track also charted #1 on the R&B charts and #2 on Pop.

On September 7, 1974, The Isley Brothers release *Live It Up* on **T-Neck Records**. They reached #1 on the Soul Album charts and #14 on Pop; it's most noted singles, *Live it Up*, #4 on R&B, and *Midnight Sky* #8 on R&B.

⇒ **TV News: On September 7, 1974,** *The Harlem Globetrotters Machine* aired on **CBS** as a Saturday morning variety show.
⇒ **Politics: On September 8, 1974, President *Gerald Ford*** pardons *former President Nixon* for any crimes that he may have committed while in office.

On September 15, 1974, Labelle releases *Nightbirds* on **Epic Records**. Their most noted single, *Lady Marmalade* reached #1 on both the R&B and Dance charts, while the album pinned a #4 spot on the R&B Album charts.

In September of 1974, Tavares releases *Hard Core Poetry* on **Capitol Records**. The album reached #11 on the R&B charts.

⇒ **Magazine News: In September of 1974, Jermaine and Hazel Jackson** land cover of *JET*.

In September of 1974, *Kool & the Gang* release *Light of Worlds* on *De-Lite Records*. Their most noted singles, *Summer Madness*, #35 on the Pop charts, *Rhyme Tyme People*, #3 on the R&B charts, and *Higher Plane* #1 on the R&B charts.

⇒ **Sports News: On October 30, 1974, *Muhammad Ali* defeats *George Foreman*** in Heavyweight Title bout known as *The Rumble in the Jungle* takes place in Kinshasa, Zaire.

⇒ **TV News—Soul Train: On October 5, 12, 19 & 26th, 1974, Michael Jackson, MDLT – The Four Tops, The New Birth, Creative Source – The Chi-Lites, Bloodstone, New York City (Tri-Boro Exchange) – Ashford & Simpson, Tavares & Little Beaver** were featured guests.

On October 25, 1974, Bob Marley releases *Natty Dread* on *Island / Tuff Gong Records*. *Natty Dread* reached #44 on the Black Albums chart. Rolling Stone magazine also placed it at #181 on its 500 Greatest albums of All Time list.

In October of 1974, *Al Green* releases *Al Green Explores Your Mind* on **Hi Records**. His most noted single, *Sha-La-La (Make Me Happy)* pinned #1 on the Soul Album charts.

In October of 1974, *Ohio Players* released *Climax* on **Westbound Records**. Climax reached #24 on the Soul LPs chart.

⇒ **Film News—Blaxploitation:** In October of 1974, **Dimension Pictures** released "*Hang up*" starring **William Elliot** and directed by *Henry Hathaway*.

⇒ **Film News—Blaxploitation:** In 1974, **Dimension Pictures** released "*Johnny Tough*" starring **Dion Gossett**.

On November 22, 1974, *Miles Davis* releases *Get Up with It* on **Columbia Records**. The album received mediocre reviews.

In November of 1974, *the Ohio Players* release *Fire* on **Mercury Records**. The album topped on both the R&B and Pop charts.

⇒ **Film News—Science Fiction Blaxploitation:** In November of 1974, *Jim Newman* produced *"Space is the Place"* starring **Sun Ra** and **Raymond Johnson**.
⇒ **Magazine News:** In November of 1974, **Marvin Gaye** lands cover of *EBONY*.
⇒ **Magazine News:** In November of 1974, **Ike and Tina Turner** land cover of Yugoslavia magazine, *Arena*.

In November of 1974, Curtis Mayfield releases *Got to Find a Way* on **Curtom Records**.

⇒ **TV News—Soul Train: On November 2, 9 & 16th, 1974, The 5th Dimension, Al Wilson, Formula IV, Mark Gordon – The Ohio Players, Ecstasy, Passion & Pain, B.T. Express – Nancy Wilson, Johnny Bristol & Mighty Clouds of Joy** were featured guests.

In December of 1974, *Blue Magic* released *The Magic of the Blue* on **Atco Records**. The album didn't do as well as their first, but did reach #14 on the R&B charts.

⇒ **TV News—Soul Train: On December 7, 14, 21 & 28th, 1974, The Moments, Labelle, Carl Carlton – The Isley Brothers – Jose Feliciano, Minnie Riperton, The Dynamic Superiors – Johnny Nash, The Commodores & Lonnie Youngblood** were featured guests.

In December of 1974, *The Spinners* released *New and Improved* on **Atlantic Records**. The album reached #9 on Billboard 200 and also pinned some hot singles, *Sadie*, and *Then Came You*.

In December of 1974, *Rufus* released *Rufusized* on **ABC Records**. Rufusized charted at #7 on Billboard.

⇒ **Politics: On December 19, 1974, Nelson Rockefeller** the former Governor of New York is sworn in as Vice President of the United States.
⇒ **Magazine News: On December 19, 1974, Red Foxx** lands cover of *JET*.

⇒ **U.S Events**: **On December 21, 1974,** it is revealed that the *CIA* has been performing illegal domestic spying. This was reported largely by the *New York Times*.

⇒ **Film News—Blaxploitation: On December 25, 1974, American International Pictures** released *"Abby"* an African American Horror Movie. The film was directed by *William Girdler* and **Carol Speed** played lead.

⇒ **TV News—Blaxploitation: In 1974, Universal Television** released *"Get Christie Love!"* as a film made just for TV. *William A. Graham* directed and **Teresa Graves** played lead in the film based on Dorothy Uhnak's novel.

1974 – Billboards Year End – Hot 100 Singles

1974	Urban Music 33% of Billboard's Hot 100 singles.	33%
3	**Love Unlimited Orchestra** – *Love's Theme*	20th Century
5	**Dancing Machine** – *The Jackson 5*	Motown
7	**TSOP (The Sound of Philadelphia)** – *MFSB*	Phila International
11	**Until You Come Back to Me (That's What I'm Gonna Do)** – *Aretha Franklin*	Atlantic
12	**Jungle Boogie** – *Kool & the Gang*	Mercury
14	**You Make Me Feel Brand New** – *The Stylistics*	Avco
15	**Show and Tell** – *Al Wilson*	Rocky Road
19	**Sideshow** – *Blue Magic*	ATCO
30	**Boogie Down** – *Eddie Kendricks*	Tamla
34	**Best Thing That Ever Happened to Me** – *Gladys Knight and the Pips*	Columbia
35	**Feel Like Makin Love** – *Roberta Flack*	Atlantic
36	**Just Don't Want to Be Lonely** – *The Main Ingredient*	Columbia
37	**Nothing from Nothing** – *Billy Preston*	A&M
38	**Rock Your Baby** – *George McCrae*	TK Records
41	**I've Got to Use My Imagination** – *Gladys Knight & the Pips*	Buddah
43	**Rock the Boat** – *The Hues Corporation*	RCA
45	**Living for the City** – *Stevie Wonder*	Tamla
47	**Then Came You** – *Dionne Warwick & The Spinners*	Atlantic
55	**Never, Never Gonna Give You Up** – *Barry White*	20th Century
56	**Tell Me Something Good** – *Rufus*	ABC
59	**Hollywood Swinging** – *Kool &the Gang*	De-Lite
60	**Be Thankful for What You Got** – *William DeVaughn*	Roxbury
61	**Hang on in There Baby** – *Johnny Bristol*	MGM
67	**Lookin for a Love** – *Bobby Womack*	UA
68	**Put Your Hands Together** – *The O'Jays*	Phila International
69	**On and On** - *Gladys Knight & the Pips*	Buddah
75	**For the Love of Money** – *The O'Jays*	Phila International
87	**Trying to Hold On to my Woman** – *Lamont Dozier*	ABC
88	**Don't You Worry 'bout a Thing** – *Stevie Wonder*	Tamla
91	**My Mistake (Was to love You)** – *Diana Ross & Marvin Gaye*	Motown
96	**Rockin' Roll Baby** – *The Stylistics*	Avco

| 100 | Mighty Love – *The Spinners* | Atlantic |

1974 – Record Labels in Urban Music

20th Century: Barry White once again brought success to the label with his Love Unlimited Orchestra's *Love's Theme* and his single, *Never, Never Gonna Give You Up* both hitting the Hot 100.

Motown: The Hitsville family charted 5 singles on the Hot 100 between the parent label and subsidiary Tamla. Diana Ross, Marvin Gaye, Stevie Wonder, Eddie Kendricks, and the Jackson 5 were becoming fixtures on the charts.

Philadelphia International: Thanks to the O'Jays and TSOP, the Philly sound had once again found its way back to the Hot 100.

Atlantic: Aretha Franklin, Roberta Flack, Dionne Warwick, and The Spinners all contributed to a great year for the label with 5 Hot 100 singles.

Mercury: Not to be left out of the growing R&B and Disco era, the label charted this year with Kool & the Gang's now classic *Jungle Boogie*.

Avco: The Stylistics charted two singles this year for the label keeping it relevant to the genre.

Rocky Road: Originally formed in 1970 and called Carousel Records, founder Marc Gordon, Motown producer, had success with Al Wilson (Show and Tell), The Outsiders, Leon Ware and more on his Rocky Road label, but it would be taken over by Bell Records later this year.

ATCO: Blue Magic's hit *Sideshow,* like some of its other hits, kept the label on the charts once again.

Columbia: Thanks to Gladys Knight & the Pips along with The Main Ingredient, the label execs insured themselves a number of hits.

A&M: With Billy Preston making consecutive hits year after year, the label found itself a hit maker that would produce several classics.

TK Records: Founded in 1973 by Henry Stone, the Miami base label was on the cusp of the disco era with artists such as, KC and the Sunshine Band and George Mcrae.

Buddah: Founded in 1967 in New York City by Art Kass who first launched Karma Sutra Records, which was distributed by MGM after a distribution disagreement with MGM, Kass started Buddah; the label was mostly known for distributing other labels such as Curtom (Curtis Mayfield), T-Neck (The Isley Brothers), Sussex (Bill Withers), Hot Wax (Holland-Dozier-Holland), and more. Most artists launching their own labels reached out to Buddah for distribution. This year however they charted two hits by Gladys Knight & the Pips, not to mention the percentage they would get from the other labels they distributed that also charted hits.

RCA: The label charted a classic with The Hues Corporation's *Rock the Boat*, one of the Disco era's biggest hits.

ABC: Founded in 1955 in New York City by the subsidiary of American Broadcasting – Paramount Theatres. Two of its artists, Rufus and Lamont Dozier charted on the Hot 100 this year giving the label a taste of success.

De-Lite: Founded in 1969 by producer Gene Redd, its first artist, Kool & the Gang, would prove to be successful beyond measures. Distributed by Pickwick from 1972 to 1977, the label would garner a number of hits.

Roxbury: Formed in 1974 by Wes Farrell, the label was a subsidiary of Los Angeles based Chelsea Records.

MGM: Johnny Bristol charted one hit this year to keep the label relevant to the genre. The label didn't fare too well when it came to R&B and Disco.

United Artist: Bobby Womack would prove to be timeless when it came to classics. Needless to say, he would be the only artist this year on the label to chart.

Circa 1975

- ⇒ **Broadway News**: **On January 5, 1975, The Wiz** (Urban version of Wizard of Oz) opens on *Broadway* at the *Majestic Theater* in New York City.
- ⇒ **TV News: On January 6, 1975,** the daytime game show *Wheel of Fortune* premieres on *NBC*.

On January 16, 1975, *Michael Jackson* releases *Forever, Michael* on **Motown Records**. Unlike his albums before, this one failed to garner the success of his previous recordings.

In January of 1975, *Gil Scott-Heron* **and** *Brian Jackson* released *The First Minute of a New Day* on **Arista Records**. The album reached #5 on the Jazz charts and #8 on the Black Albums chart.

- ⇒ **TV News – Sitcom: On January 18, 1975,** *The Jeffersons* debuted on *CBS*.
- ⇒ **TV News – Soul Train: On January 4, 11, 18 & 25, 1975, Bobby Womack, Latimore, The Kay-Gees – Graham Central Station, Zulema, Leon Haywood – Ike & Tina Turner, Lonette McKee – David Ruffin, Shirley Brown, 9th Creation and The Lockers** were featured guests.

⇒ **Protest News: On January 29, 1975, The U.S State Department** main office in Washington D.C is bombed by the *Weather Underground*, a radical left-wing party founded on the campus of the University of Michigan. Their goal was to create a revolutionary party to over throw the government.

In January of 1975, *Tower of Power* released *Urban Renewal* on **Warner Bros. Records**. This would be the last album to feature Lenny Williams as the lead singer before he embarked on his solo career.

On February 7, 1975, *Grover Washington, Jr.* releases *Mister Magic* on **Kudu Records**. The album reached #1 on the Jazz and Soul charts.

⇒ **News: On February 13, 1975,** A fire breaks out in the **World Trade Center**.
⇒ **Film News—Blaxploitation: On February 26, 1975,** *Dimension Pictures* released "*Boss N*****"* directed by *Jack Arnold* starring **Fred Williamson**.

⇒ **TV News—Soul Train:** On February 1, 8, 15 & 22, 1975, Tower of Power, The Hues Corporation, Garland Green – The Crusaders, The Whispers – Rufus featuring Chaka Khan, Gino Vanelli, Bohannon – Kool & The Gang, Charles Wright & the Watts 103rd Street Rhythm Band and The Jackson 5 were featured guests.

In February of 1975, *Dionne Warwick* released *Then Came You* on **Warner Bros. Records**. The album charted #1 in the U.S.

On March 1, 1975, *Roberta Flack* releases *Feel Like Makin' Love* on **Atlantic Records**. The title track reached #1 on the Hot 100 a few months prior to the album's release.

On March 12, 1975, *Parliament* releases *Chocolate City* on **Casablanca Records**. The album that was dedicated to D.C, aka Chocolate City, reached #18 on the soul LP charts.

On March 15, 1975, *Earth, Wind & Fire* release *That's the Way of the World* on **Columbia Records**. Originally recorded as a soundtrack for a movie of the same name, *Shining Star* reached #1 on the R&B and Pop charts, while *That's the Way of the World* reached #12 on the Pop charts. The album itself went triple platinum.

On March 25, 1975, *Barry White* releases *Just Another Way to Say I Love You* on **20th Century Records**. The album reached #17 on the Billboard 200, while its hottest singles, *What Am I Gonna Do with You* reached #1 on the R&B charts, and *I'll Do for You Anything You Want Me To* reaching #40 on the Hot 100.

⇒ **Economy**: **In March of 1975,** the recession had finally ended, but the unemployment rate would take longer to decline. This would continue to cause an influx of crime and drug abuse in America.

⇒ **Film News — Nazi Blaxploitation: In March, Bryanston Releasing** released *"The Black Gestapa"* directed by *Lee Frost* starring **Rod Perry** and **Charles Robinson**.

⇒ **Film News — Blaxploitation: On March 26, 1975, David Sheldon** produced *"Sheba, Baby"* directed by *William Girdler,* starring **Pam Grier**.

⇒ **TV News — Soul Train: On March 1, 8, 15, 22 & 29, 1975, Jimmy Ruffin, Buddy Miles, The Manhattans – Lou Rawls, The Main Ingredient, Gloria Scott – Bobby Bland, Tavares, Lyn Collins, Fred Wesley & Steam – Bloodstone, Carol Douglas, Sly Johnson – B.B. King, The Younghearts and People's Choice** were featured guests.

1975 – Urban American Grammy Award Recipients – 17th Annual

Awards, 1975: Stevie Wonder wins Album of the Year *(Fulfillingness' First Finale)*.

Awards, 1975: Richard Pryor wins Best Comedy Recording *(That N*****'s Crazy)*.

Awards, 1975: The Pointer Sisters win Best Country Vocal Performance by a Duo or Group *(Fairytale)*.

Awards, 1975: James Cleveland & the Southern California Community Choir wins Best Soul Gospel Performance *(In the Ghetto)*.

Awards, 1975: Charlie Parker wins Best Jazz Performance by a Soloist *(First Recordings!)*.

Awards, 1975: Stevie Wonder wins Best Pop Vocal Performance, Male *(Fulfillingness' First Finale)*.

Awards, 1975: Thom Bell wins Best Producer of the Year.

Awards, 1975: Aretha Franklin wins Best R&B Vocal Performance, Female *(Ain't Nothing Like the Real Thing)*.

Awards, 1975: Stevie Wonder wins Best R&B Vocal Performance, Male *(Boogie on Reggae Woman)*.

Awards, 1975: Rufus wins Best R&B Vocal Performance by a Duo, Group or Chorus *(Tell Me Something Good)*.

Awards, 1975: MFSB wins Best R&B Instrumental Performance *(The Sound of Philadelphia)*.

Awards, 1975: Stevie Wonder wins Best Rhythm & Blues Song *(Living for the City)*.

On March 26, 1975, *Smokey Robinson* releases *A Quiet Storm* on **Tamla Records**. The album reached #7 on the R&B charts, while its best single, *Baby That's Backatcha* reached #1 on the R&B charts. The album's name, *Quiet Storm*, went on to be used as a R&B musical programming format for radio stations across the globe.

On April 21, 1975, *Funkadelic* releases *Let's Take It to the Stage* on **Westbound Records**. The album reached #14 on the R&B charts.

⇒ **TV New**: On April 30, 1975 *Starsky & Hutch* debuted on *ABC*.

In April of 1975, *Al Green* releases *Al Green's Greatest Hits*; the compilation album went on to be placed #52 on Rolling Stone magazine's list of 500 Greatest Albums.

In April of 1975, *The O'Jays* release *Survival* on *Philadelphia International Records*. The album's hottest single, *Give the People What They Want*, reached #10 on the R&B Singles chart, while the album peaked at #11 on the R&B Album chart.

⇒ **TV News—Soul Train: On April 5, 12, 19 & 26, 1975, Al Green – Blue Magic, Sister Sledge, Major Harris – The Dramatics, Barbara Mason, Ben E. King – Eddie Kendricks, L.T.D and The Waters** were featured guests.

On May 10, 1975, *Stevie Wonder* performs at the Washington Monument for *Human Kindness Day* in front of 125,000 people.

On May 15, 1975, *The Jackson 5* releases *Moving Violation* on *Motown Records*. Its chart top single, *All I Do is Think of You*, was the album's crown jewel; this would also be the last time J5 recorded with Motown.

⇒ **Film News—Blaxploitation:** **American International Pictures** releases "*Cornbread, Earl and Me*, directed by *Joseph Manduke*, starring **Laurence Fishburne** and **Jamaal Wilkes**.

On May 22, 1975, *Minnie Riperton* releases *Adventures in Paradise* on **Epic Records**. The album's best single, *Inside My Love*, reached #26 on the R&B charts.

In May of 1975, the *Pointer Sisters* release *Steppin'* on **ABC/Blue Thumb Records**. Its featured single peaked at #1, *How Long (Betcha' Got a Chick on the Side)*, and also reached #20 on the Hot 100.

In May of 1975, *Curtis Mayfield* releases *There's No Place Like America Today* on **Curtom Records**.

⇒ **TV News—Soul Train:** On May 3, 10, 17 & 24, 1975, Melba Moore, Eddie Harris, Bunny Sigler – Dionne Warwick, Greg Perry, The Futures – Elton John, Mandrill, Karl Grigsby – Barry White and Love Unlimited Orchestra were featured guests.

On June 16, 1975, *WAR* releases *Why Can't We Be Friends* on **United Artist Records**. The title track, now a classic, reached #8 on the Hot 100.

On June 20, 1975, *Billy Preston* releases *It's My Pleasure* on **A&M Records**.

⇒ **Film News—Blaxploitation:** On June 25, 1975, American International Pictures releases *"Cooley High"* directed by *Michael Schultz,* starring **Glynn Turman** and **Lawrence Hilton-Jacobs**.

In June of 1975, *Average White Band* releases *Cut the Cake* on **Atlantic Records**. The title track, now a classic, reached #10 on the Pop charts.

⇒ **TV News — Soul Train: On June 7, 14 & 21, 1975, Curtis Mayfield, Leroy Hutson, Natural Four – Smokey Robinson, Betty Wright – Harold Melvin & The Blue Notes, The Southshore Commission and Richard Pryor** were featured guests.

In June of 1975, *The Isley Brothers* release *The Heat Is On* on **T-Neck/Epic Records**. The album would be the group's first #1 album, and it went on to go double platinum.

⇒ **Magazine News: In June of 1975, Atlanta Mayor, Maynard Jackson** lands cover of *Atlanta Magazine*.
⇒ **Film News — Blaxploitation: On July 2, 1975 American International Pictures** released *"Bucktown"* directed by *Arthur Marks,* starring **Fred Williamson**.

In July of 1975, *Eddie Kendricks* releases *The Hit Man* on **Tamla Records**. The album reached #9 on the R&B charts, while its hottest singles, *Happy* reached #1 on the Dance charts, and *Get The Cream Off The Top* reached #6 on the Dance charts and #7 on the R&B.

On July 6, 1975, *KC and the Sunshine Band* release their self-titled album on *TK Records*. The self-titled album produced two #1 singles, *That's the Way (I Like It)* and *Get Down Tonight*.

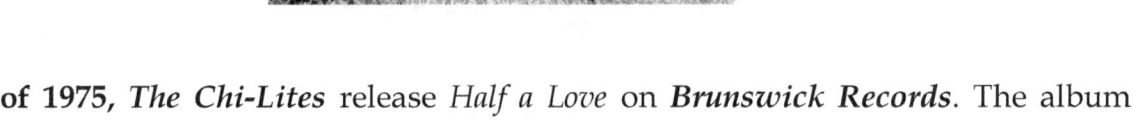

In July of 1975, *The Chi-Lites* release *Half a Love* on *Brunswick Records*. The album reached #41 on the Top Soul charts.

⇒ **Film News—Blaxploitation:** In July of 1975 **Dimension Pictures** released *"Dolemite"* directed by *D'Urville Martin*, starring **Rudy Ray Moore**.

⇒ **Film News—Blaxploitation:** On July 11, 1975, **Warner Bros**. released *Cleopatra Jones & the Casino Gold* directed by *Charles Ball*, starring **Tamara Dobson**.

⇒ **Film News—Blaxploitation:** On July 25, 1975, **Paramount Pictures** released "*Mandingo*" directed by *Richard Fleischer*, starring **James Mason**.

In July of 1975, *Tavares* releases *In the City* on **Capitol Records**. Its best single, *It Only Takes a Minute* reached #10 on the Hot 100.

⇒ **News:** On July 31, 1975, **Teamsters Union President Jimmy Hoffa** is reported missing in Detroit, MI.

On August 19, 1975, *Labelle* releases *Phoenix* on **Epic Records**. The album went to #10 on the R&B charts.

⇒ **TV News—Soul Train:** On August 23 & 30, 1975, The Supremes, Willie Hutch – Johnny Bristol and The Blackbyrds were featured guests.

⇒ **Film News—Animated Crime:** On August 20, 1975, **Bryanston Distributing Company** released "*Coonskin*" directed by *Ralph Bakshi* starring **Barry White**.

On August 22, 1975, *Herbie Hancock* releases *Man-Child* on *Columbia Records*.

On August 27, 1975, *Donna Summer* releases *Love to Love You Baby* on *Casablanca Records*. The title track reached #2 on the Hot 100.

In August of 1975, *Tina Turner* releases *Acid Queen* on *EMI (UK)* & *United Artist (US) Records*. The album consisted of several rock cover songs.

⇒ **Film News—Blaxploitation:** **Moonstone Entertainment** released *"The Candy Tangerine Man"* directed by *Matt Cimber*, starring **John Daniels**.

In August of 1975, *Al Green* releases *Al Green is Love* on **Hi Records**. Like the 5 albums before, this one also reached #1 on the R&B Soul charts.

In August of 1975, *Ohio Players* release *Honey* on **Mercury Records**. The album reached #2 on the Billboard charts.

⇒ **Magazine News:** **Pam Grier** lands the cover *Ms. Magazine*, August edition.

In August of 1975, *Quincy Jones* releases *Mellow Madness* on ***A&M Records***. The album reached #1 on the Jazz charts and #3 on the R&B charts, while its hottest single, *Is It Love That We're Missing?* reached #18 on the R&B Singles chart.

In August of 1975, *The Spinners* released *Pick of the Litter* on ***Atlantic Records***. The album reached #2 on the R&B charts and #8 on Billboard 200.

⇒ **Drugs: During 1975** drug abuse had reached an all-time high and brought on new challenges for America. In September, President Ford put in place the *Domestic Council Drug Abuse Task Force* and appointed Vice President Rockefeller to assess the extent of the abuse. During their assessment, they found marijuana was a minor problem and that cocaine wasn't a problem at all because it was not addictive and did not lead to violence. The findings led the task force to have the DEA and U.S Customs pursue heroin and more violent drugs focusing on smuggling and distribution, and choosing to turn a blind eye to both cocaine and marijuana.

In August of 1975, *Kool & The Gang* released *Spirit of the Boogie* on **De-Lite Records**. The album peaked at #5 on the R&B charts, while the title track reached #1 on the R&B Singles chart.

⇒ **Magazine News: On August 28, 1975, Bern Nadette Stanis** (Thelma from Good Times) lands cover of *JET*.

In September of 1975, *Tower of Power* releases *In the Slot* on **Warner Bros Records**.

In September of 1975, *Blue Magic* releases *Thirteen Blue Magic Lane* on **Atco Records**. The album reached #9 on the Top Soul charts, while two singles, *Chasing Rainbows* reached #17, and *What's Come Over Me* peaked at #11 on the R&B Singles chart.

⇒ **TV News—Animation: On September 6, 1975,** *The Grape Ape Show* debuted on **ABC**.

⇒ **Politics: On September the 5th and 22nd of 1975,** two assassination attempts were made on **President Gerald Ford's** life; 1st in Sacramento, California by Lynette Fromme, then again by Sara Jane Moore in San Francisco, California.

⇒ **TV News—Soul Train: On September 6, 13, 20 & 27, 1975, Joe Simon, Millie Jackson, Choice Four – The New Birth, Blue Magic, Bobby Moore – The Impressions, Ranc Allen Group – Eddie Kendricks, Tavares, and Paul Mooney** were featured guests. *The Soul Train Dance Contest* was also held on **September 20th**.

⇒ **Music News: On September 29, 1975,** while performing on stage in Cherry Hill, New Jersey, **Jackie Wilson** suffers a massive heart attack.

⇒ **Sports News: On October 1, 1975, Muhammad Ali and Joe Frazier** fight in the Philippines. Ali wins by TKO in what was known as *The Thriller in Manila*.

⇒ **TV News—Comedy: On October 11, 1975,** the very first episode of *Saturday Night Live* airs on **NBC**; *Billy Preston* was one of the shows first musical guest.

⇒ **Film News—Blaxploitation: On October 11, 1975, Warner Bros.** released *"Let's Do It Again"* directed by *Sidney Poitier*, starring **Sidney Poitier** and **Bill Cosby**.

On October 16, 1975, *Aretha Franklin* releases *You* on **Atlantic Records**. Its title track reached #15 on the R&B charts.

⇒ **Film News—Blaxploitation: On October 22, 1975 AVCO Embassy Pictures** and **Anchor Bay Entertainment** released *"Diamonds"* directed by *Menahem Golan* starring **Richard Roundtree**.

Hip Hop History — Book 1

- ⇒ **Magazine News**: **Robert Lee Elder** becomes the first African-American Golfer to play in the *1975 Masters Tournament* and lands the cover of *Sports Illustrated*.
- ⇒ **TV News — Soul Train: On October 4, 11, 18 & 25, 1975, The Pointer Sisters, B.T. Express, Ralph Carter – The O'Jays, Little Milton, Cholly Atkins – Labelle, Creative Source – Minnie Riperton and Twenty First Century** were featured guests.

In October of 1975, *The Commodores* released *Movin' On* on **Motown Records**. *Movin On* reached #9 on the R&B charts, while its single, *Sweet Love* charted at #5 on the Hot 100.

- ⇒ **TV News — Morning Show: On November 3, 1975**, *Good Morning America* debuted on **ABC**.
- ⇒ **TV News — Adventure: On November 7, 1975**, *Wonder Woman* debuted on **ABC**.

On November 11, 1975, *Earth, Wind and Fire* release *Gratitude* on **Columbia – Legacy Records**. The album peaked at #1 on the Pop charts, #1 on the Soul Black Album charts, and went triple platinum.

⇒ **TV News — Soul Train: On November 1, 8, 15, 22 & 29, 1975; Ramsey Lewis, Fantastic Four – The Spinners, Merry Clayton – WAR, The Main Ingredient – Harold Melvin & the Blue Notes, Esther Phillips – The Miracles, Poison, Quincy Jones, and Nat Adderley** were featured guests.

In November of 1975, *The O'Jays* released *Family Reunion* on **Philadelphia International Records**. The classic album peaked at #7 on the Pop charts and went platinum. It also garnered several hot singles, *I Love Music, Livin' for the Weekend, Stairway to Heaven,* and the title track, *Family Reunion*.

⇒ **Politics: On November 20, 1975, Ronald Regan**, then Governor of California, enters race for the Republican presidential nomination challenging Gerald Ford.
⇒ **Medellin Massacre: On November 22, 1975, Colombian Police** seize 600 kilos of cocaine at Cali airport from a small plane. Despite the U.S decision to ignore cocaine and marijuana use and trafficking; this would change the direction of the DEA and increased the murder rate in the drug business.
⇒ **Business News: On November 26, 1975, Bill Gates'** *"Microcomputer Software,"* aka Microsoft, becomes a registered trademark.

In November of 1975, *Rufus* releases *Rufus featuring Chaka Khan* on **ABC Records**. The album reached #7 on the Pop charts and topped the R&B charts, and went on to be certified gold, then platinum. Its most noted single, *Sweet Thing*, reached #1 on R&B Singles charts.

On December 5, 1975, *Bob Marley & The Wailers* release *Live!* on **Island Records**. The album was a live recording of the group's performance in London at the Lyceum Theater on July 19, 1975. Among the songs performed were chart toppers: *No Woman, No Cry, I Shot the Sheriff,* and *Get Up, Stand Up*.

⇒ **TV News—Soul Train: On December 6, 13, 20 & 27, 1975, Average White Band, The Undisputed Truth – Rufus featuring Chaka Khan, David Ruffin – Freda Payne, The Whispers – Billy Preston and The Sylvers** were featured guests.

On December 15, 1975, *Parliament* releases *Mothership Connection* on **Casablanca Records**. The album went platinum and featured classics such as *P. Funk (Wants to Get Funked Up), Mothership Connection (Star Child),* and *Give Up the Funk (Tear the Roof Off the Sucker).*

⇒ **Drugs: This year, Frank Lucas'** home was raided — Frank Lucas, the New York Kingpin. Officials seize more than half a million dollars in cash. Lucas is arrested and sentenced to 70 years in prison on drug related charges.

⇒ **Fashion**: Men's corduroy sport jackets, cardigan sweaters, and hounds tooth check slacks were popular among the guys, while women fancied double-knit polyester shirtdresses, corduroy pinafores, and Aztec print rain coats.

⇒ **Film News — Blaxploitation: On December 25, 1975, Columbia Pictures** released *"Aaron Loves Angela"* directed by *Gordon Parks, Jr.,* starring **Moses Gunn** and **Irene Cara**.

⇒ **Film News — Blaxploitation: In 1975, New World Pictures** released *"Darktown Strutters"* directed by *William Witney,* starring **Trina Parks**.

⇒ **Film News — Blaxploitation: On December 25, 1975, American International Pictures** released *"Friday Foster"* directed by *Arthur Marks,* starring **Pam Grier**.

⇒ **Film News — Blaxploitation: In December of 1975, Dimension Pictures** released *"Lady Cocoa"* directed by *Matt Cimber,* starring **Lola Falana**.

1975 – Billboards Year End – Hot 100 Singles

1975	Urban Music 22% of Billboard's Year-End Hot 100	22%
6	**Earth, Wind & Fire** – *Shining Star*	Columbia
13	**Minnie Riperton** – *Lovin' You*	Epic
18	**Tony Orlando and Dawn** – *He Don't Love You (Like I Love You)*	Elektra
20	**Average White Band** – *Pick Up the Pieces*	Atlantic
22	**Labelle** – *Lady Marmalade*	Epic
23	**WAR** – *Why Can't We Be Friends*	ABC
24	**Major Harris** – *Love Won't Let Me Wait*	Atlantic
25	**Stevie Wonder** – *Boogie On Reggae Woman*	Tamla
27	**The Isley Brothers** – *Fight the Power*	T-Neck
30	**Ohio Players** – *Fire*	Mercury
48	**Barry White** – *You're the First, the Last, My Everything*	20th Century
53	**Gladys Knight & the Pips** – *The Way We Were/Try to Remember*	Buddah
58	**B.T. Express** – *Express*	Scepter
59	**Earth, Wind & Fire** – *That's the Way of the World*	Columbia
64	**KC and the Sunshine Band** – *Get Down Tonight*	TK
70	**Average White Band** – *Cut the Cake*	Atlantic
75	**The Three Degrees** – *When Will I See You Again*	Philadelphia International
79	**Eddie Kendricks** – *Shoeshine Boy*	Motown
80	**B.T. Express** – *Do It ('Til You're Satisfied)*	Scepter
82	**Al Green** – *Sha-La-La (Make Me Happy)*	Hi
84	**Rufus** – *You Got the Love*	ABC
86	**Tavares** – *It Only Takes a Minute*	Capitol

1975 – Record Labels in Urban Music

Columbia: The elements of the earth, aka Earth, Wind and Fire, pinned a good year with a now classic album and two Hot 100 singles, keeping the label in the Funk business.

Epic: Now a heavyweight in the R&B, Funk, Rock and Soul business with several chart-topping acts such as Heatwave, ABBA, Sly & the Family Stone to name a few, Epic charted with singles from Labelle and Minnie Riperton hitting the Hot 100.

Elektra: Originally founded in 1950 the label focused mainly on folk and rock music. Its founder *Jac Holzman* eventually sold the label to **Kinney National Company** (*DC Comics*) in 1970. After the acquisition, KNC would combine the companies holding under one umbrella to be called **Warner-Elektra-Atlantic**. Jac Holzman, however, remained in charge of Elektra until it merged with *David Geffen's* label, **Asylum**, creating **Elektra/Asylum Records** in 1972. Holzman then became Senior VP of **Warner** during his reign; Holzman also acquired the Jazz label, **Discovery Records**, which was home to the likes of *Dizzy Gillespie*. This year they made the Hot 100 with Tony Orlando and Dawn.

Atlantic: Its funk band, Average White Band charted two singles, while R&B artist, Major Harris pinned a classic love ballad.

Motown/Tamla: This would be considered a slow year for Hitsville with only two singles making the Hot 100.

T-Neck: Founded in 1964 by The Isley Brothers, the group recorded with several other labels before releasing music on their own label. Once they decided to do so the brothers pinned several hits and this year they continued their roll, charting the Hot 100 yet again making their label a success and a force in the market.

Mercury: The Ohio Players proved, yet again, to be a success charting the Hot 100.

20th Century: The label once again banked on the maestro, Barry White, to deliver, and as always he did just that.

Buddah: In desperate need of a hit, Gladys Knight & The Pips charted a classic for their new label after leaving *Motown* and would go on to be one of the label's biggest artists.

Scepter: Founded in 1959 by Florence Greenberg, the label was launched from funds received from the sale of Tiara Records, along with its artists, The Shirelles, to *Decca Records*. Greenberg re-signed The Shirelles to her new label once Decca released them; she was also responsible for launching the careers of Tammi Terrell, The Isley Brothers, Dionne Warwick and B.T. Express to name a few.

TK: With its newfound talent, KC and the Sunshine Band, the label kept the dance floors packed and DJ's spinning.

Philadelphia International: The newfound label added another hit to their roster, and it seemed that Gamble and Huff had the Midas touch. The Three Degrees fell right in place as well releasing one of the most successful hits coming out of Phila.

ABC: With two of their biggest artists charting the Hot 100, the label proved that ABC could produce hits.

Hi: Al Green yet again delivers, and the label finds itself with another hit on the Hot 100.

Capitol: Now merged with **EMI;** the label changed its name to *Capitol Industries-EMI, Inc.* after EMI increased its holdings to 70.84%.

Circa 1976

On January 2, 1976, *Barry White* releases *Let the Music Play* on **20th Century Records**. The title track reached #4 on the R&B Top 10 charts, while the album pinned #8 on the R&B Albums chart and also charted #22 in the UK.

- ⇒ **Music Industry News: On January 7, 1976,** *Former record executive Kenneth Moss* gets sentenced to 120 days in LA County Jail for involuntary manslaughter of *Average White Band's* drummer, *Robbie McIntosh,* due to a drug induced death. Moss also received 4 years of probation.
- ⇒ **Film News – Blaxploitation: On January 9, 1976, Dimension Pictures** released *"The Human Tornado"* directed by *Cliff Roquemore* starring **Rudy Ray More** and **Ernie Hudson**.
- ⇒ **Music Industry News: On January 13, 1976,** *Seven Dakar Records'* **and** *Brunswick Records'* employees start trial. They are charged with stealing $184,000.00 in royalties from the label's artists.
- ⇒ **TV News – Adventure: On January 14, 1976,** *The Bionic Women* debuted on **ABC**.
- ⇒ **Sports News: January 18, 1976, The Pittsburgh Steelers** defeat the Dallas Cowboys in Super Bowl X at the Orange Bowl in Miami, Florida.
- ⇒ **Magazine News: January 26, 1976,** *Diana Ross* and husband *Bob Silberstein* land cover of *People*.
- ⇒ **TV News – Sitcom:** On January 27, 1976, the *Laverne & Shirley* show premiered on **ABC**.
- ⇒ **Film News – Blaxploitation: In January of 1976, Atlas Productions** released *"Adios Amigo"* directed by *Fred Williamson,* starring **Richard Pryor** and **Fred Williamson**.

⇒ **TV News — Soul Train: On January 3, 10, 17 & 24, 1976,** featured guests included, **David Bowie, Faith, Hope and Charity, Jeff Perry – The Temptations, Edwin Starr – The Staple Singers, Bobby Womack – The Jackson 5.**

On February 10, 1976, *Diana Ross* releases her self-titled album *Diana Ross* on **Motown Records**. The album pinned two chart topping singles, *Theme from Mahogany (Do You Know Where You're Going To,* and *Love Hangover*; both classics peaked at #1 on the charts. The album reached number #4 on the R&B Albums charts and broke the Top 5 in the UK.

On February 10, 1976, *Smokey Robinson* releases *Smokey's Family Robinson* on **Tamla Records**.

⇒ **Politics: February 11, 1976, Clifford Alexander, Jr.** becomes the 1st African-American Secretary of the United States Army.
⇒ **TV News — Soul Train: On February 7, 14, 21 & 28, 1976,** featured guests included, **Bill Withers, The Soul Train Gang – The Jimmy Castor Bunch, Leon Haywood, The Southshore Commission – The Commodores, George McCrae – Joe Tex, The Chi-Lites and Tom Dreesen.**

In February of 1976, *Al Green* releases *Full of Fire* on **Hi Records**. The album was produced by Willie Mitchell, and unlike his past albums, this one did not pin any chart toppers.

⇒ **Music Industry News: On February 19, 1976,** *Rick Stevens*, the former lead singer of *Tower of Power*, is arrested and charged with drug-related murders of three men in San Jose, California.

⇒ **Sports News—Boxing: March 17, 1976,** Boxer Rubin "Hurricane" Carter is arrested in New Jersey on murder charges.

⇒ **Magazine News: In March of 1976, Super Model Iman** lands cover of *Italian Vogue*.

On March 5, 1976, *Donna Summer* releases *A Love Trilogy* on *Casablanca Records*. The album went gold and also topped the Disco Charts.

⇒ **TV News—Soul Train: On March 6, 13, 20 & 27, 1976,** featured guests included, Wilson Pickett, Betty Wright, The Modulations – Eddie Kendricks, The Temprees – Johnnie Taylor, Donna Summer – The Supremes and Al Wilson.

On March 10, 1976, *The Temptations* release *Wings of Love* on **Gordy Records**. It went down as one of the Temps most unsuccessful albums.

On March 16, 1976, *Marvin Gaye* releases *I Want You* on **Tamla Records**. This album marked Gaye's change in direction to a more sensual singer.

⇒ **Magazine News: In 1976 Pam Grier** lands cover of *Players* 1976 Calendar.

In March of 1976, *Kool and The Gang* releases *Love & Understanding* on **De-Lite Records**.

⇒ **Business News: April 1, 1976, The Apple Computer Company** is formed by Steve Jobs and Steve Wozniak.

1976 – Urban American Grammy Award Recipients – 18th Annual

Awards, 1976: Natalie Cole wins Best New Artist.

Awards, 1976: Richard Pryor wins Best Comedy Recording *(Is It Something I Said)*.

Awards, 1976: Muddy Waters wins Best Ethnic or Traditional Recording *(The Muddy Waters Woodstock Album)*.

Awards, 1976: The Imperials win Best Gospel Performance (Other Than Soul Gospel) *(No Shortage)*.

Awards, 1976: Andrae Crouch wins Best Soul Gospel Performance *(Take Me Back)*.

Awards, 1976: Dizzy Gillespie wins Best Jazz Performance by a Soloist *(Oscar Peterson and Dizzy Gillespie)*.

Awards, 1976: Charlie Smalls (composer), Jerry Wexler (producer), and original cast with Stephanie Mills and Dee Dee Bridgewater, wins Best Cast Show Album *(The Wiz)*.

Awards, 1976: Jim Ladwig wins Best Album Package *(Honey by the Ohio Players)*.

Awards, 1976: Natalie Cole wins Best R&B Vocal Performance, Female *(This Will Be)*.

Awards, 1976: Ray Charles wins Best R&B Vocal Performance, Male *(Living for the City)*

Awards, 1976: Earth, Wind & Fire wins Best R&B Vocal Performance by a Duo, Group or Chorus *(Shining Star)*.

Awards, 1976: Silver Convention wins Best R&B Instrumental Performance *(Fly, Robin, Fly)*.

Awards, 1976: Betty Wright, Harry Wayne Casey, Willie Clarke and Richard Finch win Best Rhythm & Blues Song *(Where is the Love)*.

⇒ **TV News—Soul Train:** On April 3, 1976, **The Dramatics, Dorothy Moore, and Leon Thomas** were featured guests.
⇒ **Film News—Biopic:** On April 7, 1976, **Warner Bros.** released *"Sparkle"* directed by *Sam O'Steen*, starring **Irene Cara** and **Philip M. Thomas**.
⇒ **Magazine News:** On April 15, 1976, **Tina Turner** lands cover of *JET*.

On April 30, 1976, **Bob Marley & The Whalers** release *Rastaman Vibration* on **Island Records**. The album peaked at #8, and its hottest single, *Roots, Rock, Reggae* reached #51 on the Hot 100.

⇒ **Film News—Blaxploitation:** In April of 1976, **Warner Bros.** released *"Hot Potato"* directed by *Oscar Williams*, starring *Jim Kelly*.
⇒ **Magazine News:** **April/May of 1976** edition, **O.J. Simpson** lands the cover of *The Electric Company Magazine*.

On **May 4, 1976,** *The Isley Brothers* release *Harvest of the World* on their *T-Neck label*. The album reached #1 on the Soul Albums charts and #9 on Pop. The title track reached #9 on the R&B charts, while *Who Loves You Better* reached #3 on R&B, and *People of Today* reached #3 on the Dance charts.

⇒ **Politics: May 25, 1976, presidential challenger, Ronald Regan** loses in three Republican primaries to President Gerald Ford.

On May 27, 1976, Aretha Franklin releases *Sparkle* for the **Warner Bros**. *Sparkle* movie soundtrack produced by *Curtis Mayfield*. The album reached #1 on the R&B charts and #18 on Billboard 200. Its most popular single, *Something He Can Feel* reached #1 on Hot Soul Singles and #28 on the Hot 100.

In May of 1976, The Ohio Players released *Contradiction* on **Mercury Records**. The album peaked at #1 on the Soul charts, while singles, *Who'd She Coo?* reached #1 on the R&B Singles chart, and *Far East Mississippi* reached #26 on the R&B charts.

⇒ **Magazine News: In May of 1976, Diana Ross** lands cover of *Photoplay*.
⇒ **Film News—Black Biopic: On May 28, 1976, Paramount Pictures** released *"Leadbelly"* directed by *Gordon Parks*, starring **Roger E. Mosley**.
⇒ **TV News—Soul Train: On May 1, 8, 15 & 22, 1976,** featured guests included, **Kool & The Gang, Ashford & Simpson, Ronnie McNeir – The Delfonics, D.J. Rogers – Billy Paul, The Trammps – Archie Bell & The Drells and Brass Construction.**

In May of 1976, *Tavares* releases *Sky High!* on **Capitol Records**. The album reached #20 on the R&B charts and #24 on Pop.

On June 7, 1976, *Lou Rawls* releases *All Things in Time* on **Philadelphia International Records**. The album reached #1 on the R&B charts, while several singles charted; *Time* peaked at #8 on the Dance charts, *You'll Never Find Another Love Like Mine* reached #1 both on the R&B and Dance charts, and *Groovy People* reached #19 on R&B.

In June of 1976, **The Commodores** released *Hot on the Tracks* on **Motown Records**. The classic album reached #1 on the R&B charts, while singles *Just to Be Close to You* reached #1 on R&B, *Let's Get Started* reached #3 on the Dance charts, and *Fancy Dancer* reached #9 on the R&B charts.

⇒ **TV News — Game Show: On June 14, 1976,** *The Gong Show* debuted on **NBC**.

- ⇒ **TV News—Variety: On June 16, 1976,** *The Jacksons* variety show premiered on **CBS**.
- ⇒ **Sports News: June 17, 1976, The National Basketball Assoc. and American Basketball Assoc.** agree on a NBA–ABA merger.
- ⇒ **Film News—Blaxploitation: On June 30, 1976, Howard Mahler Films** released *"Velvet Smooth"* directed by *Michael L. Fink,* starring ***Johnnie Hill.***
- ⇒ **TV News—Soul Train: On June 12 & 19, 1976, Rufus feat Chaka Khan, The Checkmates, The Booty People – The 5th Dimension, The Brothers Johnson & Pat Lundy** were featured guests.
- ⇒ **TV News—Game Show:** On July 12, 1976, *Family Feud* premiered on **ABC**.
- ⇒ **Politics: July 15, 1976, Jimmy Carter** is nominated for President at the Democratic National Convention in New York City.
- ⇒ **Film News—Blaxploitation: On July 16, 1976, Universal Pictures** released *"The Bingo Long Traveling All-Stars & Motor Kings"* produced by *Motown* starring ***Billy Dee Williams, James Earl Jones*** and ***Richard Pryor.***

On July 20, 1976, *Parliament* releases *The Clones of Dr. Funkenstein* on **Casablanca Records**. George Clinton once again dropped the funk and everyone loved it! Like the albums before, this one also charted in the top 5 on the R&B charts.

On July 20, 1976, *Gloria Gaynor* releases *I've Got You* on **Polydor Records**. The album reached #40 on the R&B charts.

- ⇒ **Politics**: **On July 26, 1976, Ronald Regan,** while in Los Angeles, announces U.S Senator Richard Schweiker as his vice-presidential running mate in efforts to win the Republican party's vote over President Gerald Ford.
- ⇒ **Film News—Blaxploitation: On July 30, 1976, United Artist** released *"Drum"* directed by *Steve Carver,* starring **Warren Oates, Pamela Grier,** and **Ken Norton**.
- ⇒ **TV News—Sitcom: On August 5, 1976,** *What's Happening* premiered on **ABC**.

On August 6, 1976, Bootsy's Rubber Band releases *Stretchin' Out in Bootsy's Rubber Band* on **Warner Bros Records**. Bootsy's album went on to reach #10 on the R&B charts. His most noted singles, *I'd Rather Be With You* peaked at #25 on the R&B charts, and *Stretchin' Out (In A Rubber Band)* reached #18.

On August 8, 1976, Jermaine Jackson releases *My Name is Jermaine* on **Motown Records**. Jermaine's 3rd solo album reached #29 on the R&B charts, while its hottest single, *Let's Be Young Tonight* reached #19 on the R&B Singles chart.

- ⇒ **TV News—Musical Variety: On August 14, 1976,** *The Diahann Carroll Show* debuted on **CBS** for four episodes.

⇒ **Books**: **August 17, 1976, Alex Haley** releases <u>Roots: The Saga of an American Family</u> published by *Doubleday*. The book became a bestseller, spending 22 weeks atop of the New York Times Bestsellers List. Haley would also go on to win a Pulitzer Prize.
⇒ **Politics**: **August 19, 1976, Ronald Regan** fails to come up with enough votes to win Republican Party, leaving President Gerald Ford the nominee in Kansas City.

In August of 1976; *Herbie Hancock* released *Secrets* on **Columbia Records**.

⇒ **Film News—Blaxploitation:** On **August 25, 1976**, **American International Pictures** released *"J.D.'s Revenge"* directed by *Arthur Marks* starring **Glynn Turman, Louis Gossett, Jr.** and **Joan Pringle**.
⇒ **TV News—Sitcom:** On August 31, 1976, the sitcom **ALICE** debuted on **CBS**.
⇒ **TV News—Soul Train: On August 21 & 28, 1976,** featured guests included, **Johnnie Taylor, The Tymes – The Sylvers, Sun and Frankie Crocker**.
⇒ **Magazine News: On September 2, 1976, Jermaine Jackson** lands cover of *JET*.

On September 13, 1976, *Rose Royce* releases *Car Wash: Original Motion Picture Soundtrack* on *MCA Records*. The classic album produced by Norman Whitfield reached #2 on the Soul charts. The title track, *Car Wash*, peaked at #1 on the R&B singles chart, while "*I Wanna Get Next to you*" reached #3 on the R&B singles chart. *I'm Going Down* peaked at #10.

- ⇒ **Film News — Blaxploitation:** In 1976, **Dimension Pictures** released *"Black Shampoo"* directed by *Greydon Clark* starring **John Daniels, Tanya Boyd, Joe Ortiz** and **Skip E. Lowe**.
- ⇒ **Film News — Blaxploitation:** In 1976, **Ronald K. Goldman** produced and released *"Brotherhood of Death"* directed by *Bill Berry*, starring **Roy Jefferson, Le Tari** and **Haskell Anderson**.
- ⇒ **TV News — Sketch Comedy:** On September 19, 1976, *Cos* debuted on **ABC** hosted by *Bill Cosby*.

On September 21, 1976, *Funkadelic* releases *Tales of Kidd Funkadelic* on **Westbound Records**.

- ⇒ **TV News: On September 22, 1976,** *Charlie's Angels* debuted on **ABC**.

On September 28, 1976, *Stevie Wonder* releases *Songs in the Key of Life* on **Tamla Records**. This would be one of Stevie's best-selling albums of all time. Rolling Stone magazine placed it at #57 on its 500 Greatest Albums of all times list.

⇒ **TV News—Soul Train:** On September 4, 11, 18 & 25, 1976, featured guests included, **Melba Moore, The Whispers – The O'Jays, Thelma Houston – D.J. Rogers, The Lockers – Labelle, Brother to Brother** – Also featuring the *Soul Train National Dance Contest*.

⇒ **Film News—Blaxploitation:** In 1976, **Ramana Productions, Inc.** released *"Mean Johnny Barrows"* directed by *Fred Williamson* starring **James Brown, Elliot Gould, Stuart Whitman, Roddy McDowell,** *and* **Fred Williamson**.

In September of 1976, *Earth, Wind & Fire* release *Spirit* on **Columbia Records**. This would be the group's 7th album, and it peaked at #2 on the Pop and R&B charts.

⇒ **Film News—Blaxploitation:** On September 29, 1976, **United Artist** released *"Norman…is that You?"* directed by *George Schlatter,* starring **Redd Foxx** *and* **Pearl Bailey**.

On October 11, 1976, *Donna Summer* releases *Four Seasons of Love* on **Casablanca Records**. Donna once again hit pay dirt with her 3rd certified gold album.

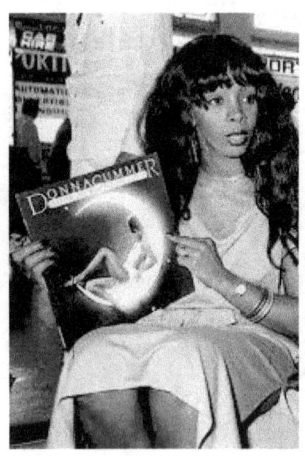

- ⇒ **TV News—Soul Train: On October 2, 9, 16 & 23, 1976,** featured guests included, **The Spinners, David Ruffin – Jermaine Jackson, Tata Vega – The Emotions, The Rimshots, The Ritchie Family – Marilyn McCoo & Billy Davis, Jr. and Denise Williams – The Undisputed Truth, Impact & Carol Douglas.**
- ⇒ **Film News—Blaxploitation: On October 22, 1976, Universal Pictures** released *Car Wash* directed by *Michael Schultz*, starring **Franklyn Ajaye, Bill Duke, Antonio Fargas, Richard Pryor, The Pointer Sisters, George Carlin** and more.

On October 29, 1976, *Funkadelic* releases *Hardcore Jollies* on **Warner Bros Records**. This was their first release for Warner Bros., and it charted #12 on the R&B charts.

In October of 1976, *KC and the Sunshine Band* released *Part 3* on **TK Records**. The classic release pinned 3 hot singles, *(Shake, Shake, Shake) Shake Your Booty, I'm Your Boogie Man,* and *Keep It Comin' Love*.

- ⇒ **Politics: November 2, 1976, Jimmy Carter** defeats Gerald Ford to become the first President from the Deep South since the Civil War.

⇒ **Film News—Drama: In November of 1976, AVCO Embassy Pictures** released *"Pipe Dreams"* directed by *Stephen F. Verona*, starring **Gladys Knight** *and* **Barry Hankerson**.

On November 5, 1976, *The Jacksons* released *The Jacksons* on **Epic Records**. This is the first album they recorded since breaking their contract with **Motown**. *Jermaine* remained with **Motown** and was replaced by Randy in this new venture with **Epic/Philadelphia International Records**. The album peaked at #6 on the Soul Album charts and produced two hit singles, *Enjoy Yourself* #2 on the R&B charts, #6 on the Hot 100, *Show You the Way to Go* #6 on the R&B charts and #28 on Billboard Hot 100.

On November 18, 1976, *Al Green* releases *Have a Good Time* on **Hi Records** produced by Willie Mitchell.

⇒ **Business News: November 26, 1976, Microsoft** is officially registered with the Secretary of State of New Mexico.

TV News — Soul Train: On November 6, 13, 20 & 27, 1976, featured guests included, **The Four Tops, Vicki Sue Robinson – Aretha Franklin, Ronnie Dyson – The Manhattans, Brass Construction, Rose Royce – K.C. and the Sunshine Band and Dee Dee Bridgewater.**

On November 30, 1976, *Barry White* releases *Is This Whatcha Wont?* on **20th Century Records**. The album reached #25 on the Soul charts.

In November of 1976, *Kool & the Gang* released *Open Sesame* on **De-Lite Records**. The title track broke the Top 10 on the R&B charts.

⇒ **Music Industry News: On December 3, 1976, In Kingston, Jamaica**, gunmen invade *Bob Marley's* home and open fire, Marley and seven others are injured.

⇒ **Magazine News: On December 16, 1976, Pam Grier** lands cover of *JET*.

⇒ **Film News—Blaxploitation:** On December 24, 1976, **American International Pictures** released *"The Monkey Hustle"* directed by *Arthur Marks*, starring **Yaphet Kotto, Kirk Calloway** and **Rudy Ray Moore.**

⇒ **TV News—Soul Train:** On December 4, 11, 18 & 25, 1976, featured guests included, **The Ohio Players, Johnny Bristol – Average White Band, The Soul Train Gang – O.C. Smith, Dorothy Moore – The Moments & Donna Summer.**

⇒ **Magazine News**: On December 30, 1976, **Marvin Gaye** lands Xmas edition of *JET*.

1976 – Billboards Year End – Hot 100 Singles

1976	Urban Music 28% of Billboards Year-End Hot 100	28%
3	Johnnie Taylor – *Disco Lady*	Columbia
5	Wild Cherry – *Play That Funky Music*	Epic
6	The Manhattans – *Kiss and Say Goodbye*	Columbia
7	The Miracles – *Love Machine*	Tamla
15	Diana Ross – *Love Hangover*	Motown
20	The Sylvers – *Boogie Fever*	Capitol
22	Hot Chocolate – *You Sexy Thing*	Big Tree
26	K.C. and the Sunshine Band – *Shake, Shake (Shake your Booty)*	TK
27	The Commodores – *Sweet Love*	Motown
28	Maxine Nightingale – *Right Back Where We Started From*	United Artist
30	The Ohio Players – *Love Rollercoaster*	Mercury
32	Lou Rawls – *You'll Never Find Another Love Like Mine*	Phila Intl.
41	Donna Summer – *Love to Love You Baby*	Oasis
43	Diana Ross – *Theme from Mahogany (Do You Know Where You're Going To)*	Motown
44	Rufus – *Sweet Thing*	ABC
45	KC and the Sunshine Band – *That's the Way (I Like It)*	TK
52	The O'Jays – *I Love Music*	Phila Intnl
59	Earth, Wind & Fire – *Sing A Song*	Columbia
60	Tavares – *Heaven Must Be Missing an Angel*	Capitol
61	The Brothers Johnson – *I'll Be Good to You*	A&M
66	The Staple Singers – *Let's Do It Again*	Curtom
69	George Benson – *This Masquerade*	Warner
73	Harold Melvin & the Blue Notes – *Wake Up Everybody*	Phila Intnl
74	WAR – *Summer*	United Artist
80	Earth, Wind & Fire – *Getaway*	Columbia
86	Ohio Players – *Who'd She Coo?*	Mercury
88	David Ruffin – *Walk Away from Love*	Motown
93	Parliament – *Give Up the Funk (Tear the Roof off the Sucker)*	Casablanca

1976 – Record Labels in Urban Music

Columbia: The label charted this year with hits from Johnnie Taylor, Earth, Wind & Fire twice, and The Manhattans. It should also be noted that this year, its Canada-based label under the same name was renamed *CBS Records*.

Epic: The label only charted with the classic, *Play That Funky Music* by Wild Cherry, although its roster included several other chart-topping acts.

Motown/Tamla: Gordy charted five singles on the Hot 100 this year proving that Hitsville through adversity could still produce hits even with some of its talent leaving to join other labels.

Capitol: Having two groups hit the Hot 100 this year, Capitol was still a proven label to be reckoned with.

Big Tree: Originally founded in 1970 by music executive Doug Morris. By this time the label had been distributed by both *Bell* and *Ampex Records* before being sold to *Atlantic* in 1974. The now Atlantic owned label charted this year with the UK band, Hot Chocolate's classic, *You Sexy Thing*.

TK: The Miami based label was still on a roll with two Hot 100 singles from K.C and the Sunshine Band.

United Artist: With only one single on the Hot 100 this year in the urban genre the label didn't fair to well against the competition.

Mercury: It seems the label hit pay dirt with two singles from its newly signed band, the Ohio Players, charting two singles on the Hot 100.

Philadelphia International: The song writer and producer duo continue to ride high with three of their artists charting the Hot 100 giving Motown a run for their money. Lou Rawls, Harold Melvin, and The Blue Notes along with The O'Jays made sure the world felt the sound of Philadelphia.

Oasis: The European label was owned by Giorgio Moroder and Pete Bellotte, who is credited for finding Donna Summer and releasing the 17-minute song, *Love to love You Baby* by the Queen of Disco.

ABC: Pinned another Hot 100 single with *Sweet Thing* by Rufus.

A&M: After a solid run with Billy Preston charting in the past, this year The Brothers Johnson would represent the label on the Hot 100.

Curtom: Curtis Mayfield's label made the charts with a classic from The Staple Singers, *Let's Do It Again*.

Warner Bros: With a hit from George Benson, the label managed to make a buzz amongst the more popular labels in the urban genre.

Casablanca: Originally founded by industry executive of Buddah Records, Neil Bogart and partners, with financing from *Warner Bros.*, they started the venture after leaving Buddah and signed groups such as Kiss, Donna Summer, Parliament, Lipps, Inc., Cher , and The Village People. To date the catalogue is under the direction of Tommy Mottola.

Circa 1977

⇒ **Politics**: **On January 20, 1977, Jimmy Carter** succeeds Gerald Ford as 39th President.

On January 21, 1977, *Ashford & Simpson* released *So So Satisfied* on **Warner Bros Records**. The album went to #30 on the R&B charts.

TV News — Soul Train: On January 1, 8, 15, 22 & 29, 1977, The Supremes, Al Hudson & the Soul Partners – The Sylvers, Donald Byrd & the Blackbyrds – Billy Paul, Brick – Lou Rawls, L.T.D. – Billy Preston and Brenda Payton were featured guests.

On February 5, 1977, *Minnie Riperton* releases *Stay in Love* on **Epic Records**. Its hottest single, *Stick Together* reached #23 on the Dance charts.

⇒ **TV News — Soul Train: On February 5, 12, 19, 26, 1977, Rufus featuring Chaka Khan, The Impressions – The Commodores, Thelma Houston – The Dramatics, Randy Crawford, Crown Heights Affair – Ashford & Simpson, and Bootsy's Rubber Band** were featured guests.

On February 18, 1977, *Gloria Gaynor* releases *Glorious* on **Polydor Records**. This was the 4th album released by Gaynor.

On February 19, Hip Hop pioneer, Prince Markie Dee of the Fat Boys turn 9 years old. *(Born 2-19-1968)*

In February of 1977, *Natalie Cole* released *Unpredictable* on **Capitol Records**. Her top selling single, *I've Got Love on My Mind*, peaked at #5 on the Hot 100.

On March 8, 1977, *The Isley Brothers* released *Go for Your Guns* on **T-Neck Records**. Like many of its prior projects, this album reached #1 on the Soul Album chart and #6 on Pop.

On March 30, 1977, The *Commodores* released *Commodores* on ***Motown Records***. The album broke top 5 on the R&B charts.

In March of 1977, *The Ohio Players* released *Angel* on ***Mercury Records***. Its top single *O-H-I-O* reached #9 on the R&B charts, while the album peaked at #9 on the Soul charts.

In March of 1977, *Tavares* released *Love Storm* on ***Capitol Records***. The album's chart-topping single, *Whodunit* peaked at #22 on the Pop charts.

⇒ **Magazine News: In March of 1977, Michael Jackson** appears on the cover JET.

1977 – Urban American
Grammy Award Recipients – 19th Annual

Awards, 1977: Stevie Wonder wins Album of the Year *(Songs in the Key of Life)*.

Awards, 1977: George Benson wins Record of the Year *(This Masquerade)*.

Awards, 1977: Richard Pryor wins Best Comedy Recording *(Bicentennial Nigger)*.

Awards, 1977: Norman Whitfield wins Best Original Score Written for a Motion Picture or Television Special. (Car Wash)

Awards, 1977: Mahalia Jackson wins Best Soul Gospel Performance *(How I Got Over)*.

Awards, 1977: Count Basie wins Best Jazz Performance by a Soloist (Instrumental) *(Basie and Zoot.*

Awards, 1977: Duke Ellington wins Best Jazz Performance by a Big Band *(The Ellington Suites)*.

Awards, 1977: Ella Fitzgerald wins Best Jazz Vocal Performance *(Fitzgerald and Pass... Again)*.

Awards, 1977: Stevie Wonder wins Best Pop Vocal Performance, Male *(Songs in the Key of Life)*.

Awards, 1977: George Benson wins Best Pop Instrumental Performance *(Breezin)*.

Awards, 1977: Stevie Wonder wins Best Producer of the Year.

Awards, 1977: Natalie Cole wins Best R&B Vocal Performance, Female *(Sophisticated Lady "She's a Different Lady")*.

Awards, 1977: Stevie Wonder wins Best R&B Vocal Performance, Male *(I Wish)*.

Awards, 1977: Billy Davis, Jr. & Marilyn McCoo win Best R&B Vocal Performance by a Duo, Group or Chorus *(You Don't Have to Be a Star "To Be in My Show)*

Awards, 1977: George Benson wins Best R&B Instrumental Performance *(Theme from Good King Bad)*

TV News—Soul Train: On March 5, 12, 19 & 26, 1977, Latimore, Shalamar, Crown Heights Affair –Natalie Cole, Arthur Prysock – Al Green, Fatback Band – Melba Moore and Joe Tex were featured guests.

On April 2, 1977, *Phyllis Hyman* releases her self-titled album *Phyllis Hyman* on **Buddah Records**. The debut album peaked at #107 on Billboard 200, and its bestselling single, *No One Can Love You More* reached #58 on the Hot Soul charts.

On April 4, 1977, *Rufus* released *Ask Rufus* on **ABC Records**. The album, like their first release, went on to reach platinum status.

⇒ **News: On April 26, 1977,** the notorious disco *Studio 54* night club opens in New York City.
⇒ **TV News—Soul Train: On April 2, 9, 16, 23 & 30, 1977, Roy Ayers Ubiquity, Lonnie Liston Smith, Gwen McCrae – B.T. Express, Letta Mbulu, Enchatment – Archie Bell & the Drells, Brainstorm – Teddy Pendergrass, Double Exposure – Smokey Robinson and Lakeside** were featured guests.

⇒ **Film News—Blaxploitation:** **In May of 1977, British Lion Films** released *"The Greatest"* directed by *Tom Gries & Monte Hellman*, starring **Muhammad Ali** and **James Earl Jones.**

On May 13, 1977;, *Donna Summer* releases *I Remember Yesterday* on **Casablanca Records**. The album reached #3 in the UK, #18 on the Billboard 200, and #11 on the R&B charts.

In May of 1977, *The O'Jays* release *Travelin' at the Speed of Thought* on **Philadelphia International Records**. The album reached #6 on the R&B charts.

⇒ **TV News—Soul Train:** **On May 7 & 14, 1977, Marvin Gaye – Harold Melvin & the Blue Notes, and Side Effect** were featured guests.

On June 3, 1977, *Bob Marley & The Wailers* released *Exodus* on *Island Records*. The album reached #15 on the R&B charts and also reached gold status in the US.

On June 8, 1977, Hip Hop producer and Rap Star, Kanye West is born.

On June 29, 1977, Jermaine Jackson releases *Feel the Fire* on **Motown Records**. This was Jermaine's 2nd solo album since he left the Jackson 5; it reached #36 on the R&B charts.

- ⇒ **Film News—Blaxploitation: On July 1, 1977, Warner Bros.** released *"Greased Lightning"* directed by *Michael Schultz*, starring **Richard Pryor, Beau Bridges** and **Pam Grier.**
- ⇒ **NYC Blackout: On July 3, 1977, New York City** blacks out with no power for 25 hours.
- ⇒ **Magazine News: On July 18, 1977, Major League Baseball player, Rod Crew** lands cover of *Time.*
- ⇒ **TV News—Soul Train: On August 20 & 27, 1977, O.C. Smith, Hot, Floaters – Jermaine Jackson, and Switch** were featured guests.

On August 30, 1977, Barry White releases *Barry White Sings for Someone You Love* on **20th Century Records**. The classic album reached #1 on the Soul charts, while singles, *Playing Your Game, Baby* reached #8 on the R&B charts, and *It's Ecstasy When You Lay Down Next to Me* reached #1.

- ⇒ **TV News—Animation: On September 10, 1977, NBC** released *I Am the Greatest: The Adventures of Muhammad Ali* created by *Fred & Kimie Calvert* starring **Muhammad Ali** as his own voice.

- ⇒ **Sports News:** On September 14, 1977, **HBO** debuts *Inside the NFL*; the show featured highlights from around the league from week to week.
- ⇒ **TV News — Soul Train:** On September 3, 10, 17 & 24, 1977, The O'Jays, Al Jarreau, Truth – Johnny Guitar Watson, The Whispers – Tyrone Davis, Dorothy Moore – The Dramatics and Tata Vega were featured guests.

On September 16, 1977, *Diana Ross* releases *Baby It's Me* on **Motown Records**. The album reached #7 on the Black Albums charts and #18 on Pop.

- ⇒ **Film News — Blaxploitation:** On October 7, 1977, **Warner Bros.** released *"A Piece of Action"* directed by *Sidney Portier,* starring **Bill Cosby, James Earl Jones** and **Sidney Portier.**

On October 8, 1977, The Jacksons released *Goin' Places* on **Epic & Philadelphia International Records**. Not considered to be one of their best bodies of work, the album peaked at #63 on the Billboard 200, but reached #11 on the R&B charts.

⇒ **TV News — Soul Train:** On October 1, 8, 15, 22 & 29, 1977, The Emotions, Maze featuring Frankie Beverly – Lamont Dozier, Phyllis Hyman, High Inergy – Smokey Robinson, Dee Dee Sharp – Tavares, David Oliver- Johnnie Taylor & Millie Jackson were featured guests.

On October 9, 1977, *Ashford & Simpson* release *Send It* on **Warner Bros. Records**. *Send it* went gold and charted #10 on the R&B charts.

On October 12, 1977, Atlanta based Rap Star, Young Jeezy is born.

⇒ **Sports News — MLB: On October 18, 1977, Reggie Jackson,** aka Mr. October, hits three home runs to lead the New York Yankees to a World Series win.

On October 25, 1977, *Donna Summer* releases *Once Upon a Time* on **Casablanca Records**. The album charted at #1 on the Dance/Disco charts and #13 on R&B.

In October of 1977, *Ray Charles* released *True to Life* on **Atlantic Records**. Compiled mostly of cover tunes this was the first album released by Ray upon his return to Atlantic.

- ⇒ **Drugs**: **In October of 1977, under President Jimmy Carter**, the U.S Senate Judiciary Committee voted to decriminalize possession of up to an ounce of marijuana for personal use.
- ⇒ **Magazine News: In October of 1977, O.J. Simpson** lands cover of *People*.
- ⇒ **Magazine News: In October of 1977, Donna Summer** lands cover of *EBONY*.
- ⇒ **Film News—Blaxploitation: On November 4, 1977, Universal Pictures** released *"Which Way Is Up"* directed by *Michael Schultz*, starring **Richard Pryor**.

On November 14, 1977, Detroit based Rap Star, Obie Trice is born.

On November 16, 1977, *Natalie Cole* releases *Thankful* on **Capitol Records**. The album peaked at #5 on the Soul charts, while the single, *Our Love* reached #1 on the R&B charts.

On November 21, 1977, *Earth, Wind & Fire* release *All 'n All* **on *Columbia Records*.** The classic album went on to reach triple platinum status.

⇒ **Film News—Blaxploitation:** In 1977, **Mirror Releasing** released *"Abar, the First Black Superman"* directed by *Frank Packard,* starring **Tobar Mayo**.

⇒ **Film News—Blaxploitation:** In November of 1977, **Burt Steiger & Theodore Toney** produced *"Petey Wheatstraw"* directed by *Cliff Roquemore,* starring **Rudy Ray Moore**.

On November 22, 1977, *Chic* released their self-titled album *Chic* **on *Atlantic Records*.** Their debut album reached #12 on the R&B charts and went on to gold status. Their most noted singles, *Dance, Dance, Dance (Yowsah, Yowsah, Yowsah)* charted #1 on the club charts, while *Everybody Dance* also peaked at #1 on the club charts.

⇒ **TV News—Soul Train: On November 5, 12, 19 & 26, 1977, Teddy Pendergrass, Rose Royce – Barry White, Love Unlimited – Lou Rawls, The Ritchie Family – The Manhattans & Kellee Patterson** were featured guests.

On November 28, 1977, *Parliament* released *Funkentelechy Vs. the Placebo Syndrome* on *Casablanca Records*. Its most noted single, *Flash Light* reached #1 on the R&B charts.

⇒ **Magazine News: In November of 1977, Willona (Ja'Net DuBois)** and **Penny (Janet Jackson)** of the sitcom *Good Times* appear on the cover of *JET*.
⇒ **TV News—Soul Train: On December 3, 10, 17, 24 & 31, 1977, Deniece Williams, Mother's Finest – Ashford & Simpson, Ronnie Dyson – The Spinners, Hodges, James & Smith – Brick, Sister Sledge – Philippe' Wynne, Side Effect, Al Hudson & the Soul Partners** were featured guests.

On December 6, 1977, *Al Green* released *The Belle Album* on **Hi Records**. This would be last album recorded by Green before he became an ordained minister and started to release gospel music.

On December 13, 1977, **Roberta Flack** released *Blue Lights in the Basement* on **Atlantic Records**. The album reached #5 on the R&B charts and #8 on the Pop.

In December of 1977, *The Ohio Players* released *Mr. Mean* on **Mercury Records**. The album reached #11 on the Soul charts.

⇒ **Film News—Disco: On December 14, 1977, Paramount Pictures** released *"Saturday Night Fever"* directed by *Robert Stigwood* and *Kevin McCormick*, starring **John Travolta**.

Underneath the smooth sounds of R&B, the electric vibes of funk, and vibrant seduction of disco, a new genre of music was being created by the African American youth of the New York (Bronx) ghettos. Any fan of music outside of the city had no idea, but the suits and all their counterparts in NYC who played major roles in bringing music to the masses were well aware. Not even Jesus Christ himself could have prepared them for what lay ahead. It started early in the 1970's as a source of entertainment, summer block parties at the park with kids dancing to the hottest music being played by their local DJ's.

Those kids all contributed to the culture, whether fan, B-Boy, DJ, Tagger, or MC, the culmination of their talents, relentless drive, and originality would give birth to a new way of life, an unforgiving culture where your street credibility or name carried weight amongst its peers; this was the true core of the movement that spawned the four core elements of Hip Hop.

4 Elements of Hip Hop

Graffiti, 1970-1977: Before the MC (Rapper) ever made his/her mark, the tagger or bomber was putting in work. Like the music side of Hip Hop, these artists also expressed themselves through their talent. It is safe to say that the elaborate murals on the New York subway trains and walls of its Burroughs was the back drop for our culture, rightfully taking its place as one of the four core elements of Hip Hop—Tagging, Rapping, DeeJaying, and Breakdancing.

Deejaying, 1970-1977: At the center of the Hip Hop movement was the DJ. South Bronx DJ's like *Kool Herc* and *Afrika Bambaataa* would throw block parties at the parks while jacking power from the street light poles to power their equipment. People would gather to dance to the hippest music, among them were the Graffiti Artists, B-Boys, and the MC all accompanying the DJ Crew to hype up the DJ to the crowd.

Break Dancing, 1970-1977: Dance crews like the *Rock Steady Crew* would battle other dance crews at block parties, clubs, or where ever they could find room. Dance crews battled each other in dance instead of fighting to stop and/or minimize the gang violence.

Rapping, 1970-1977: In the beginning, MC's entertained party crowds by hyping their DJ, but as the culture progressed, these hype men turned into story tellers, aka *Rappers*. It was at this point where four elements merge together through the rapper's delivery, detailing a vivid picture of the ghetto and how its negativity inspired a movement. Their voices carried these images outside of New York City via mix tapes, word of mouth, and underground radio shows. Soon every ghetto in every city, state, and country fell in line and supported the Hip Hop movement. We walked the walk, talked the talk, dressed how we wanted, and no one was going to stop us; Hip Hop's foundation was now set and for better or worse there would be no turning back. The energy was being felt by the masses, including those who held the keys to the Music Industry; they would try to resist, but soon they would have to give the people what they wanted and learn the true meaning of "*Hip Hop, can't Stop, won't Stop!*"

For a more detailed look into the four elements of Hip Hop and its players before the incorporation of Hip Hop, you should read: <u>Can't Stop, Won't Stop</u> by Jeff Chang and <u>That's the Joint</u> by Murray Forman and Mark Anthony Neal.

1977 – Billboards Year End – Hot 100 Singles

1977	Urban Music 21% of Billboard's Year-End Hot 100	21%
3	The Emotions – Best of My Love	Columbia
7	Thelma Houston – Don't Leave Me This Way	Motown
11	KC and the Sunshine Band – I'm Your Boogie Man	TK
18	Stevie Wonder – Sir Duke	Tamla
20	Marvin Gaye – Got to Give it Up	Tamla
25	The Sylvers – Hot Line	Capitol
26	Rose Royce – Car Wash	MCA
27	Marilyn McCoo & Billy Davis Jr. – You Don't Have to Be a Star Baby (To Be in My Show)	ABC
33	Commodores – Easy	Motown
35	Natalie Cole – I've Got Love on My Mind	Capitol
40	The Jacksons – Enjoy Yourself	Philadelphia International
41	Brick – Jazz	Bang
51	Stevie Wonder – I Wish	Tamla
54	The Brothers Johnson – Strawberry Letter 23	A&M
72	The Floaters – Float On	ABC
75	KC and the Sunshine Band – Keep it Comin Love	TK
81	The Spinners – The Rubber band Man	Atlantic
84	The Sylvers – High School Dance	Capitol
86	Joe Tex – Ain't Gonna Bump No More (With No Big Fat Woman)	Tree Productions/ Epic
87	Rose Royce – I Wanna Get Next to You	MCA/Whitfield
93	Heatwave – Boogie Nights	GTO

1977 – Record Labels in Urban Music

Columbia: As the number of urban singles decreased on the Hot 100 charts, Columbia and producers Maurice White and Al McKay of Earth, Wind & Fire pinned a hit with The Emotions single, *Best of My Love*.

Philadelphia International: The sound of Philadelphia continued to roll with two singles hitting the Hot 100, again proving their staying power. The original single, *Don't Leave Me This Way*, was released first by Harold Melvin & the Blue Notes before *Motown's* Thelma Houston made it a disco hit.

Motown/Tamla: With 5 singles on the Hot 100 this year from 4 different artists, Gordy and his prolific roster of talent were kings of the hill once again.

TK: Still riding the wave of Disco, the label pinned two Hot 100 classics from its hottest group, KC and the Sunshine Band.

Capitol: With 3 singles on the Hot 100 from two different artists, the label continued to make a name for itself in the urban arena.

Bang: Originally founded in 1965 by Bert Bern's and fellow execs from Atlantic Records, Ahmet Artegon, Nesuhi Artegon, and Jerry Wexler. The label name comes from the first letters of their names using Gerald for Jerry. B-A-N-G

MCA: With the help of Norman Whitfield and Rose Royce, the label was responsible for releasing the classic soundtrack album *Car Wash*, which pinned 2 Hot 100 singles this year.

ABC: The Floaters pinned a hit, and the classic from Billy Davis, Jr. and Marilyn McCoo assured the labels place in the urban genre.

A&M: The label had only one single to hit the 100 this year, but it would go on to be a platinum success for The Brother's Johnson.

Atlantic: The Spinners, like they did so many times before, made the Hot 100 yet again, making the label relevant to the urban genre.

GTO: Originally founded in 1974 by Laurence Myers, the UK based label signed such acts as Billy Ocean and Heatwave. They were also responsible for releasing Donna Summer's albums in the UK.

Circa 1978

On January 27, 1978, *Bootsy's Rubber band* released *Bootsy? Player of the Year* on **Warner Bros. Records**. The album reached #1 on the Soul Album charts while its hottest single, *Bugzilla* peaked at #1 on the Hot Soul charts.

In January of 1978; *Muddy Waters* released *I'm Ready* on **Blue Sky Records**. The album consisted of several chart-topping singles, and earned the Chicago Jazz musician a Grammy.

In January of 1978, *Rufus* released *Street Player* on **ABC Records**. This album would be the 3rd one to go gold as it top the R&B charts with Chaka Khan on lead vocals.

- ⇒ **TV News—Soul Train: On January 7, 14, 21 & 28, 1978, Brothers Johnson, Foster Sylvers – Freda Payne, Ronnie Laws, Morris Jefferson – The Sylvers, Lawrence Hilton-Jacobs – Bill Withers & Odyssey** were featured guests.
- ⇒ **Film News—Blaxploitation: On February 3, 1978, New World Pictures** released *"A Hero Aint Nothin' But A Sandwich"* directed by *Ralph Nelson*, starring **Cicely Tyson** and **Paul Winfield**.
- ⇒ **Sports News—Boxing: On February 15, 1978, Leon Spinks** wins the heavyweight title in a 15-round decision against *Muhammad Ali*.
- ⇒ **TV News—Soul Train: On February 4, 11, 18 & 25, 1978, L.T.D, Michael Henderson – The Temptations, William Bell, Pattie Brooks – WAR, Eloise Laws – Billy Preston & Esther Phillips** were featured guest.

On **March 23, 1978**, *Bob Marley & The Wailers* release *"Kaya"* on *Tuff Gong/Island Records*. The album broke the Top 5 on the UK charts.

- ⇒ **Magazine News: In March of 1978, Donna Summer** lands the cover of *Rolling Stone*.
- ⇒ **Magazine News: In March of 1978, Richard Pryor** lands cover of *People*.
- ⇒ **TV News—Super Hero: On March 10, 1978, CBS** debuts *The Incredible Hulk* starring **Bill Bixby** and **Lou Ferrigno**.
- ⇒ **TV News—Soul Train: (Soul Train): On March 4, 11, 18 & 25, 1978, Lonnie Jordan, Brass Construction, Pattie Brooks – The Four Tops, Con Funk Shun – Bobby Womack, Denise LaSalle – Marilyn McCoo, Billy Davis, Jr., Cheryl Barnes & Stargard** were featured guest.
- ⇒ **Magazine News: In April of 1978, Herbie Hancock** lands cover of *Black Music & Jazz Review*.
- ⇒ **TV News—Soap Opera: On April 2, 1978, CBS** debuts *Dallas* starring **Linda Gray, Patrick Duffy** and **Larry Hagman**.

⇒ **TV News—Soul Train: (Soul Train)**: On April 1, 8, 15, 22 & 29, 1978, **Harold Melvin & The Blue Notes, Roy Ayers – Johnny Mathis, Deniece Williams – Enchantment, Wild Cherry, Bunny Sigler – Herb Alpert & Hugh Masekela, Aalon – The 5th Dimension & Mandrill** were feature guests.

On April 7, 1978, *Prince* releases his debut album *For You* on **Warner Bros. Records**. Most noted singles, *Soft and Wet* reached #92 on the Hot 100 and #12 on Hot Soul Singles charts, while *Just as Long as We're Together* reached #91 on the R&B charts.

On April 13, 1978, *Aretha Franklin* releases *Almighty Fire* on **Atlantic Records**. This album didn't do as well as her prior classics mostly because the musical climate was being overtaken by the new Disco era. The Queen of soul did manage to reach #12 on the R&B charts with the title single.

On April 20, 1978, *Rick James* releases his debut album *Come Get It* on **Gordy Records**. Out of the gate the album's two most noted singles, You *and I*, and *Mary Jane* pinned Rick James' first album double platinum.

Evolution of Hip Hop, 1978: As a young African American, Latino or Caribbean during this time in the late 70's, most of us aspired to be like the local street hustlers, pimps or athletes in our poverty-stricken neighborhoods. The Rick James, Curtis Mayfield's, Marvin Gaye's, George Clinton's, Rose Royce's and Brother Johnson to name a few, only magnified the ghetto lifestyle through their music. It seemed that everywhere we looked our lives were being exploited in song and in Blaxploitation films on the movie screen. So, it was only natural for us to emulate what we'd seen and heard; Hip Hop would combine the flashy clothes, disco moves, poverty, the street names like Supa Fly and Mack, with the life of our neighborhood drug dealer, pimp and hustler to create a compelling persona. Once that MC grabbed the mic and started telling fables and sometimes even truth over the hottest instrumentals being spun by the DJ, the most influential element of Hip Hop was born, and it would ride into the music industry on the shoulders of giants.

1978 – Urban America

Grammy Award Recipients – 20th Annual

Awards, 1978: Muddy Waters wins Best Ethnic or Traditional Recording *(Hard Again)*.

Awards, 1978: James Cleveland wins Best Soul Gospel Performance, Traditional *(James Cleveland Live at Carnegie Hall)*.

Awards, 1978: Oscar Peterson wins Best Performance by a Soloist *(The Giants)*.

Awards, 1978: Count Basie wins Best Jazz Performance by a Big Band *(Prime Time)*.

Awards, 1978: Al Jarreau wins Best Jazz Vocal Performance *(Look to the Rainbow)*.

Awards, 1978: Thelma Houston wins Best R&B Vocal Performance, Female *(Don't Leave Me This Way)*.

Awards, 1978: Lou Rawls wins Best R&B Vocal Performance, Male *(Unmistakably Lou)*.

Awards, 1978: The Emotions win Best R&B Vocal Performance by a Duo, Group or Chorus *(Best of My Love)*.

Awards, 1978: The Brothers Johnson wins Best R&B Instrumental Performance *(Q)*.

On April 25, 1978, *The Isley Brothers* release *Showdown* on **T-Neck Records**. The album reached #1 on the Soul charts, #4 on the Pop.

In April of 1978, *Tavares* releases *Future Bound* on ***Capitol Records***. Their remake of the Bee Gees, *More Than a Woman*, reached #32 on the Hot 100 and was also featured on the *Saturday Night Fever* soundtrack.

⇒ **Film News — Martial Arts Blaxploitation: In April of 1978, Leo Fong** produced *"Blind Rage"* starring ***Fred Williamson***.

In May of 1978, the *Commodores* released *Natural High* on ***Motown Records***. The albums single, *Three Times a Lady* peaked at #1 on the Hot 100, while the album also reached #1 on the R&B charts and #3 on Pop.

Film News: On May 24, 1978, American International Pictures released *"Youngblood"* directed by *Noel Nosseck*, starring ***Lawrence Hilton-Jacobs***.

TV News — Soul Train: On May 6 & 13, 1978, Smokey Robinson, Patti Austin – Cuba Gooding & Lenny Williams were featured guests.

On June 7, 1978, *Grace Jones* released *Fame* on **Island Records**. Capitalizing on the Disco era, Jones' album charted across the country placing #5 in Canada, #15 in Italy, #22 in Sweden, #57 on the U.S. Top R&B/Black Albums, and #59 in Australia.

On June 15, 1978, *Herbie Hancock* released *Sunlight* on **Columbia Records**. This would be the first time Hancock's vocals were heard through the vocoder (synthesizer).

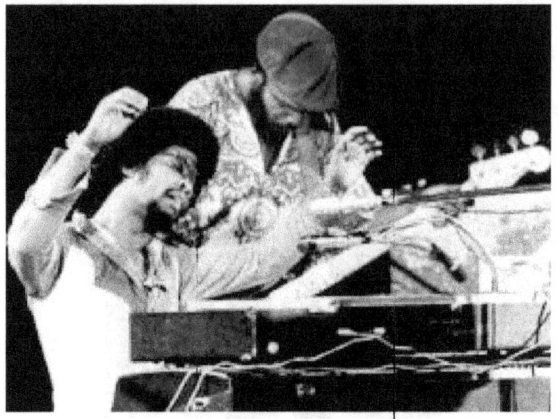

On July 17, 1978, *Cheryl Lynn* releases her debut album *Cheryl Lynn* on **Columbia Records**. Her debut release reached #5 on the R&B charts, while the single *Got To Be Real* reached #1 on the R&B Single charts.

In July of 1978, *Norma Jean Wright* released *Norma Jean* on **Bearsville Records**. The album pinned a Top 20 R&B hit with *Saturday* reaching #15 on the charts.

On August 7, 1978, *Roberta Flack* released *Roberta Flack* on **Atlantic Records**. The album charted with single, *If Ever I See You Again* peaking at #1 on the Adult Contemporary charts.

On August 11, 1978, *Chic* releases *C'est Chic* on **Atlantic Records**. The hottest single on the album, *Le Freak*, went on to sell 6 million albums in the U.S. The sophomore album reached #4 on the album charts and currently holds the record for best-selling single ever for its respective labels.

In August of 1978, Curtis Mayfield releases *Do It All Night* on **Curtom Records**.

In August of 1978, *Ashford & Simpson* release *Is It Still Good to Ya* on **Warner Bros. Records**. The album peaked at #1 on the R&B charts and reached gold status.

In August of 1978, the *Ohio Players* release *Jass-Ay-Lay-Dee* on **Mercury Records**. This would be the last album recorded on the *Mercury* label, and it reached #15 on the Soul charts.

TV News—Soul Train: On August 19 & 26, 1978, The O'Jays, Etta James – Brothers Johnson, and The Dells were featured guests.

On August 11, 1978, *Rose Royce* releases *Rose Royce III* on **Whitfield Records**. The junior album reached #4 on the Soul charts, #7 in the UK, while the hit single, *Love Don't Live Here Anymore* peaked at #2 in the UK and #5 in the U.S.

In August of 1978, *KC and the Sunshine Band* release *Who Do Ya (Love)* on **TK Records**. Only one of its singles reached the charts, *It's the Same Old Song*, an original Four Tops track placed on the Hot 100.

⇒ **Magazine News**: **In August of 1978, George E. Johnson**, President of Johnson Products Co., Inc. lands cover of *Black Enterprise*.

⇒ **Drugs—Government:** *Asset Forfeiture* is amended into the Comprehensive Drug Abuse Prevention and Control Act. This allows law enforcement *"to seize all money and/or other things of value furnished or intended to be furnished by any person in exchange for a controlled substance and all proceeds traceable to such an exchange"*.

On September 3, 1978, *Diana Ross* releases *Ross* on **Motown Records**. The album reached #32 on the Black Album charts and #49 on Billboard 200.

On September 11, 1978, *Funkadelic* releases *One Nation Under a Groove* on **Warner Bros. Records**. Noted as one of the best funk albums of all time, it was also ranked #177 on Rolling Stone magazine's list of the 500 Greatest Albums of All Time.

⇒ **Sports News — Boxing:** On September 15, 1978, **Muhammad Ali** recovers the heavyweight title a third time by decision in his rematch against *Leon Spinks*.

On September 19, 1978, *Al Jarreau* releases *All Fly Home* on **Warner Bros. records**. The album reached #2 on the Jazz charts and #27 on R&B.

On September 22, 1978, *Barry White* releases *The Man* on *20th Century Fox Records*. The album reached #1 on the Soul charts, while the single *Your Sweetness Is My Weakness* peaked at #2 on the R&B charts.

In September of 1978, *Tina Turner* releases *Rough* on **United Artist Records**. This was Tina's debut solo album.

⇒ **TV News — Soul Train:** On September 2, 9, 16, 23 & 30, 1978; **The Emotions, Randy Jackson, Hal Jackson Talented Teen – The Sylvers, Kenny Brawner & Raw Sugar – Earth Wind & Fire, Heaven & Earth – Rose Royce, D.J. Rogers – Peabo Bryson and Stargard** were featured guests.

⇒ **Film News — Musical Adventure:** On October 24, 1978, **Motown Productions & Universal Pictures** released *"The Wiz"* directed by *Sidney Lumet,* starring **Diana Ross, Michael Jackson, Lena Horne, Richard Pryor, Theresa Merritt, Thelma Carpenter,** *and* **Nipsey Russell.**

On October 12, 1978, *Chaka Khan* releases *Chaka* on **Warner Bros Records**. This would be Chaka's debut solo album; she pinned a hit single with the classic, *I'm Every Woman*, which peaked at #1 on the Soul charts.

In October of 1978, *The Bar-Kays* released *Money Talks* on **Stax Records**. The album peaked at #21 on the Soul charts.

In October of 1978, *The Three Degrees* released *New Dimensions* on **Ariola Records**. The album consisted of three hot singles breaking the Top 20 in the UK, *The Runner* at #10, *Giving Up, Giving In* at #12, and *Woman in Love* at #3.

⇒ **TV News — Soul Train:** On October 7, 14, 21 & 28, 1978, **Larry Graham & Graham Central Station, Charles Jackson – The Whispers, Gil Scott-Heroin, Evelyn "Champagne" King – Melba Moore, Michael Henderson – Freda Payne and Atlantic Starr** were featured guests.

⇒ **TV News — Sitcom:** On November 3, 1978, **NBC** debuts *Diff'rent Strokes* starring *Gary Coleman* and *Todd Bridges*.

⇒ **Events:** November 18, 1978, *Jonestown Mass Murder/Suicide*, under the direction of Jim Jones 909 Americans collectively committed suicide.

On November 20, 1978, Parliament releases *Motor Booty Affair* on **Casablanca Records**. Its most noted single, *Aqua Boogie*, peaked at #1 on the Soul charts.

On November 27, 1978, Gloria Gaynor releases *Love Tracks* on **Polydor Records**. This album pinned the classic #1 Disco single, *I Will Survive*, which went on to platinum status.

⇒ **TV News — Soul Train:** On November 4, 11, 18 & 25, 1978, **The Trammps, Shalamar, Norma Jean Wright – Frankie Valli, Crème D' Coca – Jerry Butler, Rick James – Lenny Williams, Mother's Finest and Cheech & Chong** were featured guests.

In November of 1978, *Peabo Bryson* released *Crosswinds* on *Capitol Records*. The junior album peaked at #3 on the R&B charts.

⇒ **TV News — Drama: On November 27, 1978, CBS** debuts *The White Shadow* starring *Byron Stewart, Thomas Carter, Timothy Van Patten* and several other characters.

In November of 1978, *The Pointer Sisters* released *Energy* on *Planet Records*. The album reached #9 on the Soul charts and #13 on Top LP's, with *Fire* being its best-selling single reaching #2 on the Pop charts and going certified gold.

⇒ **TV News — Soul Train: On December 2, 9, 16, 23 & 30, 1978, Johnny Guitar Watson, Jean Carne – Stylistics, Sun – Barry White, Danny Pearson – Switch, The McCrays – The Temptations and Randy Brown** were featured guests.

On December 1, 1978, *Herbie Hancock* releases *Directstep* on **Columbia Records**. Hancock only released this album in Japan, and it would be one of the first albums to be released on CD.

On December 15, 1978, *Marvin Gaye* releases *Here, My Dear* on **Tamla Records**. The album went on to reach #4 on the Black Album charts.

On December 17, 1978, *The Jacksons* released *Destiny* on **Epic Records**. The Jackson's had proven their production capabilities with this album as it went on to sell over 4 million copies worldwide.

1978 – Billboards Year End – Hot 100 Singles

1978	Urban Music 16% of Billboards Year-End Hot 100	16%
9	**A Taste of Honey** – *Boogie Oogie Oogie*	Capitol
10	**Commodores** – *Three Times A Lady*	Motown
20	**Chic** – *Dance, Dance, Dance (Yowsah, Yowsah, Yowsah)*	Buddah/Atlantic
34	**Donna Summer** – *Last Dance*	Casablanca
38	**Roberta Flack & Donny Hathaway** – *The Closer I Get to You*	Atlantic
42	**The O'Jays** – *Use ta Be My Girl*	Philadelphia International
43	**Natalie Cole** – *Our Love*	Capitol
49	**Heatwave** – *The Groove Line*	GTO
54	**The Trammps** – *Disco Inferno*	Atlantic
55	**George Benson** – *On Broadway*	Atlantic
57	**L.T.D.** – *(Every Time I Turn Around) Back in Love Again*	A&M
64	**Evelyn "Champagne" King** – *Shame*	RCA
75	**Heatwave** – *Always and Forever*	GTO/Epic
76	**Rick James** – *You and I*	Gordy
77	**Earth Wind & Fire** – *Serpentine Fire*	Columbia
85	**Foxy** – *Get Off*	Dash/TK
92	**Parliament** – *Flashlight*	Casablanca

1978 – Record Labels in Urban Music

Capitol: With hits from Natalie Cole and the hot disco group, Taste of Honey, the label pinned two Hot 100 Singles this year that went on to be classics.

Motown/Gordy: Both Rick James and the Commodores continued to usher in new found success for the iconic label.

Atlantic: Seventy-eight was a great year for the label, with four Hot 100 Singles from four different artists, proving once again that they could recruit and manage good talent; all this accomplished even while they were in the process of building their Rock & Roll catalogue.

Philadelphia International: The sound of Phila only charted one Hot 100 Single this year from the O'Jays, but like all the prior hits before this one, it too kept us dancing.

Casablanca: The Queen of Disco, Donna Summer along with Parliament continued to keep the label relevant and atop of the disco and funk era. *Polygram* would share in the success due to the 50% stake they acquired a year before.

GTO: Thanks to Heatwave's continued string of hits, the label enjoyed two Hot 100 Singles this year. Because of this success, major record companies came calling, which led to GTO being purchased by *CBS* records this year.

A&M: With a classic hit from L.T.D., the label managed to pin one slot on the Hot 100 this year even though its roster consisted mostly of Rock bands.

RCA: The young Evelyn "Champagne" King hit the charts with her smash single, *Shame*, making the others take notice.

Columbia: The three elements, Earth Wind & Fire carried the label this year with another classic hit.

Dash/TK: *Dash*, a subsidiary label under TK was created to release just singles; the label is credited for signing the Blue Notes before they signed with *Philadelphia International Records*, when their name changed to *Harold Melvin & The Blue Notes* with *Teddy Pendergrass* singing lead. The rest is history. Dash did however manage to top the charts for the first time this year with a Cuban group who was exiled from Cuba by Castro called *Foxy*; they would go on to release the labels top selling single to date, *Get Off* which went on to be a Disco classic.

Sylvia Robinson

As Rap Music became more popular in the streets of New York it would be a platinum selling female vocalist and producer who would take the first step in bringing the new genre to the masses. Sylvia Robinson and husband Joe launched the first successful rap label and named it after an artistic neighborhood in Harlem, New York—the genesis of **Sugar Hill Records**. Sylvia started in the industry as a young kid and sold millions of records throughout her career. It was this experience that proved successful in releasing *Rappers Delight* by **The Sugar Hill Gang**, *The Message* by **Grandmaster Flash and the Furious Five,** and *Funk U Up* by **The Sequence**. Robinson would lay the blue print that her protégés would take to unspeakable levels, which unfortunately would shorten her reign.

Joe and Sylvia Robinson, founders of Sugar Hill Records

Home: Englewood, New Jersey

Sylvia Robinson, aka Mother of Hip Hop

R.I.P.

March 6, 1936 – September 29, 2011

Circa 1979

Hip Hop Goes Main Stream

The consistency of block parties in the New York City parks, along with night club performances throughout the city, and DJ crews battling for name recognition in their Burroughs all found their ways into an industry that quite frankly had no idea what to make of Hip Hop. Media, at this time, was calling the culture a fad and said it too would fade away. Man, were they wrong! Enter Russell Simmons, a Queens, New York club and party promoter who fell in love with the Hip Hop culture. Inspired by the performances and charisma of pioneering MC's, Artists, DJ's, and Entertainers such as *Eddie Cheba* and *Melle Mel* to name a few, it would be Russell's relentless drive and business savvy that would pioneer the Hip Hop culture into a billion-dollar brand. Russell grabbed the bull by the horns and started managing and developing rap artists, *Kurtis Blow*, the *Beastie Boys* of which *Rick Rubin* was a member, and *RUN DMC*, which included his brother RUN as an MC. He later produced a single featuring Kurtis Blow called *Christmas Rappin* this year that generated a huge street buzz and became a Hip Hop culture favorite, and still remains so today.

Russell Simmons

Home: Queens, New York.

Hip Hop Godfather

On January 1, 1979, *Herbie Hancock* releases *Feets, Don't Fail Me Now* on **Columbia Records**. This would be the 27th album for the prolific and ever-changing musician.

On January 26, 1979, *Rick James* releases *Bustin' Out of L Seven* on **Gordy records**. James' sophomore release reached #2 on the R&B charts while his hit single *Bustin' Out (On Funk)* peaked at #8 on the R&B charts.

⇒ **TV News — Soul Train: On January 6, 13, 20 & 27, 1979, Marilyn McCoo, Billy Davis, Jr., Lakeside – Roy Ayers & Ubiquity, Sarah Dash – Gene Chandler, Chic – Brass Construction, Peaches & Herb and Captain Sky** were featured guests.
⇒ **New York News: On January 13, 1979, Atlantic Records** recording artist, *Donny Hathaway* dies after falling 15 stories from his Essex House hotel room window.

In January of 1979, *Tavares* releases *Madam Butterfly* on **Capitol Records**. The album reached #13 on the R&B charts, while its most noted single, *Never Had a Love Like This Before* peaked at #5 on the R&B charts.

In January of 1979, *Sister Sledge* releases *We Are Family* on **Cotillion records**. The classic album pinned four hit singles and peaked at #1 on the Soul Album charts. Its singles, *He's the Greatest Dancer*, and *We are Family* both peaked at #1 on the R&B charts. The album was written and produced by *Nile Rodgers* and *Bernard Edwards* of *Chic*.

⇒ **Magazine News: In February of 1979, Gary Coleman** lands the cover of ***Ebony***.
⇒ **TV News — Sitcom: On January 26, 1979, CBS** debuts *The Dukes of Hazzard*.
⇒ **TV News — Soul Train: On February 3, 10, 17 & 24, 1979, The Jacksons – Pattie Brooks, David Oliver – Joe Simon, Cheryl Lynn – Edwin Starr, The Jimmy Castor Bunch and Grace Jones** were featured guests.
⇒ **TV News — Soul Train: On March 3. 10, 17, 24 and 31, 1979, Bonnie Pointer, Dan Hartman – Gino Vanelli, Gloria Gaynor – The Bar-Kays, Arpeggio – Isaac Hayes, Tasha Thomas – Instant Funk and Cerrone** were featured guests.

On March 25, 1979, the *Fatback Band* releases *King Tim III (Personality Jock)* on *Spring/Polydor records*. In some circles, this single is considered to be the first Hip Hop single released on a label. It also peaked at #26 on the R&B charts.

In March of 1979, *Natalie Cole* released *I Love You So* on *Capitol records*. The album reached #11 on the R&B charts and would be nominated for a Grammy.

On April 10, 1979, *Barry White* releases *I Love to Sing the Songs I Sing* on *20th Century - Fox records*. This would be the last project White recorded with 20th Century-Fox. It reached #40 on the R&B charts and pinned no other hits with any singles, unlike his previous work.

On April 25, 1979, *Donna Summer* releases *Bad Girls* on **Casablanca records**. This would be Summer's bestselling album to date reaching double platinum status. The album peaked at #1 on the Billboard 200, R&B, and Canadian RPM Hot 100.

⇒ **Magazine News: On April 2, 1979, Donna Summer** lands the cover of *Newsweek*.
⇒ **TV News—Soul Train: On April 7, 14, 21 and 28, 1979, Billy Preston, Syreeta Wright, Chuck Brown & The Soul Searchers – Curtis Mayfield, Linda Clifford, Keith Barrow – Amil Stewart, Boney M – Hamilton Bohannon and The Raes** were featured guests.
⇒ **Magazine News: In April of 1979, Muhammad Ali** lands the cover of *Sports Illustrated*.

On May 22, 1979, *Smokey Robinson* releases *Where There's Smoke* on **Tamla records**. The album pinned a top 10 hit with *Cruisin'*, and reached #8 on the R&B charts.

1979 – Urban American
Grammy Award Recipients – 21st Annual

Awards, 1979: A Taste of Honey wins Best New Artist.

Awards, 1979: Quincy Jones & Robert Freedman win Best Instrumental Arrangement *(The Wiz)*.

Awards, 1979: Maurice White wins Best Arrangement Accompanying Vocals *(Got to Get You into My Life performed by Earth, Wind & Fire)*.

Awards, 1979: Muddy Waters win Best Ethnic or Traditional Recording *(I'm Ready)*.

Awards, 1979: Mighty Clouds of Joy win Best Soul Gospel Performance, Traditional *(Live and Direct)*.

Awards, 1979: Andrae Crouch win Best Soul Performance, Contemporary *(Live in London performed by Andrae Crouch & the Disciples)*.

Awards, 1979: Oscar Peterson wins Best Jazz Instrumental Performance, Soloist *(Oscar Peterson Jam – Montreux)*.

Awards, 1979: Al Jarreau wins Best Jazz Vocal Performance *(All Fly Home)*.

Awards, 1979: Donna Summer wins Best R&B Vocal Performance, Female *(Last Dance)*.

Awards, 1979: George Benson wins Best R&B Vocal Performance, Male *(On Broadway)*.

Awards, 1979: Earth, Wind & Fire win Best R&B Vocal Performance by a Duo, Group or Chorus *(All 'n All)*.

Awards, 1979: Earth, Wind & Fire win Best R&B Instrumental Performance *(Runnin')*.

On May 23, 1979, *Diana Ross* releases *The Boss* on ***Motown records***. The title track peaked at #12 on the R&B charts, #14 on Billboard and the album went certified gold.

⇒ **TV News—Soul Train:** On May 5, 12 and 15, 1979, Third World, Danny Pearson – Tyrone Davis, Gary's Gang – Carrie Lucas, GQ, and The Gap Band were featured guests.

⇒ **Magazine News:** In 1979, **Richard Pryor** landed the cover of *Rolling Stone*.

Hip-Hop (Rap Music): In 1979, *Sugar Hill Records* released their second single *Funk U Up"* by *The Sequence,* the first female rap group to release an album which peaked at #15 on the Black Singles chart.

City: Columbia, S.C. **Members**: Cheryl Cook (Cheryl The Pearl), Gwendolyn Chisolm (Blondie), and Angie Brown Stone (Angie B). **Producer**: Sylvia Robinson

On June 1, 1979, *Bootsy's Rubber Band* released *The Boot Is Made for Fonk-N* on **Warner Bros. Records**.

On June 9, 1979, *Earth, Wind & Fire* release *I Am* on **CBS Records**. The album peaked at #1 on the Black Album charts and #3 on pop, while reaching double platinum status.

In June of 1979, *A Taste of Honey* release *Another Taste* on **Capitol records**. The album reached #26 on the R&B charts.

⇒ **Magazine News**: **In July of 1979, Rick James** lands the cover of *JET*.

Disco Demolition Night: On the night of July 12, 1979, Anti-Disco fans were admitted into Chicago's Comiskey Park, on this night the White Sox played the Detroit Tigers. In a promotion sponsored by *97.9 FM (WLUP)* Disc Jockey, *Steve Dahl,* any anti-disco fan with a disco record and 98 cents were admitted into the two-night doubleheader. In between games, Dahl collected all the disco records and placed them in a crate on the field then lit a fuse and watched them explode. Thousands of anti-disco fans stormed the field in excitement. Disco would never recover from this spectacle.

On July 30, 1979, *Chic* released *Risque'* on **Atlantic Records**. The album went on to reach platinum status with several hit tracks. The most noted single, *Good Times*, peaked at #1 on the Pop and R&B charts.

In July of 1979, the *Commodores* release *Midnight Magic* on **Motown Records**. The album pinned a #1 hit with *Still,* while *Sail On* reached #4.

⇒ **L.A News: On August 9, 1979,** co-founder of the Crips, Raymond Lee Washington was shot and killed several months after he was arrested for quadruple murder.

On August 10, 1979, *Michael Jackson* releases *Off the Wall* on **Epic records**. This would be Michael's 5th solo album, and it went on to be a classic. It went 8x platinum in the U.S., 6x in the UK, 6x in New Zealand, Diamond+ 2x Platinum in Mexico, 2x Platinum in Japan, 7x Platinum in Italy, 4x Platinum in Europe, 3x Platinum in Canada, and 5x Platinum in Australia.

⇒ **TV News—Soul Train: On September 15, 22 & 29,** The show did a tribute to *Minnie Riperton* featuring **Stevie Wonder, Wintley Phipps, Lorraine Fields and Larry Vickers** on 9-15-1979 – **Deniece Williams, Apollo – Shalamar and Tata Vega** were also featured guests this month.

On September 6, 1979, *Kool & the Gang* release *Ladies Night* on **De-Lite records**. This was the 11th album by the group, and all of the tracks went on to reach the Top 5 on the Disco chart, while the album peaked at #1 on the R&B charts.

⇒ **Film News—Blaxploitation: In September of 1979, Transvue Pictures** released *"Disco Godfather"* starring *Rudy Ray Moore*, directed by *J. Robert Wagner*.

On September 6, 1979, *Aretha Franklin* released *La Diva* on **Atlantic Records**. The album only peaked at #146 on the Billboard charts marking the end of a long run for the Queen of Soul as the music landscape geared towards Disco and a new form of music called Hip Hop.

⇒ **TV News—Sitcom: On September 13, 1979, ABC** debuts *"Benson"* starring *Robert Guillaume* as an African American butler for a dysfunctional Caucasian family.

Hip-Hop (Rap Music): On September 16, 1979; *The Sugarhill Gang* release *Rapper's Delight* on **Sugar Hill Records**. The rap single was the first of its kind to reach the Top 40 on Billboard's Hot 100. The track was recorded over *Chic's* instrumental hit record, *Good Times*, a single from this year's platinum-selling record, paving the way for a new genre to enter the music industry. As the saying goes, "Once a Hit, Always a Hit," and in Hip Hop this would hold true. The debut Rap Album peaked at #4 on the R&B charts, #3 in the UK, #18 in New Zealand, #36 in the U.S., and #14 on the U.S. Club Play charts; a great look for Hip Hop. (*This format would later reward all contributors*) **The Blueprint, aka Remix.**

Members: Big Bank Hank, Wonder Mike, & Master Gee. **City**: New York **Producers**: Bernard Edwards & Nile Rodgers **Executive Producer**: Sylvia Robinson

On September 21, 1979, *Funkadelic* releases *Uncle Jam Wants You* on **Warner Bros. Records**. The album went on to reach #2 on the Soul charts and went certified gold.

⇒ **TV News—Animation: On September 22, 1979, NBC** debuts *The Super Globetrotters*, based on the African-American characters of the famed *Harlem Globetrotters*.

On October 16, 1979, *Rick James* releases *Fire it Up* on **Gordy Records**. The album peaked at #5 on the R&B charts and went certified gold.

On October 16, 1979, *Barry White* releases *The Message is Love* on **Unlimited Gold Records**. Unlike his previous projects, this album didn't pin any hit singles, but would reach #14 on the R&B charts.

On October 19, 1979, *Prince* releases *Prince* on **Warner Bros. Records**. Although the album pinned some classic tracks, it failed to produce any top hits other than *Soft and Wet* reaching #12 on the R&B charts.

⇒ **TV News — Soul Train:** On October 6, 13, 20 & 27, 1979, **Bonnie Pointer, Switch – David Ruffin, Heatwave – Rick James & the Stone City Band, Teena Marie – Billy Preston and Crème d' Coca** were featured guests.

On November 28, 1979, Parliament released *Gloryhallastoopid* on Casablanca records.

⇒ **TV News—Soul Train: On November 3, 10, 17 & 24, 1979, The Bar-Kays, McFadden & Whitehead – Herb Alpert, Dynasty – Keith & Darrell – The Whispers, Vernon Burch, and comedian, Tom Dreesen** were featured guests.

In November of 1979, *Rufus featuring Chaka Khan* release *Masterjam* on **MCA records**. The album reached #1 on the Soul charts and also pinned the #1 hit single *Do You Love What You Feel*.

⇒ **New Jersey News: On November 2, 1979, Assata Shakur,** former *Black Panther*, after being charged with murder, was being held in a Clinton, New Jersey prison when she escaped and fled to Cuba where she remains under political asylum.
⇒ **Film News—Blaxploitation: On November 21, 1979, The Jerry Gross Organization** released *"Penitentiary"* starring **Leon Isaac Kennedy**.

⇒ **TV News—Soul Train: On December 1, 8 & 15, 1979, The Commodores - Johnnie Taylor, and Lakeside** were featured guests.
⇒ **TV News—Soap Opera: On December 27, 1979, CBS** debuts *Knots Landing*, a spin-off of the popular *Dallas* series.

Hip-Hop (Rap Music): In 1979 Eddie Cheba releases *Lookin' Good (Shake Your Body)* on ***Tree Line Records***. No stranger to the stage, club, parks, or the Hip Hop culture, Cheba, one of the original pioneers of Hip Hop, influenced many rappers and fans alike with his showmanship and ability to move the New York crowds and beyond.

1979 – Billboards Year End – Hot 100 Singles

1979	Urban Music 25% of Billboards Year-End Hot 100	25%
2	**Donna Summer** – *Bad Girls*	Casablanca
3	**Chic** – *Le Freak*	Atlantic
5	**Peaches & Herb** – *Reunited*	Polydor
6	**Gloria Gaynor** – *I Will Survive*	Polydor
7	**Donna Summer** – *Hot Stuff*	Casablanca
9	**Anita Ward** – *Ring My Bell*	Juana
12	**Donna Summer** – *MacArthur Park*	Casablanca
15	**The Pointer Sisters** – *Fire*	Planet
20	**Chic** – *Good Times*	Atlantic
22	**Amii Stewart** – *Knock on Wood*	Ariola
25	**The Jacksons** – *Shake Your Body (Down to the Ground)*	Epic
31	**Peaches & Herb** – *Shake Your Groove Thang*	Polydor
32	**Dionne Warwick** – *I'll Never Love This Way Again*	Arista
38	**Earth, Wind & Fire** – *After the Love Has Gone*	Columbia
39	**Donna Summer & Brooklyn Dreams** – *Heaven Knows*	Casablanca
45	**Sister Sledge** – *He's the Greatest Dancer*	Cotillion
55	**Hot Chocolate** – *Every 1's a Winner*	RAK/Infinity
57	**Earth, Wind & Fire** – *Boogie Wonderland*	Columbia
62	**Chic** – *I Want Your Love*	Atlantic
65	**McFadden & Whitehead** – *Ain't No Stoppin' Us Now*	Philadelphia International
69	**Cheryl Lynn** – *Got to Be Real*	Columbia
78	**Earth, Wind & Fire** – *September*	Columbia
91	**Michael Jackson** – *Don't Stop 'til You Get Enough*	Epic
97	**Diana Ross** – *The Boss*	Motown
98	**Commodores** – *Sail On*	Motown

1979 – Record Labels in Urban Music

MCA: On January 15, 1979 the label purchases *RCA* records for 20 million dollars and on November 16, 1979, *Infinity* records is shut down and absorbed into *MCA* records. Both of these acquisitions increased the labels catalogue and power in the industry.

Casablanca: Noted as one of the top selling Disco labels, the company lit up the charts this year with four hits from Donna Summer, pinning spots 2, 7, 12, and 39 on the Hot 100.

Atlantic: The platinum selling group, Chic, landed 3 hits on the Hot 100 keeping the label relevant in the disco era.

Polydor: Not to be excluded from the Disco movement, the label pinned a few classics of their own from artists, Peaches & Herb and Gloria Gaynor both with Top 10 hits on the Hot 100.

Juana: Another subsidiary label under the Miami based *TK records* pinned their only #1 hit with the Anita Ward classic, *Ring My Bell*.

Planet: Founded by record executive Richard Perry in 1978 as a new talent label. Perry hit pay dirt this year with the release of *Fire* by the *Pointer Sisters* who would become the label's bestselling artist. The label was also distributed by *Elektra/Asylum records*.

Ariola: A German based label founded in 1975 in Los Angeles made good this year with new artist Amii Stewart's cover of *Knock on Wood*, a **Stax Records** original by Eddie Floyd. Stewart's version would go on to be certified platinum.

Epic: The label cashed in on the Jackson family this year with the #25 hit *Shake Your Body (Down to the Ground)* from the group, and the #1 Hot 100 single, *Don't Stop til You Get Enough* by Michael Jackson.

Arista: When it seemed that the R&B ballads had faded, Dionne Warwick pinned a hit with *I'll Never Love this Way Again*, the label's only urban single to hit the year-end Hot 100.

Columbia: Platinum selling group, Earth, Wind & Fire would again deliver classic hits with two landing on this year's Hot 100 while on the Columbia label.

Cotillion: The label was a subsidiary of Atlantic records and focused on blues and deep southern soul music. They won this year with the release of a classis Disco hit by Sister Sledge called *He's the Greatest Dancer*.

RAK: Founded by record producer Mickie Most as a British label and distributed by **EMI Records,** the label made the Hot 100 this year with a hot single from its British Soul band, Hot Chocolate's track, *Every 1's a Winner*.

Philadelphia International: The sound of Phila pinned one hit on the year-end Hot 100 with a release from their newest act McFadden & Whitehead's single, *Ain't No Stoppin' Us Now*.

Motown: At this time, the music landscape had changed and the one-time giant who concurred most of the genre was now a big fish among many, some of them were even prior Motown artists and execs, but Gordy had found a way to change with the times. Hot 100 hits from Diana Ross and the Commodores showed the mogul was still relevant.

Circa 1980

These are The Breaks

TV News—Black Entertainment Television: On January 25, 1980, Robert L. Johnson launches *BET* as a block of programming on *Nickelodeon*. The original broadcast block was only for 2 hours a week. (For more on the BET story, I recommend <u>The Billion Dollar BET</u> by Brett Pulley).

In January of 1980, *Lou Rawls* releases *Sit Down and Talk to Me* on **Philadelphia International Records**. The album reached #19 on the R&B charts.

⇒ **Magazine News: In January of 1980, model Beverly Johnson** lands the cover of UK based *Company* magazine.

⇒ **TV News—Soul Train: On February 2 & 9, 1980, WAR – Chic, High Energy, and Dick Gregory** were show guests.

Hip Hop (Rap Music): On February 7, 1980, *The Sugarhill Gang* release their debut self-titled album after the success of the 1st ever released certified gold, Hip Hop single, *Rappers Delight* on **Sugar Hill Records**. No category existed for Hip Hop or Rap at this time, so the album competed in the R&B genre, where it peaked at #4 on the U.S R&B charts.

Producers: Sylvia Robinson, Billy Jones and Nate Edmonds

On February 14, 1980, *Teena Marie* releases *Lady T* on **Gordy records.** The album peaked at #18 on the Top Soul album charts.

1980 – Urban American

Grammy Award Recipients – 22nd Annual

Awards, 1980: George Benson and Claus Ogerman win Best Instrumental Arrangement *(Soulful Strut)*.

Awards, 1980: Gloria Gaynor wins Best Disco Recording *(I Will Survive)*. *This would be the first and last time the award was ever given.

Awards, 1980: Muddy Waters win Best Ethnic or Traditional Recording *(Muddy "Mississippi" Waters Live)*.

Awards, 1980: The Imperials win Best Gospel Performance, Contemporary *(Heed the Call)*.

Awards, 1980: Mighty Clouds of Joy win Best Soul Gospel Performance, Traditional *(Changing Times)*.

Awards, 1980: Andrae Crouch wins Best Soul Gospel Performance, Contemporary *(I'll Be Thinking of You)*.

Awards, 1980: Oscar Peterson wins Best Jazz Instrumental Performance, Soloist *(Jousts)*.

Awards, 1980: Duke Ellington wins Best Jazz Instrumental Performance, Big Band *(Duke Ellington at Fargo, 1940 Live)*.

Awards, 1980: Ella Fitzgerald wins Best Jazz Vocal Performance *(Fine and Mellow)*.

Awards, 1980: Dionne Warwick wins Best Pop Vocal Performance, female *(I'll Never Love This Way Again)*.

Awards, 1980: Dionne Warwick wins Best R&B Vocal Performance, Female *(Deja-Vu)*.

Awards, 1980: Michael Jackson wins Best R&B Vocal Performance, Male *(Don't Stop 'til You Get Enough)*.

Awards, 1980: Earth, Wind & Fire wins Best R&B Vocal Performance by a Duo, Group or Chorus *(After the Love is Gone)*.

Awards, 1980: Earth, Wind & Fire wins Best R&B Instrumental Performance *(Boogie Wonderland)*.

Awards, 1980: Earth, Wind & Fire wins Best R&B Song *(After the Love is Gone)*.

Awards, 1980: Donna Summer wins Best Rock Vocal Performance, Female *(Hot Stuff)*.

On February 25, 1980, *Smokey Robinson* releases *Warm Thoughts* on *Motown Records*. Smokey would pin another hit album for the Motown label peaking at #4 on the R&B charts.

In February of 1980, *Tavares* releases *Supercharged* on *Capitol Records*. The album would put the group back on the R&B charts, peaking at #20.

⇒ TV News — Soul Train: On March 1, 8, 15, 22 & 29, 1980; Lou Rawls, Narada Michael Walden – Shalamar, The Gap Band – The Whispers, Patrice Rushen – L.T.D, Cheryl Lynn – Harold Melvin & the Blue Notes, and Brass Construction were featured guests.

On **March 3, 1980, *Roberta Flack*** released *Roberta Flack featuring Donny Hathaway* on ***Atlantic Records***. The album included two singles she previously recorded with Hathaway before his death, which were *Back Together Again* and *You Are My Heaven*.

⇒ **L.A News: Musician & Record Producer, Quincy Jones** receives a Star on the *Hollywood Walk of Fame*.

On **March 17, 1980, *Jermaine Jackson*** releases *Let's Get Serious* on ***Motown Records***. The title track was the biggest soul single of the year and pushed the album to #1 on the R&B charts.

On March 26, 1980, *Chaka Khan* releases *Naughty* on **Warner Bros. Records**. The album's most noted track, *Clouds*, featured *Whitney Houston* at the age of 16 singing background vocals on the #10 R&B hit single.

⇒ **TV News—Soul Train: On April 5, 12, 19 and 26, 1980, Sister Sledge, Randy Brown – The Spinners, Con Funk Shun – Captain & Tennille, The Ritchie Family, The Electric Boogaloos – Stephanie Mills, and Roy Ayers** were featured guests.

On April 24, 1980, *Cameo* releases *Cameosis* on **Chocolate City Records**. The album's hit single, *Shake Your Pants*, helped push the album to #1 on the R&B charts.

⇒ **TV News—Soul Train: On May 3, 10, 17, 24 & 31, 1980; Village People, Side Effect – Jermaine Jackson, Dramatics – Ray, Goodman & Brown, Ray Parker, Jr. & Raydio – Syreeta Wright** were featured guests.

On May 9, 1980, *Grace Jones* releases *Warm Leatherette* on **Island records**. Unlike some of her earlier work, this album went in a Reggae direction instead of Disco, peaking at #132 in the U.S and #45 in the U.K.

On May 22, 1980, *Diana Ross* releases *Diana* on **Motown Records**. Diana's best-selling album pinned several singles and peaked at #1 on the Dance charts.

⇒ **TV News—Soul Train: On June 7, 1980, Leon Haywood and L.A Boppers** were featured guests.

On June 10, 1980, *Bob Marley & The Wailers* release *Uprising* on *Tuff Gong Records*. With its hottest single *Could You be Loved* reaching #6 on the Club Singles charts, this album was an instant classic.

⇒ **Music News**: **On June 25, 1980, The Sony Walkman** is released on the U.S market.

On June 30, 1980, *Chic* releases *Real People* on *Atlantic Records*. The album reached #8 on the R&B charts.

On July 16, 1980, *Rick James* releases *Garden of Love* on **Gordy Records**. Unlike his previous hit albums, this one only peaked at #17 on the Top Soul charts falling short of his previous #1 hits.

On July 25, 1980, *Teddy Pendergrass* releases *TP* on **Philadelphia International Records**. His most noted single, *Love T.K.O.*, helped push the album to #3 on the R&B charts, while the single peaked at #1 on the R&B charts.

On July 28, 1980, *Zapp* released their self-titled album on *Warner Bros. Records*. The album reached #2 on the Hot R&B Tracks charts and was certified gold less than 120 days after its release.

On August 9, 1980, *George Benson* releases *Give Me the Night* on *Qwest Records/Warner Bros. Records*. It's title track peaked at #1 on the Soul Singles charts and propelled the album to platinum status.

On August 13, 1980, *The S.O.S. Band* releases *S.O.S.* on **Tabu records**. This would be the group's debut album and they hit the ground running with the Hot Club hit, *Take Your Time (Do It Right)* reaching #1 on the R&B Hit charts. *S.O.S.* the album peaked at #2 on the R&B charts.

In August of 1980, *The Pointer Sisters* release *Special Things* on **Planet records**. Like their previous projects, the sisters pinned another hit, *He's So Shy*, which helped the album reach certified gold status.

⇒ **TV News—Music Series: On September 13, 1980, Solid Gold** premieres in syndication and was hosted by *Dionne Warwick* for the first season. The show featured musical guests and performances by the *Solid Gold Dancers*.

⇒ **TV News—Soul Train: On September 20 & 27, 1980, Brothers Johnson, Rockie Robbins – L.T.D., Stevie Wonder, and Kurtis Blow** were featured guests.

On September 26, 1980, *The Jacksons* released *Triumph* on **Epic Records**. The album reached #10 in the U.S and went certified platinum.

On September 29, 1980, *Kool & the Gang* release *Celebrate!* on **De-Lite Records**. Their hottest track, *Celebration* reached #1 on the R&B charts as did the album.

On September 29, 1980, *Stevie Wonder* releases *Hotter Than July* on **Tamla records**. Like so many times before, Stevie pinned another platinum-selling album that reached #3 in the U.S.

Hip-Hop (Rap Music): On September 29, 1980, *Kurtis Blow* releases his debut self-titled album *Kurtis Blow* on **Mercury records**. This would be only the 2nd Rap album publicly released from the new culture called Hip Hop. His most noted single, **The Breaks** went certified gold and the album reached #87 on the Billboard Hot 100, #4 on the R&B charts, and #9 on the Dance charts. Blow also made history by being the second artist to sell over 500,000, 12-inch singles pinning a gold certification from the Recording Industry Association of America. He came second to Donna Summers and Barbra Streisand's hit single, *No More Tears (Enough Is Enough)*. Kurtis Blow's charisma, word play, and originality laid the foundation for a new music genre on a huge scale. If the Music industry wasn't paying attention before, they were now, with two certified gold albums from the Hip Hop culture in as many years from two different artists.

City: Harlem, New York   **Producers**: J.B. Moore, Robert Ford, Larry Smith, Russell Simmons, Joseph Simmons, and Kurtis Blow.

In September of 1980, *Herbie Hancock* releases *Mr. Hands* on **Columbia Records**. This album didn't pin any hits, but would mark another significant change in the Jazz musician's prolific catalogue.

On October 14, 1980, *Earth, Wind & Fire* release *Faces* on **ARC/Columbia Records**. The platinum-selling band, now on their 10th album, had struck certified gold with this one as the album peaked at #2 on the Black Album charts.

On October 20, 1980, *Donna Summer* releases *The Wanderer* on **Geffen Records**. This was Donna's first release for her new label, and like her previous projects, this too would top the charts.

On October 25, 1980, *Aretha Franklin* releases *Aretha* on **Arista records**. The album was the first she recorded for Arista, and it peaked at #47 on the Billboard Album chart.

⇒ **TV News — Soul Train: On October 4, 11, 18 and 25, 1980, Larry Graham, Irene Cara – Rick James, The S.O.S. Band – Tyrone Davis, Teena Marie, Tom Dreesen – Teddy Pendergrass, and The Jones Girls** were featured guests.

In October of 1980; *Bootsy Collins* releases *Ultra Wave* on **Warner Bros. Records**. This would be the 5th album released by the funk musician.

In November of 1980, *Slave* releases *Stone Jam* on ***Cotillion records***. The album went certified Gold and peaked at #5 on the R&B charts.

⇒ **TV News — Soul Train:** On November 1, 8, 15, 22 & 29, 1980, Cameo, Edmund Sylvers, Kim Fields – Michael Henderson, La Toya Jackson – Shalamar, Mtume – Lakeside, Geraldine Hunt – Lenny Williams, and Yellow Magic Orchestra were featured guests.

⇒ **Politics**: On November 4, 1980, former California Governor, *Ronald Regan* wins the Presidential election.

On December 5, 1980; *Parliament* release *Trombipulation* on *Casablanca Records*. Keeping true to form, this album, like previous releases, experimented with different musical directions from other producers outside of George Clinton.

In December of 1980, *Tavares* releases *Love Uprising* on *Capitol Records*. Unlike previous projects, this one failed to break the Top 100.

⇒ **TV News—Soul Train**: On December 6, 1980, Ray, Goodman & Brown, and Gently were featured guests.
⇒ **Magazine News**: In December of 1980, Bill Cosby appears on the cover of *Ebony*.
⇒ **New York News**: On December 8, 1980, John Lennon, co-founder of the famous English band, *The Beatles*, was shot four times in the back by Mark David Chapman. Lennon was pronounced D.O.A. at Roosevelt Hospital.

1980 – Billboards Year End – Hot 100 Singles

1980	Urban Music 28% of Billboards Year-End Hot 100	28%
4	**Michael Jackson** – *Rock with You*	Epic
8	**Lipps Inc** – *Funkytown*	Casablanca
13	**Smokey Robinson** – *Cruisin'*	Motown
14	**The Spinners** – *Working My Way Back to You/Forgive Me, Girl*	Atlantic
18	**Diana Ross** – *Upside Down*	Motown
19	**KC and the Sunshine Band** – *Please Don't Go*	TK
21	**Billy Preston & Syreeta** – *With You I'm Born Again*	Motown
22	**The Manhattans** – *Shinning Star*	Columbia
23	**Commodores** – *Still*	Motown
29	**The Spinners** – *Cupid/I've Loved You for a Long Time*	Atlantic
30	**Jermaine Jackson** – *Let's Get Serious*	Motown
35	**Kool and the Gang** – *Ladies Night*	DeLite
36	**Kool and the Gang** – *Too Hot*	DeLite
37	**The SOS Band** – *Take Your Time (Do It Right)*	Tabu
38	**Donna Summer & Barbra Streisand** *No More Tears (Enough Is Enough)*	Casablanca/ Columbia
42	**Ray, Goodman & Brown** – *Special Lady*	Polydor
43	**Stevie Wonder** – *Send One Your Love*	Motown
44	**Shalamar** – *The Second Time Around*	Solar
47	**The Brothers Johnson** – *Stomp!*	A&M
52	**Donna Summer** – *On the Radio*	Casablanca
63	**Isaac Hayes** – *Don't Let Go*	Polydor
65	**Michael Jackson** – *She's Out of My Life*	Epic
66	**Irene Cara** – *Fame*	RSO
74	**Donna Summer** – *Dim All the Lights*	Casablanca
79	**Michael Jackson** – *Off the Wall*	Epic
80	**Peaches & Herb** – *I Pledge My Love*	MVP Polydor
84	**Dionne Warwick** – *I*	Arista
95	**Prince** – *I Wanna Be Your Lover*	Warner Bros

1980 – Record Labels in Urban Music

Epic: Michael Jackson made history yet again for the label with his platinum selling album *Off the Wall*, as several of his singles landed on the Hot 100.

Casablanca: The Queen of Disco managed to land 3 singles on the Hot 100 as Disco was nearing its end; Donna Summer carried much of the load for the label, but they did score another hit from one of their newer groups Lipps Inc with *Funkytown*. Unfortunately, this was Summer's last year on the label as she would later sign with *Geffen records*.

Motown: Not to be forgotten, Gordy's label landed several hits this year from several artists, proving that they still had the Midas touch even in Hollywood.

TK: During the downfall of Disco, the label did manage to land one hit on the Hot 100, but would eventually be sold this year to Morris Levy's *Roulette Records* because of financial troubles.

Columbia: With the smash hit from the Manhattans, the historic label enjoyed much success as the single *Shining Star* made its way up the charts.

Atlantic: Thanks to the Spinners, the label proved competitive in the R&B genre this year with two Hot 100 singles.

DeLite: Their most noted act, Kool and the Gang, would bring home the hits yet again with two classic singles that would stand the test of time.

Tabu: The R&B Funk label was founded in 1975 by Clarence Avant and pinned success this year with a hit from the S.O.S. Band, *Take Your Time (Do it Right)*, which reached #1.

Polydor: With several noted acts on its roster, the label charted three Hot 100 Singles this year improving their R&B track record.

Solar: Originally founded in 1975 by *Don Cornelius* and *Dick Griffey* as *Soul Train Records* after the *Soul Train* TV show, it would later be renamed in 1977 after Don Cornelius parted ways with Griffey to *Solar Records*, aka *Sound of Los Angeles Records*. It would be, however, a group that was created by Griffey and Cornelius to take advantage of the Disco era they called *Shalamar* that landed the label its first #1 hit, *The Second Time Around*.

A&M: The label hit pay dirt this year with a catchy hit *Stomp!* from The Brothers Johnson that topped several charts.

RSO: The Robert Stigwood Organization, aka *RSO Records* was founded in 1973 by Robert Stigwood. The label was known for releasing several movie soundtracks and hit the charts this year with the FAME soundtrack, landing on the Hot 100 with its title track.

Warner Bros: With one of their newly signed artists, PRINCE, who didn't fare so well with his debut album, the A&R's summoned a follow up album that gave the artist his 1st hit, *I Wanna Be Your Lover,* cementing what would become a legendary career.

Circa 1981

Reganomics

On January 15, 1981, *Marvin Gaye* releases *In Our Lifetime* on **Tamla Records**. This would be Marvin's final album recorded with **Motown**; it peaked at #6 on the Black Albums chart.

In January of 1980, *B.B. King* releases *There Must Be a Better World Somewhere* on **MCA Records**. King would later win a Grammy for his 27th album.

⇒ **Politics: On January 20, 1981, former Sports Radio show announcer, Hollywood Actor and California Governor, Ronald Regan** officially becomes the 40th American President succeeding Jimmy Carter. Regan elected George H.W Bush as his Vice President. (*Reagan graduated with a Bachelor of Arts degree in Social Science and Economics from Eureka College in 1932, and was an active member of Tau Kappa Epsilon fraternity – TKE.*)

- ⇒ **Sports News—NFL: On January 25, 1981, The Oakland Raiders** defeat the Philadelphia Eagles in Super Bowl XV 27-10 at the New Orleans, Louisiana Superdome.
- ⇒ **TV News—Soul Train: On January 10, 17, 24 & 31, 1981, Al Green, The Dells – Dynasty, Tierra – The Stylistics, Spyro Gyra – The Ch-Lites, and Patrice Rushen** were featured guests.

On February 17, 1981, *Smokey Robinson* released *Being With You* on **Motown Records**. The title track went platinum and reached #1 on the charts.

On February 17, 1981, *Diana Ross* releases *To Love Again* on **Motown Records**. The album reached #16 on the R&B charts.

1981 – Urban American
Grammy Award Recipients – 23rd Annual

Awards, 1981: James Cleveland & the Charles Ford Singers win Best Soul Gospel Performance, Traditional *(Lord, Let Me Be an Instrument)*.

Awards, 1981: Shirley Caesar wins Best Soul Gospel Performance, Contemporary *(Rejoice)*.

Awards, 1981: Ella Fitzgerald wins Best Jazz Vocal Performance, Female *(A Perfect Match)*.

Awards, 1981: George Benson wins Best Jazz Vocal Performance, Female *(Moody's Mood)*.

Awards, 1981: Count Basie wins Best Instrumental Jazz Performance, Big Band *(On the Road)*.

Awards, 1981: Stephanie Mills wins Best R&B Vocal Performance, Female *(Never Knew Love Like This Before)*.

Awards, 1981: George Benson wins Best R&B Performance, Male *(Give Me the Night)*.

Awards, 1981: The Manhattans win Best R&B Performance by a Duo or Group with Vocal *(Shining Star)*.

Awards, 1981: George Benson wins Best R&B Instrumental Performance *(Off Broadway)*.

Awards, 1981: James Mtume & Reggie Lucas win Best R&B Song *(Songwriters, Never Knew Love Like This Before)* performed by **Stephanie Mills**.

In March of 1981, *Miles Davis* releases *Directions* on **Columbia Records**. The album, however, received mediocre reviews.

In March of 1981, *Quincy Jones* releases *The Dude* on **A&M Records**. The album won several awards and also introduced James Ingram to the world.

⇒ **Film News — Comedy: On March 6, 1981, Walt Disney Productions** released *"The Devil and Max Devlin"* starring **Bill Cosby**, directed by *Steven Hillard Stern*.

On March 18, 1981, Female MC Queen Latifah turns 11 years old. (*Born 3-18-1970*)

⇒ **D.C. News — Politics: On March 30, 1981,** an assassination attempt was made on President *Ronald Reagan* by John Hinckley who shot the President in the chest and injured U.S. Press Secretary, James Brady and two police officers in the process, outside of the Washington Hilton Hotel in Washington, D.C. Reagan suffered a punctured lung and some internal bleeding, but would recover due to prompt medical attention.

In March of 1981, *The Isley Brothers* release *Grand Slam* on **T-Neck records**. The album went certified gold and peaked at #3 on the R&B charts.

In March of 1981, *Rufus* releases *Party 'Til You're Broke* on **MCA records**. The album reached #24 on the R&B charts.

⇒ **TV News—Soul Train: On March 7, 14, 21 & 28, 1981, Deniece Williams, The Gap Band – The Bar-Kays, Yarbrough & Peoples, Robert Winters – The Pointer Sisters, Con Funk Shun – The Whispers, and Carrie Lucas** were featured guests.

In March of 1981, *Ray Parker, Jr.* and *Raydio* release *A Woman Needs Love* on *Arista Records*. The album peaked at #1 on the Hot Soul Singles and R&B charts.

⇒ **Magazine News**: **In March of 1981, Black Supermodel, Beverly Johnson** lands cover of *UK Cosmopolitan*.

⇒ **Magazine News**: In March of 1981, Black Pitcher, J.R. Richard lands cover of *Sports Illustrated.*

On April 6, 1981, *DeBarge* releases *The DeBarges* on *Gordy Records*. This was the first album released by the group, but it failed to chart.

⇒ **TV News — Soul Train: On April 4, 11, 18 & 25, 1981, Rufus, Dee Dee Sharp – Billy Preston, Lakeside – Shalamar, Teena Marie – A Taste of Honey, and Jerry Knight** were featured guests.

On April 7 1981, *Rick James* releases *Street Songs* on **Gordy Records**. James pinned several classic hits with *Super Freak*, *Ghetto Life*, and *Give It to Me Baby*, which helped push the album to #1 on the R&B charts.

On April 15, 1981, *Chaka Khan* released *What Cha' Gonna Do for Me* on **Warner Bros. Records**. The album sold over 500,000 copies making it certified gold.

On April 29, 1981, *Funkadelic* releases *The Electric Spanking of War Babies* on **Warner Bros. Records**.

On May 11, 1981, *Grace Jones* releases *Nightclubbing* on *Island Records*. Like her previous albums, Jones topped the charts in several countries, earning a platinum certification in Australia.

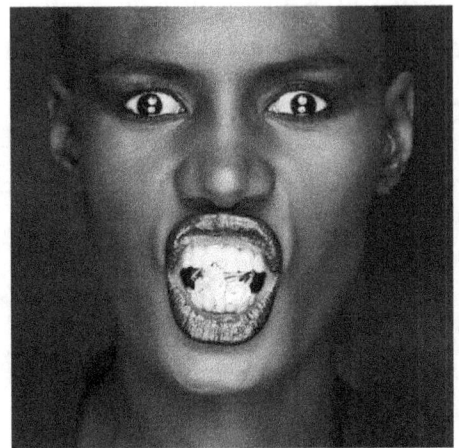

⇒ **Miami News**: **On May 11, 1981, Reggae legend, Bob Marley** dies from cancer due to melanoma which spread to his lungs and brain.

⇒ **Music News**: **On May 14, 1981, Diana Ross** signs the largest record deal to date with **RCA Records** for $20,000,000.00; the deal also included that her albums would be released internationally through *EMI Records*. Diana spent 20 years with *Motown records* prior to signing with RCA/EMI.

⇒ **TV News — Soul Train: On May 2, 9, 16, 23 and 30, 1981; Sister Sledge, Atlantic Starr – The Spinners, Skyy, Arsenio Hall – Sugarhill Gang, Patrice Rushen – Betty Wright, Funkadelic – Bill Withers, and Side Effect** were featured guests.

⇒ **Magazine News: In May of 1981, Black Supermodel, Beverly Johnson** lands cover of *Glamour*.

On May 14, 1981, *Teena Marie* releases *It Must Be Magic* on **Gordy records**. The album peaked at #2 on the R&B charts and featured the hit single *Square Biz*.

On May 18, 1981, *Cameo* releases *Knights of the Sound Table* on **Chocolate City Records**. The album peaked at #2 on the R&B charts.

⇒ **Film News—Comedy:** On May 22, 1981, **Universal Pictures** releases *Bustin' Loose* starring **Richard Pryor**, directed by *Oz Scott* and *Michael Schultz*.

⇒ **Economy: In June of 1981, the United States** enters a recession with unemployment rates reaching 7.2%.

⇒ **L.A News: In June of 1981,** the first case of **AIDS** is reported by the Centers for Disease Control and Prevention when they discover five homosexual men in Los Angeles, California with a form of pneumonia that weakens the immune system.

Hip-Hop (Rap Music): On June 15, 1981, *Kurtis Blow* releases his second album *Deuce* on *Mercury Records*. The album reached #35 on the R&B charts, unlike his debut album that went certified gold, but the release showed consistency and would help establish a foundation for the Hip Hop culture.

Producers: *Kurtis Blow, Robert Ford, Jr., J.B. Moore, Jimmy Bralower, Dean Swenson, Larry Smith, William Whiting, Seth Glassman, David Reeves, and Russell Simmons.*

On June 15, 1981, Rapper Ice Cube of *NWA* turns 12 years old. (*Born 6-15-1969*)

⇒ **Atlanta News**: In the case of the Atlanta Child Murders, a suspect is taken into custody and charged initially with the murder of two African American children; Wayne Williams, 23 at the time, is later charged with 28 additional child murders.

On June 30, 1981, *Al Jarreau* releases *Breakin' Away* on **Warner Bros. Records**. The album peaked at #1 on the Jazz charts and was certified platinum.

In June of 1981, *The Pointer Sisters* release *Black & White* on **Planet Records**. They peaked at #9 on the R&B charts.

In June of 1981, the *Commodores* release *In the Pocket* on **Motown Records**. This would be Lionel Richie's last album with the group before he embarked on his solo career.

⇒ **TV News—Soul Train:** On June 6, 13 and 20, 1981, Jermaine Jackson, T-Connection , Marsha Warfield – Rick James, Brenda Russell – Cameo, and **Mantra** were featured guests.

⇒ **Magazine News:** In July of 1981, Actress and Model, **Jayne Kennedy** lands cover of *Playboy Mexico*.

On July 21, 1981, *Luther Vandross* releases *Never Too Much* on *Epic records*. This was Luther's first album, and it peaked at #1 on the R&B charts and earned a double platinum certification.

On July 29, 1981, *The Time* release their self-titled debut album *The Time* on *Warner Bros. Records*. The album pinned three hits with, *Girl*, *Get It Up*, and *Cool*.

- ⇒ **TV News — Music: On August 1, 1981, MTV,** aka *Music Television* debuts on cable TV, broadcasting music videos 24 hours a day in the U.S.
- ⇒ **Magazine News**: In August of 1981, Jermaine Jackson and wife Hazel land cover of *Ebony*.

In August of 1981, *Aretha Franklin* releases *Love All the Hurt Away* on **Arista Records**. The album didn't sell as many copies as her previous hits, but did win her a Grammy for Best R&B Vocal Performance.

On September 4, 1981, *Diana Ross* releases *Why Do Fools Fall in Love* on **RCA Records**. Ross left her home label, *Motown*, this year and signed a $20 Million deal with *RCA*; upon arrival she produced her first album and proved to be successful as it went certified platinum.

On September 17, 1981, MC Steady B turns 12 years old. (*Born 9-17-1969*)

On September 24, 1981; *Kool & the Gang* release *Something Special* on **De-Lite Records**. The album peaked at #1 on the Top Soul charts.

⇒ **Film News—Comedy: On September 25, 1981, Avco Embassy Pictures/MGM** released "*Carbon Copy*" which debuted **Denzel Washington**, directed by *Michael Schultz*.

On September 29, 1981, *Herbie Hancock* releases *Magic Windows* on **Columbia Records**.

⇒ **TV News—Soul Train: On September 19 and 26, 1981, Barry White, Goldean White – Phyllis Hyman, Carl Carlton, and Mike Weaver** were featured guests.
⇒ **Magazine News: In September of 1981, Black Supermodel, Iman** lands cover of *Essence.*

On October 11, 1981, Female Rap Star, MC Lyte turns 11 years old. *(Born 10-1-1970)*

On October 14, 1981, *Prince* releases *Controversy* on **Warner Bros. Records**. After a slow starting debut album, Prince started to come into his own with this platinum-selling release that peaked at #3 on the R&B charts.

In October of 1981, *The Isley Brothers* release *Inside You* on **T-Neck Records**. The album reached #8 on the Top Soul charts.

- ⇒ **TV News—Soul Train: On October 3, 10, 17, 24 & 31, 1981, Deniece Williams, Richard "Dimples" Fields – Brothers Johnson, La Toya Jackson – The Four Tops, Stacy Lattisaw, Arsenio Hall – Jose' Feliciano, and Stone City Band** were featured guests.
- ⇒ **TV News—Sitcom: Sitcom: On October 29, 1970, NBC** released *Gimmie a Break* starring **Nell Carter** as a housekeeper, created by *Mort Lachman* and *Sy Rosen*.

On November 14, 1981, *Earth, Wind & Fire* released *Raise!* on **ARC/Columbia Records**. With several chart toppers and a Grammy, the album was a platinum success.

On November 16, 1981, *Chic* released *Take it Off* on **Atlantic Records**. Unlike their previous projects, this album didn't top the charts, but peaked #35 on the R&B.

⇒ **Politics — Iran Contra Scandal: On November 23, 1981, Ronald Regan** signs the top secret NSDD-17 (*National Security Decision Directive 17*). The directive gave the CIA (*Central Intelligence Agency*) authority to recruit and support Contra rebels in Nicaragua. The initiative was initially put into play to secretly facilitate the sale of weapons to Iran in hopes of freeing several American Hostages, but will evolve into an entirely different animal that will involve *Crack* Cocaine, *Freeway Ricky Ross,* and an American Drug epidemic.

In November of 1981, *Bobby Womack* releases *The Poet* on *Beverly Glen Music Records*. The album reached #1 on the Top Black Album charts with the success of his most noted single, *If You Think You're Lonely Now* reaching #3 on the R&B charts.

⇒ **TV News—Soul Train: On November 7, 14 and 21, 1981, Brick, Frankie Smith – Patti LaBelle, The Time, James Wesley Jackson – George Benson, and Patti Austin** were featured guests.

Hip Hop (Electro, Boogie, Funk): In November of 1981, **Afrika Bambaataa & the Jazzy Five** released *Jazzy Sensation* on **Tommy Boy Records**; the album was the label's first rap single.

Members: Afrika Bambaataa, MC Sundance, Disco King Mario, Charlie Choo, Master Bee & DJ Jazzy Jay. **Producer**: Tom Silverman **City**: South Bronx, New York

⇒ **Sports News—Boxing: On December 11; 1981, Muhammad Ali** would fight his last bout, when he is defeated by Trevor Berbick in a 10-round unanimous decision.

⇒ **TV News—Soul Train: On December 12 & 19, 1981, The Spinners, Bobby Womack, Hal Jackson's Talented Teens – Rockie Robbins, and Slave** were featured guests.

1981 – Billboard's Year End – Hot 100 Singles

1981	Urban Music 11% of Billboard's Year-End Hot 100	11%
2	**Diana Ross & Lionel Richie** – *Endless Love*	Motown
6	**Kool & the Gang** - *Celebration*	De-Lite
13	**Smokey Robinson** – *Being with You*	Motown
16	**Raydio** – *A Woman Needs Love (Just Like You Do)*	Arista
18	**Grover Washington, Jr. & Bill Withers** – *Just the Two of Us*	Elektra
19	**The Pointer Sisters** – *Slow Hand*	Planet
22	**A Taste of Honey** - *Sukiyaki*	Capitol
39	**Commodores** – *Lady (You Bring Me Up)*	Motown
42	**Diana Ross** – *It's My Turn*	Motown
68	**Stevie Wonder** – *Master Blaster (Jammin)*	Tamla
98	**Diana Ross** – *I'm Coming Out*	Motown

1981 – Record labels in Urban Music

Motown: Gordy dominated the genre this year largely due to Diana Ross' last recorded album with the label before she moved to RCA. The Commodores, Stevie Wonder, and Smokey Robinson remained true to form landing hits on the charts as usual.

De-Lite: Kool & the Gang pinned another classic charting in the Top 10 with *Celebration,* bringing yet another hit to the small label.

Arista: With new found fame from its newest band, the label enjoyed a Top 20 hit pinned by Raydio.

Elektra: The label broke the Top 20 with a smooth ballad performed by Grover Washington, Jr. and Bill Withers.

Planet: The Pointer Sisters continued to make a name for themselves and the label with another hit song.

Capitol: It would be a cover song for the ages that would place the seasoned label on the charts. Kyu Sakamoto's *Sukiyaki* remains a classic.

Circa 1982

And You Don't Stop

⇒ **TV News—Drama/Musical: On January 7, 1982, NBC** debuts *FAME*, starring *Debbie Allen, Nia Peeples, Jesse Borrego*, and several others. The series was based on the film of the same name and centers around students in school for the Performing Arts; created by *Christopher Gore*.

Hip Hop (Rap Music): In 1982, **Dr. Jeckyll & Mr. Hyde** released *"Genius Rap"* on *Profile Records*. The group brought a new twist to the Rap genre incorporating designer suits and ties into their image. The track was inspired by *Genius of Love* by the *Tom Tom Club*.

Members: Andre Harrell & Alonzo Brown, aka *Harlem World Crew*.

City: Harlem, New York.

In January of 1982; *Sister Sledge* releases *The Sisters* on **Atlantic Records**. The self-produced album pinned a #14 single on the R&B charts with *My Guy*.

⇒ **Magazine News:** In January of 1982, Boxer, **Tommy Hearns** lands cover of *Ring*.
⇒ **TV News — Soul Train:** On January 9, 16, 23 and 30, 1982, **Skyy, O' Bryan, Tim O'Brien, Ken Sevara – L.T.D., James Ingram – Syreeta, and Zoom** were featured guests.

In January of 1982, *Smokey Robinson* releases *Yes It's You Lady* on **Motown Records**, pinning several hit singles including the now classic, *Tell Me Tomorrow*.

In January of 1982, *Irene Cara* releases her debut album *Anyone Can See* on **Network Records**. The album reached #42 on the R&B charts.

⇒ **Philadelphia News: On March 18, 1982, R&B Singer, Teddy Pendergrass** becomes paralyzed from the waist down due to a severe car accident.

⇒ **TV News — Soul Train: On March 27, 1982, Irene Cara and Andrae Crouch**, were featured guests.

1982 – Urban American
Grammy Award Recipients – 24th Annual

Awards, 1982: Richard Pryor wins Best Comedy Recording *(Rev. Du Rite)*.

Awards, 1982: Quincy Jones & Johnny Mandel win Best Instrumental Arrangement *(Velas)*.

Awards, 1982: Quincy Jones & Jerry Hey win Best Instrumental Arrangement Accompanying Vocals *(Ai No Corrida)*.

Awards, 1982: B.B. King wins Best Ethnic or Traditional Recording *(There Must Be a Better World Somewhere)*.

Awards, 1982: Al Green wins Best Soul Gospel Performance, Traditional *(The Lord Will Make a Way)*.

Awards, 1982: Andrae Crouch wins Best Soul Gospel Performance, Contemporary (*Don't Give Up*).

Awards, 1982: Ella Fitzgerald wins Best Jazz Vocal Performance, Female (*Digital III at Montreux*).

Awards, 1982: Al Jarreau wins Best Jazz Vocal Performance, Male (*Round, Round, Round*), Blue Rondo a' la' Turk'.

Awards, 1982: John Coltrane wins Best Jazz Instrumental Performance, Soloist (*Bye Bye Blackbird*).

Awards, 1982: Grover Washington, Jr. wins Best Jazz Fusion Performance, Vocal or Instrumental (*Winelight*).

Awards, 1982: Quincy Jones & Lena Horne win Best Cast Show Album (*The Lady and Her Music*).

Awards, 1982: Lena Horne wins Best Pop Vocal Performance, Female (*The Lady and Her Music*).

Awards, 1982: Al Jarreau wins Best Pop Vocal Performance, Male (*Breakin' Away*).

Awards, 1982: Quincy Jones wins Producer of the Year.

Awards, 1982: Aretha Franklin wins Best R&B Vocal Performance, Female (*Hold On I'm Comin'*).

Awards, 1982: James Ingram wins Best R&B Vocal Performance, Male (*One Hundred Ways*).

Awards, 1982: Quincy Jones wins Best R&B Vocal Performance by a Duo or Group with Vocal (*The Dude*).

Awards, 1982: Bill Withers, Ralph MacDonald & William Salter win Best Rhythm & Blues Song (*Just the Two of Us*).

⇒ **Atlanta News: On February 27, 1982, Wayne Williams** is sentenced to two life terms for the Atlanta Child murders.

On March 22, 1982, *Cameo* releases *Alligator Woman* on *Casablanca Records*. Unlike their previous projects, the album didn't top the charts, but produced a few classics.

⇒ **Music Industry News**: Due to a fall-out over his *Far Cry* album that was released without his permission under Motown, *Marvin Gaye* vowed to never release another album with Motown. Allegedly, masters of the album were stolen from him in London and delivered illegally to Motown in California. On March 23, 1982, **Motown** and **CBS records** negotiated Gaye's release from his longtime label.

In March of 1982, *Atlantic Starr* releases *Brilliance* on *A&M Records*; it's most noted single, *Circles* peaked at #2 on the Hot Black Singles chart.

⇒ **Film News—Stand-Up Comedy**: On March 24, 1982, *Warner Bros.* released "*Richard Pryor: Live on Sunset Strip*", produced by *Richard Pryor* and *Biff Dawes*.

⇒ **Magazine News**: In March of 1982, Supermodel *Iman* lands cover of *Cosmopolitan France.*

In April of 1982, *Ray Parker, Jr.* releases *The Other Woman* on **Arista Records**. The album went gold and peaked #1 on the R&B charts.

⇒ **Magazine News**: **In April of 1982, Quincy Jones** lands cover of *JET*.

Hip-Hop (Rap/Electro Funk Music): April 17, 1982, **DJ & Producer, Afrika Bambaataa & the Soul Sonic Force** released *Planet Rock* on **Tommy BoyRrecords**. The iconic track peaked at #4 on the Soul charts and went hand-in-hand with the evolution of the Breakdance crews. The album proved yet again that Hip Hop was here to stay and could venture in several genres.

City: Bronx, New York **Founder**: Zulu Nation (Hip Hop Awareness Group)

- ⇒ **TV News—Soul Train: On April 3, 10, 17 and 24, 1982, Al Jarreau, Aurra – The Whispers, Mary Wells – The Chi-Lites, Bill Summers & Summer Heat – Betty Lavette** were featured guests.
- ⇒ **Magazine News: On May 3, 1982, Sheila De Windt** lands cover of *JET*.

On May 13, 1982, *Rick James* releases *Throwin' Down* on **Gordy Records**. Its most popular single *Dance Wit' Me* helped push the album to gold status.

On May of 1982, *D. Train* releases their debut self-titled album on **Prelude Records** in the U.S and on **Epic records** in the UK. The album reached #16 on the U.S R&B charts and #72 in the UK.

- ⇒ **TV News—Soul Train: On May 1, 8, 15, 22 and 29, 1982, Sister Sledge, Ray Parker Jr. – Lakeside, Sheree Brown – George Duke, D-Train – WAR, O'Bryan – Ronnie Dyson, The Dazz Band & the Ebony Fashion Fair Models** were featured guests.

In May of 1982, William "Bootsy "Collins releases the final album *The One Giveth, the Count Taketh Away*; he would record on **Warner Bros. Records**.

In May of 1982, *Ashford & Simpson* released *Street Opera* on *Capitol Records* which peaked at #5 on the R&B charts.

On July 9, 1982, *Jermaine Jackson* releases *Let Me Tickle Your Fancy* on **Motown Records**. The album peaked at #9 on the R&B charts and was also the album he would record with Motown.

⇒ **TV News—Soul Train: On June 5, 12, 19 and 26, 1982, Al Green, Third World – Deniece Williams, Junior – Cameo, Patrice Rushen – Bobby Womack, and The Gap Band** were featured guests.

Hip-Hop (Hardcore punk): In July of 1982, **the Beastie Boys** released *"Polly Wog Stew"* on ***Rat Cage Records***. This is one of the groups earlier hardcore punk projects before the Hip Hop infusion.

City: New York City. **Members**: Mike D, MCA, and Ad-Rock

On July 19, 1982, *Donna Summer* releases her self-titled album on ***Geffen records***. Donna topped several charts to include, #20 in the U.S., #2 in Sweden, #3 in Norway, #3 in the Netherlands, and #13 in the UK.

In July of 1982, *Aretha Franklin* releases *Jump to It* on **Arista records**. The title track peaked at #1 on Billboard and helped earn the album gold Status.

In July of 1982, *The Pointer Sisters* release *So Excited* on **Planet Records**. The album peaked at #24 on the R&B charts.

TV News — Soul Train: On July 3 and 10, 1982, The O'Jays, Gene Chandler – A Taste of Honey, and Jeffrey Osborne were featured guests.

On August 11, 1982, *Vanity 6* debuts their self-titled album on **Warner Bros. Records**. Originally created and produced by Prince, the group would top the charts with a funk classic, *Nasty Girl*, which peaked at #6 on the R&B charts.

On August 25, 1982, *The Time* release *What Time is It?* on **Warner Bros. Records**. Their most noted singles, *777-9311*, *Gigolos Get Lonely Too*, and *The Walk* would go on to be classics.

Hip-Hop (Rap Music): This year in Hip Hop, **Kurtis Blow** released his 3rd album *Tough* on *Mercury Records*. The album reached #37 on the Black Singles chart and #38 on the Black Albums chart.

On September 7, 1982: *Kool & The Gang* release *As One* on **De-Lite Records**. The album's most noted single, *Let's Go Dancin'*, reached #7 on the R&B charts.

On September 10, 1982, *Diana Ross* releases *Silk Electric* on **RCA Records (North America) / Capitol Records (Europe)**. The album peaked at #5 on the R&B chart and her top 10 single, *Muscles*, which was written and produced by Michael Jackson, was nominated for a Grammy.

On September 21, 1982, *Janet Jackson* releases her self-titled debut album on *A&M Records*. The debut album peaked at #6 on the R&B chart.

On September 21, 1982, *Luther Vandross* releases *Forever, For Always, For Love* on *Epic Records,* which went on to be certified platinum.

On October 1, 1982, *Marvin Gaye* releases his 1st album on *Columbia Records* after leaving *Motown* earlier this year. Gaye signed a deal with Columbia in March and released *Midnight Love*. This project pinned the classic, *Sexual Healing*, which pushed the album to triple platinum status and won two Grammy awards.

Hip-Hop (Rap Music): October 3, 1982, **Grandmaster Flash and the Furious Five** released their debut album *The Message* on *Sugar Hill Records*. The album peaked at #8 in the U.S., #14 in New Zealand, #77 in the UK, and placed at #53 on the Billboard 200. This was the 3rd Rap group to be released on the Sugar Hill label, and like its predecessors, it too made some noise on the charts further solidifying the new Rap genre and Hip Hop Culture.

City: South Bronx, New York. **Members**: DJ Grandmaster Flash, Melle Mel, The Kidd Creole, Keith Cowboy, Mr. Ness/Scorpio and Rahiem

Producers: Jigsaw Productions, Sylvia Robinson

⇒ **Politics — President's Radion Address:** On October 2, 1982, President Reagan and his wife address the nation on the drug problem in America via radio broadcast. The President announced that he would be rolling out a new drug administration to prevent drug use and trafficking, and stated that the crusade will start where the problem was worst, *South Florida*.

⇒ **TV News — Soul Train:** On October 16, 23 & 30, 1982, Barry White – Evelyn 'Champagne' King, Glen Edward Thomas, Alice Arthur – DeBarge were featured guests.

On October 6, 1982, *Lionel Richie* releases his self-titled debut album on *Motown Records*. Richie pinned several chart toppers reaching Billboard Hot 100.

On October 14, 1982, *Zapp* releases *Zapp II* on *Warner Bros. Records*. The group's sophomore album reached #2 on the R&B charts and #25 on Billboard 200.

⇒ **Politics—The War on Drugs: On October 14, 1982, President Ronald Reagan** declares a War on Drugs, claiming illicit drugs to be a threat to U.S. National Security. The 1st lady Nancy Reagan went on to lead the *Just Say No* campaign to discourage people from engaging in illegal drug use and the President followed up on his prior promise to take action.
⇒ **Sports News—MLB: On October 20, 1982, the St. Louis Cardinals** defeat the Milwaukee Brewers 6-3 in game 7 of the World Series.

On October 27, 1982, Prince releases *1999* on ***Warner Bros. Records***. The album reached #9 in the U.S. and was certified multi-platinum, making this Prince's first Top 10 project.

In October of 1982, *Musical Youth* releases *The Youth of Today* on *MCA Records*. Their most noted single, *Pass the Dutchie*, peaked at #10 in the U.S. and #1 in the UK going certified gold in both Canada and the UK.

On November 7, 1982, *Grace Jones* releases *Living My Life* on *Island Records*. Like previous albums, this one too charted across the globe, #7 in Sweden, #19 R&B in the U.S., #15 in the UK, #3 in New Zealand, #18 in the Netherlands, #13 in Norway, and #46 in Germany.

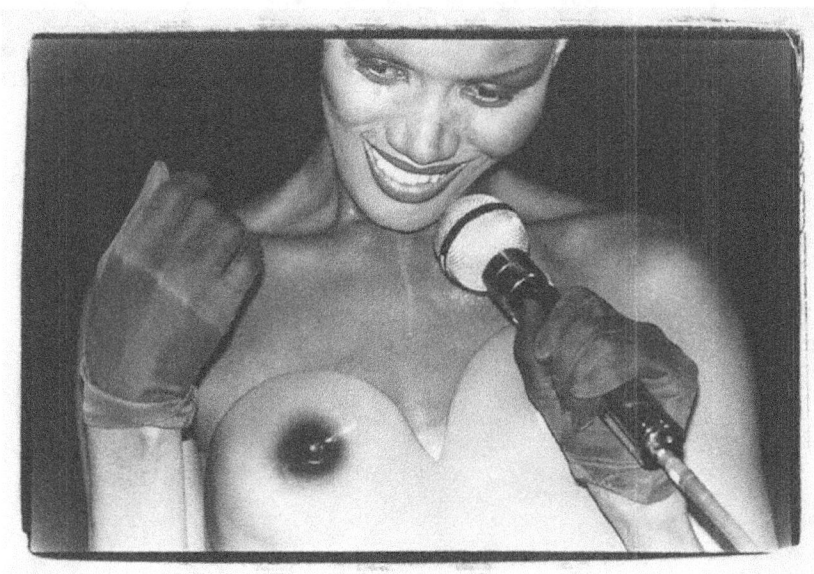

Hip Hop History — Book 1

Hip-Hop (Rap Music): November 24, 1982, **the Sugar Hill Gang** released *8th Wonder* on *Sugar Hill Records*. It's most noted single, *Apache*, peaked at #13 on the R&B charts.

Producers: Sylvia Robinson, James Cullimore

On November 30, 1982, *Michael Jackson* released *Thriller* on **Epic Records**. Jackson's sophomore solo album topped his previous *Off The Wall* release by selling over 65 million records worldwide. *Thriller* charted #1 in the U.S., #1 in the UK, #1 in the Netherlands, #1 in Italy, #1 in France, #1 in Canada, #1 Austria, #1 in Australia, #2 in Germany, and #6 in Japan.

⇒ **TV News—Soul Train:** On November 6, 13, 20 & 27, 1982, **Larry Graham, The Busboys – Hal Jackson's Talented Teens – Jerry Butler, Daryl Hall & John Oates – Luther Vandross, and Cheryl Lynn** were featured guests.

⇒ **Medical News—Utah:** On December 2, 1982 at the University of Utah, **Barney Clark**, a 61 year old dentist becomes the first person to receive a permanent artificial heart and lives for 112 days with the device.

⇒ **Film News—Comedy:** On December 8, 1982, **Paramount Pictures** released *"48hrs"* starring **Eddie Murphy** and **Nick Nolte.** Directed by *Walter Hill*; Produced by *Lawrence Gordon* and *Joel Silver*.

⇒ **TV News—Soul Train:** (Soul Train): On December 4, 11, 18 & 25, 1982, **Johnnie Taylor, Tavares – Chuck Mangione, Howard Johnson – Michael McDonald, Janet Jackson – The Time, and Magic Lady** were featured guests.

1982 – Billboards Year End – Hot 100 Singles

1982	Urban Music 16% of Billboard's Year-End Hot 100	16%
24	Dazz Band – Let it Whip	Motown
26	Ray Parker, Jr. – The Other Woman	Arista
27	George Benson – Turn Your Love Around	Warner Bros.
33	Earth Wind & Fire – Let's Groove	Columbia
43	Stevie Wonder – That Girl	Tamla
46	Roberta Flack – Making Love	Atlantic
54	Diana Ross – Why Do Fools Fall in Love	RCA/Capitol
59	Donna Summer – Love is in Control (Finger on the Trigger)	Geffen/Warner
61	Quincy Jones feat James Ingram – One Hundred Ways	A&M
69	Commodores – Oh No	Motown
71	Deniece Williams – It's Gonna Take a Miracle	ARC
82	Kool & the Gang – Get Down on it	De-Lite
85	Kool & the Gang – Take My Heart (You Can Have it if You Want it)	De-Lite
86	Diana Ross – Mirror Mirror	RCA
89	The Pointer Sisters – Should I Do it	Planet
95	Stevie Wonder – Do I Do	Tamla

1982 – Record Labels in Urban Music

Tommy Boy Records: Founded in 1981 in New York City by *Tom Silverman* as an independent label, Tommy Boy released legendary Hip Hop artists, such as Afrikaa Bambaataa and Soulsonic Force, but this would only be the beginning, as the independent label took its place among the new Hip Hop Culture.

Geffen Records: Founded in 1981 by *David Geffen* who also founded *Asylum Records* in the early 70's, the label was financed by *Warner Bros.* and distributed by *Epic Records*; with all the major pieces in place, David would lead the label to the top of the industry, while attracting super star talent along the way, like: Donna Summer, John Lennon, Yoko Ono, Cher, Irene Cara, and Elton John to name a few.

Circa 1983

Electro Funk

Hip-Hop (Electro, Boogie, Funk): In 1983, **West Street Mob** released *Break Dance – Electric Boogie* on **Sugar Hill Records**. The album peaked at #37 on the R&B charts. The track was inspired by *Apache* by Michael Viner's Incredible Bongo Band.

Members: Warren Moore, Joey Robinson, Jr. & Sabrina Gillison.

⇒ **News**: **On January 19, 1983, Apple Inc.** releases their personal computer called Apple Lisa.
⇒ **TV News—Soul Train: On January 1, 1983, Vanity 6 and Carl Carlton** were featured guests.
⇒ **Sports News—NFL: On January 30, 1983, Super Bowl XVII, the Washington Redskins** defeat the *Miami Dolphins* 27-17.

On February 3, 1983, *Earth, Wind & Fire* release *Powerlight* on **Columbia Records**. The album peaked at #4 on the R&B charts and went on to be certified gold.

⇒ **Sports News—NBA:** On February 13, 1983; before the NBA All-Star game *Marvin Gaye* sings the "*Star-Spangled Banner*

1983 – Urban American
Grammy Award Recipients – 25th Annual

Awards, 1983: Richard Pryor wins Best Comedy Recording *(Live on the Sunset Strip)*.

Awards, 1983: Queen Ida wins Best Ethnic or Traditional Folk Recording *(Queen Ida & the Bon Temps Zydeco Band Tour)*.

Awards, 1983: Al Green wins Best Soul Gospel Performance, Traditional *(Precious Lord)*.

Awards, 1983: Al Green wins Best Soul Gospel Performance, Contemporary *(HigherPlane)*.

Awards, 1983: Sarah Vaughn wins Best Jazz Vocal Performance, Female *(Gershwin Live!)*

Awards, 1983: Miles Davis wins Best Jazz Instrumental Performance, Soloist *(We Want Miles)*

Awards, 1983: Count Basie wins Best Jazz Instrumental Performance, Big Band *(Warm Breeze)*.

Awards, 1983: Lionel Richie wins Best Pop Vocal Performance, Male *(Truly)*

Awards, 1983: Jennifer Holiday wins Best R&B Vocal Performance, Female *(And I Am Telling You "I'm Not Going")*.

Awards, 1983: Marvin Gaye wins Best R&B Vocal Performance, Male *(Sexual Healing)*.

Awards, 1983: Dazz Band wins Best R&B Performance by a Duo or Group with Vocal *(Let it Whip)*.

Awards, 1983: Earth, Wind & Fire wins Best R&B Performance by a Duo or Group with Vocal *(Wanna Be With You)*.

Awards, 1983: Marvin Gaye wins Best R&B Instrumental Performance *(Sexual Healing)*.

⇒ **Magazine News: On February 17, 1983, Michael Jackson** lands the cover of *Rolling Stone*.

Hip-Hop (Graffiti): During this era *Jean-Michael Basquiat,* as an artist would use graffiti art to spread conscious messages throughout the city. Though mostly canvassing the walls and subways of the lower east side of Manhattan, Basquiat's art cemented a place in the Hip Hop culture initially when he and high school friend, *AL Diaz,* tagged their art pieces with "*SAMO,*" meaning "Same-old-sh**," at that time referring to marijuana as he and Diaz smoked regularly. He later transformed his work onto paper and canvas.

⇒ **Music Industry News: On March 2, 1983, Compact Disc, aka CD's** go on sale in the United States and begin to phase out Vinyl albums and record players, ushering in the digital age of music.

On March 15, 1983, *New Edition* releases their debut album *Candy Girl* on **Streetwise Records**. The album didn't reach the top 10, but pinned several classics like, *Jealous Girl, Popcorn Love, Is This the End*, and the title track, *Candy Girl*.

On March 28, 1983, *Al Jarreau* releases *Jarreau* on **Warner Bro. Records**. The album peaked at #1 on the Jazz charts and #4 on R&B and went to garner platinum status.

Hip-Hop (Music Videos): In 1983, **Ralph McDaniels and Lionel C. Martin** released "*Video Music Box*" on **WNYC-TV,** a New York City public television station. The show featured Hip Hop artists' music videos as well as social commentary.

Hip-Hop (Rap Music): In 1983, *Kurtis Blow* released *Party Time?* on **Mercury Records**. The Rap album peaked at #36 on the R&B charts and solidified another year for the Hip Hop Culture and new music genre.

Producer: Kurtis Blow

Hip-Hop (Rap Music): **In 1983, the Crash Crew** released *We Are Known As Emcees (We Turn Party's Out)* on *Sugar Hill Records*.

Members: G. Man, La Shubee, Barry Bistro, EK Mike C, Reggie Reg & Dj Daryll C.

City: Harlem, New York.

Hip-Hop (Electro): In 1983, **G.L.O.B.E. & Whiz Kid** released *"Play That Beat Mr. D.J."* on *Tommy Boy Records*. The track became an instant classic and tool for DJ's across the globe without being released nationally.

Producers: Craig Harris, Tom Silverman

TV News—Soul Train: On April 30, 1983, The Bar-Kays, O'Bryan and Magic Johnson & Norm Nixon of the Los Angeles Lakers were featured guests.

On April 13, 1983, the *Mary Jane Girls* release their debut self-titled album on ***Gordy Records***. Produced by *Rick James*, the group came out of the gate with several hits, *Candy Man*, *Boys*, and *All Night Long*, all peaking at #8 on the Dance charts.

⇒ **TV News—Soul Train:** On May 7, 14, 21 & 28, 1983, The Gap Band, Yarbrough & Peoples, Robert "Goodie" Whitfield – DeBarge, Champaign – Grandmaster Flash & the Furious Five, Evelyn "Champagne" King – Angela Bofill, and Con Funk Shun were featured guest.

On May 10, 1983, *Donna Summer* releases *She Works Hard for the Money* on ***Mercury Records***. Pushed by the title track, this became one of her most successful albums, peaking at #9 on the Top 200.

⇒ **Music News—Performance:** On May 16, 1983, **Michael Jackson** unleashes his dance move the *"moonwalk"* during the ***Motown 25*** special while performing *Billie Jean*.

⇒ **Movie News — Comedy: On June 10, 1983, Paramount Pictures** released "*Trading Places*" starring **Eddie Murphy**, directed by *John Landis*, written by *Timothy Harris* and *Herschel Weingrod*.

Hip-Hop (Rap Music): July 8, 1983, **Whodini** released their self-titled debut album on *Jive Records*, which was based out of London at the time. The rap pioneers would pin a string of hits further garnishing international status for the Hip Hop genre across the globe.

Members: DJ Grandmaster Dee, Ecstasy, Jalil **City**: Brooklyn, New York

On July 11, 1983, *Shalamar* releases *The Look* on *SOLAR Records*. The album reached #13 on the R&B charts and peaked at #7 in the UK.

In July of 1983, the Queen of Soul, *Aretha Franklin* releases *Get It Right* on **Arista Records**. The album was produced by *Luther Vandross* and its title track reached #1 on the Billboard charts.

⇒ **TV News — Music:** On July 22, 1983, **WABC-TV** released video show, *New York Hot Tracks* on WABC-TV. The show featured artists, such as ***Janet Jackson, the Beastie Boys, Anita Baker* and *RUN-D.M.C*** to name a few.

⇒ **TV News — Soul Train:** On July 2, 9 & 16, 1983, **Lakeside, High Energy – Thelma Houston, The System – O'Bryan, and Imagination** were featured guests.

⇒ **Magazine News:** On August 22, 1983, Democratic presidential candidate; **Jesse Jackson** lands cover of *TIME*.

On August 5, 1983, *Rick James* releases *Cold Blooded* on **Gordy records**. It's most noted tracks were, *Ebony Eyes,* a duet with label mate, *Smokey Robinson,* and the classic title track.

⇒ **Movie News—Comedy/Stand-Up: On August 9, 1983, Richard Pryor** released *"Here and Now"* on ***Warner Bros***. which was also released as a live album.

Hip-Hop (Electro, Funk): In August of 1983, **Herbie Hancock** released *Future Shock* on ***Columbia Records***. Never shying away from a challenge, the legendary Jazz musician teamed up with producer *Bill Laswell* and Dj *Grand Mixer DXT* to produce a HipHop classic, **Rock It**, that would further cement the genre. Hip Hop was here to stay!

⇒ **National News—Miss America: On September 17, 1983, Vanessa Lynn Williams** becomes the first African American woman to be crowned Miss America in Atlantic City, New Jersey.
⇒ **TV News—Music: In September of 1983, Bob Banner Associates** released *Star Search* in syndication. The show featured contestants competing in the genres of vocalist, dance, and comedy.

On October 11, 1983, *Lionel Richie* releases *Can't Slow Down* on **Motown Records**. The album pinned several hits and peaked at #1 in the US, UK and Australia, while making Diamond status in the US & Canada, 3x platinum in the UK, platinum in Finland & Hong Kong, and gold in France and Germany.

Hip-Hop (Rap Music): October 24, 1983, **Too Short** released his debut album *Don't Stop Rappin* on **75 Girls Records & Tapes**. Short brought the West Coast style of Rap to the new genre with his Playboy, Hustler, Pimp Story Telling from the streets of Oakland, California. Too Short solidified the West Coast as a force in the new genre.

City: Oakland, California **Producers**: Todd Shaw, D. Hodges

⇒ **TV News — Soul Train: On October 15, 22 & 29, 1983, Manhattan's Philip Bailey – Jeffrey Osborne, Midnight Starr, T.K. Carter – Al Green & Planet Patrol** were featured guests.

On November 2, 1983, *Irene Cara* releases *What A Feelin'* on ***Network Records***. The album peaked at #45 on the R&B charts with the title track reaching #1 on the charts.

⇒ **Civil Rights News: On November 2, 1983, President Ronald Reagan** signs a bill creating a federal holiday to honor *Dr. Martin Luther King, Jr*. The date was set to be the third Monday of every January starting in 1986.

⇒ **Politics: On November 3, 1983, the Rev. Jesse Jackson** announces his candidacy for the 1984 Democratic Party presidential nomination.

On November 4, 1983, *Earth, Wind & Fire* release *Electric Universe* on **Columbia Records**. The album peaked at #8 on the R&B charts.

On November 6, 1983, the *Pointer Sisters* released *Break Out* on **Planet Records**. The album peaked at #6 on the R&B charts going 3x platinum, winning two Grammy Awards, and an American Music Award.

On November 14, 1983, *Chic* released *Believer* on **Atlantic Records**. This would be the last album recorded by Chic's original members.

- ⇒ **TV News — Soul Train: On November 5, 12, 19 & 26, 1983, The S.O.S. Band, Mary Jane Girls – The Gap Band, Michael Sembello – Sister Sledge, Lillo Thomas – Jennifer Holiday & Klique** were featured guests.
- ⇒ **Movie News — Crime/Drugs: On December 1, 1983, Universal Pictures** released "*Scarface*" starring **Al Pacino**, screen play by *Oliver Stone*, directed by *Brian De Palma*.
- ⇒ **Music News: On December 2, 1983, Michael Jackson's** *Thriller* video airs for the first time on **MTV**. It would be the station's very first world premiere video, and it had a run time of 13 minutes and 43 seconds.
- ⇒ **TV News — Soul Train: On December 3, 10, 17, 24 & 31, 1983, Kashif, The Manhattan Transfer – Herbie Hancock, DeBarge – Kool & the Gang, Tavares – The Commodores, Anita Baker – Atlantic Starr & James Ingram** were featured guests.
- ⇒ **L.A. News: In 1983, Danilo Blandon and Norwin Menesses** were the main distributors of cocaine, supplying *Freeway Ricky Ross* with 100 kilos a week. During this time Ross began making what he called "*Ready Rock*," a cheaper form of cocaine which came to be known as crack. This union between the gentlemen came about to raise cash to support what was known as Ronald Reagan's Secret War. (The CIA and DEA needed the money to train and support the Nicaraguan Contra Army.) So, Blandon and Norwin Menesses came up with the "*Great!*" idea to sell drugs and guns to black street gangs in L.A. and Miami to finance the president's secret war. *All of this information is available in Ricky Ross's drug trial public court records from 1996. It may sound like a movie, but it really happened and it involved a US President, CIA, DEA, Drug Lords, and Gangsters. This started the CRACK Epidemic, which led to the downfall of millions of black families, neighborhoods, and countless lives lost to gun violence. Out of the three men responsible, Ricky Ross ended up being the only*

one doing time, while Blandon remained a DEA informant and Menesses has never spent a day behind US bars.

⇒ **Economy**: Fresh out of a long and unforgiving recession, **1983** was the beginning of economic growth; annual inflation rates dropped below 5% during the Regan era, but unemployment was still a problem that needed to be addressed.

Hip-Hop (Rap Music/Novelty/Parody): This year Shawn Brown released the *Rappin' Duke* on **JWP records**. Shawn rapped in the voice of legendary actor John Wayne who was also known as the Duke. The single was a first for the new culture, but quickly gained notoriety across the country. *Produced by H. B. Barnum*

1983 – Billboards Year End – Hot 100 Singles

1983	Urban Music 21% of Billboard's Year-End Hot 100	21%
2	Michael Jackson – *Billy Jean*	Epic
3	Irene Cara – *Flashdance…What A Feeling*	Casablanca
5	Michael Jackson – *Beat It*	Epic
8	Patti Austin & James Ingram – *Baby, Come to Me*	Qwest
15	Donna Summer – *She Works Hard for the Money*	Mercury
22	Eddie Grant – *Electric Avenue*	Portrait
25	Prince – *Little Red Corvette*	Warner Bros.
29	Lionel Richie – *You Are*	Motown
32	Marvin Gaye – *Sexual Healing*	Columbia
41	Prince – *1999*	Warner Bros
47	Lionel Richie – *Truly*	Motown
49	Michael Jackson & Paul McCartney – *The Girl is Mine*	Epic
68	Michael Jackson – *Wanna Be Startin Somethin*	Epic
73	Lionel Richie – *My Love*	Motown
78	DeBarge – *All This Love*	Gordy
80	Dionne Warwick – *Heartbreaker*	Arista
86	Shalamar – *Dead Giveaway*	Solar
89	Michael Jackson – *Human Nature*	Epic
91	Musical Youth – *Pass the Dutchie*	MCA
96	Roberta Flack & Peabo Bryson – *Tonight I Celebrate My Love*	Capitol
100	Earth, Wind & Fire – *Fall in Love with Me*	Columbia

1983 – Record Labels in Hip Hop Music

Sugar Hill Records: Riding high on the success of Hip Hop, the label released new rap albums from *West Street Mob* and the *Crash Crew* this year. Both albums generated some heat with the Hip Hop Culture.

Mercury Records: The label enjoyed the best of both worlds with a Disco hit album from *Donna Summer,* and the success of *Kurtis Blow*'s newly released Rap album.

Tommy Boy Records: Tommy Boy released a Hip Hop classic with *G.L.O.B.E & Whiz Kid's* Dee Jay masterpiece, *Play that Beat Mr. D.J.*

Jive Records: Originally formed by **Zomba Records** in 1981, Jive label heads, Clive Calder and Barry Weiss took advantage of the exploding Hip Hop scene by developing a group of musicians who came to be known as *Whodini*. The group's debut album dropped this year and cemented Hip Hop History.

Circa 1984

Sucker M.C.'s

Hip-Hop (New School Rap): March 27, 1984, **RUN-D.M.C.** released their debut self-titled album on *Profile Records*. The trio merged the Rap style of their predecessors with loud and rifting Rock & Roll-like beats; the tag team delivery of vocals from Run and D.M.C. struck a chord with the Hip Hop Culture by rapping about everyday life and social consciousness, while still maintaining the savvy street style of the genre. Their most noted singles, *Hard Times, Rock Box, Sucker M.C.'s,* and *It's Like That,* broke ground in the mainstream and played a huge part in pushing Rap music past the then popular Disco sound, which Hip Hop actually used to enter the DJ booths of the radio jocks and get air play. Now with MTV and the popularity of music videos on the rise, the trio aired *Rock Box* for the world to see Rap and its bold new sound; Hip Hop was becoming the new kid on the block and Run-D.M.C. was proof that we were playing for keeps.

Members: Jam Master Jay, RUN, D.M.C. **City**: Hollis Queens, New York

Producers: R. Simmons, J. Simmons, J. Mizell, D. McDaniels, N.S. Hardy, Bralower, Moore, Smith, Waring, Jr. and Hayden

⇒ **Music Industry News: On April 1, in the city of Los Angeles, R&B singer Marvin Gaye** is shot and killed by his father during an argument.

On April 10, Rapper Q-Tip of *A Tribe called Quest* turns 14 years old. (*Born 4-10-1970*)

On April 14, 1984, *Jermaine Jackson* released his self-titled album on *Arista Records*. It would be the first he released since leaving *Motown*. The album also featured appearances from his brother Michael, Randy, and Tito and would go on to be certified gold.

Hip-Hop (Rap Music): In 1984, **the Sugarhill Gang** released their third album *Livin' in the Fast Lane* on *Sugar Hill records*; unfortunately, it didn't garner any hits like their Freshman and Sophomore albums. Amidst the New School Rap that was beginning to claim its stake in the game, Sugar Hill found themselves in a new competitive arena.

Hip-Hop (Rap Music): In 1984 **Grandmaster Melle Mel & the Furious Five** released their self-titled album on *Sugar Hill Records*. The album was released after Melle Mel and Flash parted ways; the most noted track was *White Lines*.

Hip-Hop (Electro Rap): In 1984, **Newcleus** released *Jam On Revenge (The Wikki-Wikki Song)* on *Mayhew Records*. The track became a favorite and broke the top 40 on the R&B charts; Newcleus had taken Rap to a new frontier, further cementing the genre.

Members: Fresh Kid, Niecey D, Tracy G, Nikki D, Chilly B, Lady E, Cozmo D

City: Brooklyn, New York

Hip-Hop (Rap Music): In 1984, **The Treacherous Three** released their self-titled album on *Sugar Hill Records*. Prior to this release, the MC's released several singles such as *Whip It* and *Yes We Can-Can*; they also released *Xmas Rap*, which went on to be a Hip Hop classic.

Members: DJ Easy Lee, Kool Moe Dee, L.A. Sunshine, Special K & Spoonie Gee

City: Harlem, New York

On May 29, 1984, *Tina Turner* releases *Private Dancer* on **Capitol Records**. The album produced top selling singles, *What's Love Got to Do with It*, *Private Dancer*, and *You Better Be Good to Me*.

⇒ **Movie News—Hip Hop:** On June 4, 1984, **MGM** released *"Breakin"* directed by *Joel Silberg*, produced by *Allen DeBevoise* and *David Zito*, starring **Shabba Doo and Boogaloo Shrimp**. The movie captured our culture through the eyes of two Break Dancers earning $38.7 million at the box offices and cost only $1.2 million to make.

On June 5, 1984, *Shelia E* released her debut self-titled album on **Warner Bros. Records**. Shelia, also known for her skills as a drummer/percussionist, came out swinging, pinning a spot in the Top 10 with *Glamorous Life*.

⇒ **Movie News—Hip Hop:** On June 8, 1984, **Orion Pictures** released *"Beat Street"*, directed by *Stan Lathan*, produced by *Harry Belafonte* and *David V. Picker*. The movie focused on Break Dance and the Hip Hop Culture, earning $16,595,791.00 at the box office.

Birthday: June 16, 1984; rapper, **Tupac Shakur** turns 13 years old. (*Born 6-16-71*)

On June 25, 1984, *Prince and the Revolution* release *Purple Rain* on **Warner Bros. Records**. The album and movie soundtrack pinned several hit singles, *When Doves Cry, Let's Go Crazy,* and *Purple Rain*; the title track reached #2 on the Hot 100 and sells over *20 million copies*, while the movie earned *$68.4 million* at the box office.

On July 2, 1984, *The Time* released *Ice Cream Castles* on **Warner Bros. Records**. The albums most noted tracks, *Jungle Love, The Bird*, and the title track, all placed on the Pop and R&B charts, *Jungle Love* pinning the highest with #6 on the R&B charts.

On July 2, 1984, *The Jacksons* released *Victory* on **Epic Records**. The album reached #4 on the Billboard 200 and went on to sell 7 million copies.

On July 16, 1984, *Sade* released their debut album *Diamond Life* on *Epic records* **(UK)**. Many think that Sade is a solo artist, but the truth is that, *Sade* is actually an English band consisting of members, *Sade Adu, Paul Anthony Cook, Paul Denman,* and *Stuart Matthewman*. The chart-topping singles, *Hang On to Your Love, Your Love is King*, and *Smooth Operator*, helped launch the band into stardom.

On July 20, Rapper, Kool G Rap of the rap duo, *Kool G Rap and Polo* turns 16 years old. (*Born 7-20-1968*)

On August 6, 1984, *New Edition* releases their self-titled album on *MCA Records*. The group's sophomore album reached #1 on the R&B charts and went on to sell millions.

Birthday: August 20, 1984; rapper, **Busta Rhymes** of *L.O.N.S (Leaders Of the New School)* turns 12 years old. (*Born 8-20-1972*)

⇒ **Music Industry News**: **On September 7, Janet Jackson** elopes with *James DeBarge* of el Debarge.

On September 11, 1986, *Donna Summer* releases *Cats Without Claws* on **Geffen Records**. The album reached #40 on the Billboard Album chart.

On September 12, 1984, *Billy Ocean* releases *Suddenly* on *Jive Records*. Ocean shot to #1 on the Hot 100 with his hit single, *Caribbean Queen*.

On September 13, 1984, *Diana Ross* releases *Swept Away* on **Capitol Records**. The album spawned several hit singles and reached #26 on the Pop charts, while earning gold status.

⇒ **Music News: On September 14, the 1st annual MTV Video Music Awards** are held in New York City. *Herbie Hancock* stole the night with 5 awards.

On October 1, 1984, *Chaka Khan* releases *I Feel for You* on **Warner Bros. Records**. The platinum selling album was a huge success and played a large part on the Hip Hop scene in the element of Break Dancing.

Hip-Hop (Rap Music): October 17, 1984, **Whodini** released their sophomore album *Escape* on **Jive Records**. The album produced several hits, *Friends, Five Minutes of Funk, Big Mouth,* and *Freaks Come Out at Night,* all which resonated with the Hip Hop culture, cementing *Whodini* as Rap legends.

On October 23, 1984, *Janet Jackson* releases her sophomore album *Dream Street* on *A&M Records*. The album only had moderate success, but Janet wasn't about to be stopped.

On November 11, 1984, *Midnight Star* released *Planetary Vision* on **Solar Records**. The album reached #7 on the R&B charts, pushed by its lead single, *Operator*.

On November 15, 1984, *Kool & the Gang* released *Emergency* on **De-Lite Records**. The album produced several hits that pushed it to double platinum status.

On November 20, Rapper, Phife Dog the 5 foota of **A Tribe Called Quest** turns 14 years old. (*Born 11-20-1970*)

⇒ **Music Industry News: On November 20, Michael Jackson** receives a star on the *Hollywood Walk of Fame*.

Hip-Hop (Electro): November 30, 1984, **Egyptian Lover** released *On the Nile* on **Egyptian Empire Records**. The West Coast producer was a staple on the Hip Hop scene among the fans and break dance crews alike, with hot dance tracks in the lane of *Planet Rock* and *Newcleus*, but with a West Coast funk to it.

City: Los Angeles, California.

Hip-Hop (Rap Music): On December 18, 1984; *The Fat Boys* released their debut self-titled album on **Sutra Records**. The album pinned several HipHop classics, but most noted was the *Human Beat Box* featuring Buff Love, and the title track *Fat Boys*. The group branded themselves as three guys who loved to eat and owned the image. (Also known as the *Disco 3*.)

Members: Kool Rock-Ski, Buff Love, aka *Human Beat Box*, Prince Markie Dee

City: Brooklyn, New York. **Producer**: Kurtis Blow

Hip-Hop (Rap Music): This year in Hip Hop, **Rock Master Scott & the Dynamic Three** released the hit singles, *Request Line* & *The Roof is on Fire* on **Reality Records**. *The Roof is on Fire* reached #5 on the R&B/Hip Hop charts.

City: Bronx, New York   **Members**: Rock Master Scott, Slick Rick, MBG & Charlie Prince

"DJ please, pick up your phone/ I'm on the request line

Hello, what is your name and what would you like to hear?

Hi, my name is Joanne, I'm from down south & I'd like to talk to one of the Dynamic Three?

Here's Charlie Prince!

Hey! Charlie Prince on your request line, I'd like to know your name & your zodiac sign

Say What?! You a Scorpio just like me, and I'd like to let you know that I'm nasty

If you give me a chance with you fly girl, I bet you any amount of money

That I can rock your world"

-Charlie Prince (Request Line)

⇒ **Movie News—Hip Hop:** **On December 21, 1984, TriStar Pictures** released *"Breakin 2: Electric Boogaloo"* directed by *Sam Firstenberg,* produced by *Yoram Globus, Menahem Golan* and *Pieter Jan Brugge,* starring **Adolfo "Shabba Doo" Quinones** and **Michael "Boogaloo Shrimp" Chambers**. The sequel to "Breakin" cashed in with $15,101,131.00 at the box office. The surge of culturally-based movies was a clear sign that Hip Hop was now a household brand worth million's.

1984

MTV Video Music Awards – 1st Annual

Video of the Year – *The Cars* "You Might Think"

Best Male Video – *David Bowie* "China Girl"

Best Female Video – *Cyndi Lauper* "Girls Just Want to Have Fun"

Best Group Video – *ZZ Top* "Legs"

Best New Artist in a Video – *Eurythmics* "Sweet Dreams (Are Made of This)"

Best Concept Video – *Herbie Hancock* "Rock It"

Most Experimental Video – *Herbie Hancock* "Rock It"

Best Stage Performance Video – *Van Halen* "Jump"

Best Overall Performance in a Video – *Michael Jackson* "Thriller"

Best Direction in a Video – *ZZ Top* "Sharp Dressed Man" *Director: Tim Newman*

Best Choreography in a Video – *Michael Jackson* "Thriller" *Choreographers: Michael Jackson and Michael Peters*

Best Special Effects in a Video – *Herbie Hancock* "Rock It" *Special Effects: Godley & Crème*

Best Art Direction in a Video – *Herbie Hancock* "Rock It" *Art Director: Jim Whiting and Godley & Crème*

Best Editing in a Video – *Herbie Hancock* "Rock it" *Editors: Roo Aiken and Godley & Crème*

Best Cinematography in a Video – *The Police* "Every Breath You Take" *Director of Photography: Daniel Pearl*

Viewer's Choice – *Michael Jackson* "Thriller"

Video Vanguard Award – *The Beatles, David Bowie & Richard Lester*

Special Recognition Award – *Quincy Jones*

1984 – Billboard's Year End – Hot 100 Singles

1984	Urban Music 27% of Billboard's Year-End Hot 100	27%
1	Prince – *When Dove's Cry*	Warner Bros.
2	Tina Turner – *What's Love Got to Do with It*	Capitol
3	Michael Jackson & Paul McCartney – *Say Say Say*	Columbia
7	Lionel Richie – *Hello*	Motown
9	Ray Parker, Jr. – *Ghostbusters*	Arista
12	Lionel Richie – *All Night Long (All Night)*	Motown
13	Deniece Williams – *Let's Hear it for the Boy*	Columbia
18	Pointer Sisters – *Jump (For My Love)*	Planet
21	Prince and The Revolution – *Let's Go Crazy*	Warner Bros.
24	Kool and the Gang – *Joanna*	Polygram
25	Stevie Wonder – *I Just Called to Say I Love You*	Motown
26	Rockwell – *Somebody's Watching Me*	Motown
30	Shelia E – *Glamorous Life*	Warner Bros.
32	Lionel Richie – *Stuck on You*	Motown
47	Peabo Bryson – *If Ever You're in My Arms Again*	Elektra
48	Pointer Sisters – *Automatic*	Planet
49	Shannon – *Let the Music Play*	Mirage
51	Billy Ocean – *Caribbean Queen*	Jive
53	Lionel Richie – *Running with the Night*	Motown
61	The Jacksons – *State of Shock*	Epic
69	Breakdance – *Irene Cara*	Geffen
76	Pointer Sisters – *I'm So Excited*	Planet
77	Ray Parker, Jr. – *I Still Can't Get Over Loving You*	Arista
78	Michael Jackson – *Thriller*	Epic
84	DeBarge – *Time Will Reveal*	Gordy
90	Kool and the Gang – *Tonight*	Polygram
92	Shalamar – *Dancing in the Sheets*	Columbia

1984 – Record Labels in Hip Hop Music

Profile Records: Founded in 1980 by Cory Robbins and Steve Plotnicki in New York City, the label's first successful act was *Dr. Jeckyll & Mr. Hyde* with the hit Rap single *Genius Rap*. **Profile** would go on to sign more rap acts and is noted as one of the most prolific independent rap labels in the industry. Their most popular group, *RUN-D.M.C.* took the Rap game by storm this year with their self-titled debut album.

Sugar Hill Records: Sugar Hill continued to release rap albums as the genre grew to new heights. This year marked the release of the *Treacherous Three, Melle Mel & The Furious Five (Post Grandmaster Flash)*, and a new album from the *Sugar Hill Gang*.

Jive Records: This year Jive would forever leave their mark on the Hip Hop Culture with the release of *Whodini's* second album *Escape*. The album went platinum and produced several Hip Hop classics, *Five Minutes of Funk, Friends, Big Mouth, & The Freaks Come Out at Night*.

Egyptian Empire Records: Founded in California by DJ and Producer *Egyptian Lover*, one of the first Afro American label owners. Egyptian Empire made its mark with funky electro beats that kept the dance floors packed and car speakers thumping.

Sutra Records: Originally founded as Kama Sutra records in 1964 by Arthur Ripp, Hy Mizrahi and Phil Steinberg. The label defunct in the mid 70's, but restarted as *Sutra Records* in 1981. This year the label capitalized on the Hip Hop genre by releasing the *Fat Boys* debut self-titled album, which was produced by *Kurtis Blow*.

1984 – Urban American

Grammy Award Recipients – 26th Annual

Awards, 1984: Michael Jackson wins Record of the Year *(Beat It)*, Produced by Michael Jackson & Quincy Jones.

Awards, 1984: Michael Jackson wins Album of the Year *(Thriller)*, Produced by Michael Jackson & Quincy Jones.

Awards, 1984: Quincy Jones & Michael Jackson win Best Recording for Children *(E.T. the Extra-Terrestrial)*.

Awards, 1984: Eddie Murphy wins Best Comedy Recording *(Eddie Murphy)*.

Awards, 1984: Sandra Crouch wins Best Soul Gospel Performance, Female *(We Sing Praises)*.

Awards, 1984: Al Green wins Best Soul Gospel Performance, Male *(I'll Rise Again)*.

Awards, 1984: Donna Summer wins Best Inspirational Performance *(He's A Rebel)*.

Awards, 1984: Ella Fitzgerald wins Best Jazz Vocal Performance, Female *(The Best Is Yet to Come)*.

Awards, 1984: Wynton Marsalis win Best Jazz Instrumental Performance, Soloist. (Think of One)

Awards, 1984: Irene Cara wins Best Pop Vocal Performance, Female *(Flashdance.. What a Feeling)*.

Awards, 1984: Michael Jackson wins Best Pop Vocal Performance, Male *(Thriller)*.

Awards, 1984: George Benson wins Best Pop Instrumental Performance *(Being With You)*.

Awards, 1984: Michael Jackson & Quincy Jones win Best Producers of the Year *(Non-Classical)*.

Awards, 1984: Chaka Khan wins Best R&B Vocal Performance, Female *(Chaka Khan)*.

Awards, 1984: Michael Jackson wins Best R&B Vocal Performance, Male *(Billie Jean)*.

Awards, 1984: Chaka Khan & Rufus win Best R&B Performance by a Duo or Group with Vocal *(Ain't Nobody)*.

Awards, 1984: Herbie Hancock wins Best R&B Instrumental Performance *(Rock It)*

Awards, 1984: Michael Jackson wins Best R&B Song *(Billie Jean)*.

Awards, 1984: Michael Jackson wins Best Rock Vocal Performance, Male *(Beat It)*.

Circa 1985

Def Jam

Hip Hop (Music TV): On January 1, 1985, a new music video channel, **VH1** starts broadcasting in America on cable television. The first video aired was *Marvin Gaye's* version of "*The Star-Spangled Banner.*"

- ⇒ **TV News — Soul Train: On January 5, 1985, The Fat Boys** were featured guests on Soul Train, and **Whodini** performed on January 12.
- ⇒ **Politics: On January 20, 1985, President Ronald Regan and Vice President George Bush** were sworn in for their 2nd term of office.

Hip-Hop (Rap Music): February 5, 1985, rap trio **RUN D.M.C** released their sophomore album *King of Rock* on ***Profile Records***. The rock and roll influenced album played an important role in the main stream acceptance of our new genre. *(Hip Hop)* Chart topping singles like the title track, *King of Rock, You Talk Too Much,* and *Can You Rock it Like This,* showed the trio's diversity and the resolve of Hip Hop.

Producers: Russell Simmons and Larry Smith.

- ⇒ **World News: On February 27, 1985, in San Francisco, California** the *Irwin Memorial Blood Bank* said that 80 Bay Area residents received blood since 1979 from donors who are known to have contracted AIDS.
- ⇒ **Magazine News: February 1985, Mr. Olympia (1984), Lee Haney** lands cover of *Muscle & Fitness*.

⇒ **World News: On March 2, 1985, the US Government** approved a screening test for AIDS that detected antibodies to the virus, to exclude contaminated blood from the blood supply.

Birthday: March 19, 1985, rapper, **Bun B** of *UGK* turns 12 years old. (Born 3-19-1973)

⇒ **Music Industry News: On March 27, 1985, The South African Broadcasting Corporation** bans *Stevie Wonder's* music because he dedicated an award he won to *Nelson Mandela*.

⇒ **Film News — Martial Arts: On March 22, 1985, TriStar Pictures** released the *"Last Dragon"* starring **Taimak and Vanity**. *Berry Gordy* along with *Rupert Hitzig* and *Joseph Caracciolo* produced the classic for **Motown Productions**. The film grossed $25.7 Million; Directed by *Michael Schultz*.

Hip-Hop (Rap Music): April 26, 1985, **Grandmaster Flash** released *They Said It Couldn't Be Done* following the break of the Furious 5 on **Elektra Records**. One of its most noted tracks, *Sign of the Times* went on to be a classic.

Producers: Grandmaster Flash (The Group) & Gavin Christopher

⇒ **World News: On May 2, 1985, US Financial Firm E.F. Hutton** pleads guilty to charges that it carried out a large check-kiting scam.

⇒ **Magazine News: In April of 1985, Michael Jackson** and **Lionel Richie** land cover *JET*.

⇒ **Sports News — NBA: On May 16, 1985, Michael Jordan** of the Chicago Bulls was named NBA Rookie of the Year.

⇒ **Entertainment: Nintendo Co. of Japan** launched its first video game console (*The Nintendo Entertainment System*).

Hip-Hop (Rap Music): May 27, 1985, bay Area rapper, **Too Short** releases his sophomore album *Players* on **75 Girls Records**. Short continued to deliver his street tales of pimps, drug dealers, and prostitutes further branding his style of West Coast Hip Hop.

Produced by D. Hodges.

⇒ **Politics: On June 12, 1985, the US House of Representatives** approved $27 million in aid to the Nicaraguan contras.

On June 16, 1985; California Rapper, MC Ren of *NWA* turns 16 years old. (Born 6-16-1969)

⇒ **Politics: On June 27, 1985, the US House of Representatives** voted to limit the use of combat troops in Nicaragua.
⇒ **Magazine News: This year Prince** lands the cover of *Rolling Stone*.
⇒ **Magazine News: In June of 1985, Grace Jones** lands the cover of *ESSENCE*.
⇒ **Magazine News: In June of 1985, Prince** lands the cover of *EBONY*.

Hip-Hop (Rap Music): This year in Hip Hop, rap trio **The Fat Boys** released their sophomore album *The Fat Boys are Back* on **Sutra Records**. The title track, *The Fat Boys are Back* peaked at #27 on the Hot Black Singles charts, while the album reached #11 on Billboard Top R&B Albums charts, again proving to the main stream that Hip Hop was indeed here to stay.

Producer: Kurtis Blow.

"When it was held, the party of the year

Everybody was there, cold funky fresh gear

Dressed in suede, my girl in silk

Stepped straight to the bar, grabbed a glass of milk

Grabbed my girl, stepped to the floor

Did the Pee Wee Herman, until my feet got sore

Left the floor, grabbed a seat, relaxed and listened to this funky beat"

-Prince Markie Dee of the Fat Boys (In the House)

⇒ **Magazine News: This year Bill Cosby** lands the cover of *Time* as America's Funniest Father.

Hip-Hop (Rap/Dance/Electro): This year in Hip Hop, West Coast electro group, **World Class Wreckin' Cru** released their debut album *World Class* on **Kru-Cut Records**. The group delivered a sound compiled with funk, drums, and heavy vocals from Michelle' le among others.

Members: Dr. Dre, Dj Yella, Dr. Rock, Alonzo Williams, Shakespeare, Cli-N-Tel, Michelle' le and Mona Lisa. **City**: Compton, California. **Producers**: Dr. Dre & DJ Yella

Hip-Hop (Rap Music): This year **the Boogie Boys** released their debut album *City Life* on *Capitol Records*. Their most popular track, *A Fly Girl* helped push the album to #10 on the R&B charts.

City: Harlem, New York   **Members**: Boogie Knight, Romeo J.D, Lil Raheim

Hip-Hop (Rap Music): This year in Hip Hop, New York rap group, **UTFO** released their debut self-titled album on **Select Records**. The album featured a Hip Hop classic, one to publicly carve a new lane in our genre that came to be known as "Battle Rap". UTFO's smash hit *Roxanne, Roxanne* sparked several female MC's to respond with answer records creating a whole new scene for Hip Hop and opening the door for even more female MC's to get in the battle. The whole Roxanne movement gave the mainstream an inside look at what went on during battles on the stages at Hip Hop clubs, block parties, parks, and city street corners. The Art of Rap had shown the world yet another side of itself.

Members: Educated Rapper, MixMaster Ice, Kangol Kid & Doctor Ice

Producers: Full Force   **City**: Brooklyn, New York.

"Yo Kango, I don't think you're dense

But you went about the matter with no experience

You should know, she doesn't need a guy like you

She needs a guy like me, with a high IQ"

-The Educated Rapper MD of UTFO (Roxanne, Roxanne)

Hip-Hop (Rap Music): This year New York, Queensbridge rapper, **Roxanne Shante'** released her underground single *Roxanne's Revenge*, a response rap track to U.T.F.O's hit single, *Roxanne, Roxanne*. Her new single sold over 250,000 copies out of the gate before going national; this would be the beginning of the historic Hip Hop Roxanne Wars.

Producer: Marley Marl

(*Juice Crew*)

◊ **Hip-Hop (Fashion)**: The culture brought its own look along with the music, below a young *Kool Moe Dee* rocks the Bomber jacket and Name belt.

Hip-Hop (Rap/Electro-Funk): This year New York based group, **Mantronix** released their self-titled debut album on *Sleeping Bag Records*. Their hit single *Fresh Is the Word* was a culture smash hit and peaked at #16 on Billboard Hot Dance charts. Rap, although still new, was quickly gaining ground and attracting fans from all walks of life.

Members: MC Tee and Kurtis Mantronik **Producers**: Mantronik, MC Tee
City: Flatbush, Brooklyn, New York

Hip-Hop (The Boombox): The radio to the Hip Hop culture was just as important as turntables to a Dee Jay, a microphone to an MC, or spray paint to a Graffiti artist. Every crew had someone that had a Big Ass Radio! On the block, we called it the Boombox, we listened to the hottest radio stations, mix tapes, rap tracks, or our own demo tapes. Your crew was whack, if you didn't have a Box.

Hip-Hop (Rap Music): This year in Hip Hop, Philadelphia rapper, **Schoolly D** released his debut self-titled album on *Schoolly D Records*. Schoolly D scored success with his hot street tracks, *Gucci Time,* and *P.S.K. What Does it Mean?*

City: Philadelphia, Penn. **Producers**: Schoolly D & DJ Code Money

"Driving in my car down the avenue

Toking on a j, sipping on some brew

Turned around, see the fly young lady

Pull to the curb and park my Mercedes

Said "Fly lady, now you're looking real nice

Sweeter than honey, sugar and spice"

Told her my name was MC Schoolly D

All about making that cash money"

-Schoolly D (PSK 'What Does It Mean?')

Hip-Hop (Rap, Electro-Funk): This year in Hip Hop **the West Coast Crew** released *In The Mix* on **KMA records.** The Los Angeles based group scored numerous cult hits, tattooing the West Coast place in Hip Hop even further.

Members: David Wooley, James Magee, Russell Smith and Willie Lemon

City: Los Angeles, California **Producers**: Jam Power Productions

◊ **Hip-Hop (Fashion):** On the West Coast the culture rocked the **Chuck Taylor** sneakers with Jeans and Khaki's as part of their Hip Hop gear.

Hip-Hop (Rap, Electro-Funk): This year in Hip Hop, **Newcleus** released their sophomore album *Space is the Place* on **Mayhew Records**.

Producers: Jam On Productions

◊ **Music News: On September 6, 1985, Michael Jackson** purchases the publishing rights for most of *The Beatles* catalog for $47 Million.

◊ **TV News—Music:** On September 13, 1985; **MTV** debut its new half hour dance club themed television show "*Club MTV*" hosted by Video Jock "*Downtown Judy Brown*". The show was largely formatted after American Bandstand and feat industry guest such as Jody Watley, Vanessa Williams, Sheena Easton and more.

◊ **TV News—Sitcom: On September 14, 1985, NBC** released *227* starring **Marla Gibbs** produced by *Embassy Television*.

Birthday: September 25, 1985, Philadelphia rapper, **Fresh Prince (Will Smith)** of *Jazzy Jeff and the Fresh Prince* turns 17 years old. (Born 9-25-1968)

⇒ **Entertainment News: On October 2, 1985,** movie star Rock Hudsoon dies of AIDS at age 59; he is the first star to die from the disease.

⇒ **Magazine News: This year,** Pro Football player & Actor, **O.J Simpson** lands cover of *EBONY*.

Hip-Hop (Rap Music): In October of this year **Kurtis Blow** released his sixth album, *America* on **Mercury Records**. The album's most noted track, *If I Ruled the World*, topped the charts in the UK, and is a Hip Hop classic.

Producer: Kurtis Blow

⇒ **Movie News—Hip Hop:** On October 25, 1985, **Krush Groove** was released by **Warner Bros**. The film is based on the early beginnings of **Def Jam Records** and *Russell Simmons*; Industry legends, **RUN-D.M.C., Sheila E, Kurtis Blow, The Fat Boys, New Edition, LL Cool J,** *and actor,* **Blair Underwood** starred in the Hip Hop classic. Written by *Ralph Farquhar*, Directed by *Michael Schultz* and Produced by *Russell Simmons, George Jackson and Michael Schultz*.

⇒ **Magazine News:** In October of 1985, **SADE** lands the cover of ***Cosmopolitan***.

On November 9, 1985; Texas Rapper, Scarface of the *Geto Boys* turns 15 years old. (Born 11-9-1970)

⇒ **Magazine News: On November 11, 1985, Maurice White** of *Earth, Wind & Fire* lands the cover of ***JET***.

Hip-Hop (Rap Music): November 18, 1985, **New York based rapper, LL Cool J** releases his debut album *Radio* on *Def Jam Records*. This would be the first full length album released by Def Jam. LL's debut album climbed the Billboard charts, later earning him platinum status.

City: Hollis, Queens, New York   **Producers**: Rick Rubin & Jazzy Jay

"Yo Yvette, there's a lot of rumors goin' around

They're so bad, baby you might have to skip town

See something's smellin' fishy and they say it's you

All I know is that you made it with the whole damn crew"

- LL Cool J (Dear Yvette)

⇒ **Magazine News: On November 18, 1985, Walter Payton** lands the cover of *JET*.
⇒ **TV News — Soul Train: On November 19, 1985, U.T.F.O.** were featured guests on Soul Train.

Hip-Hop (Rap Music): This year in Hip Hop, DJ and Producer, **Marley Marl** released *Marley Marl featuring MC Shan - Marley Marl Scratch"* on **NIA Records**. The album displayed the DJ skills of Marley Marl, the flows of MC Shan, and snippets of a young M.C and beat boxer by the name of *Biz Markie*.

City: Queens, New York   (*Mr. Majic along with Marley launched the Juice Crew*)

⇒ **Magazine News: This year, boxer, Thomas "Hit Man" Hearns** lands cover of the ***RING*** as *Fighter of the Year*.

⇒ **TV News—Soul Train: On December 14, 1985, Doug E. Fresh** was a featured guest on Soul Train.

Birthday: December 29, 1985, Texas rapper, **Pimp C** of *UGK* turns 12 years old. (Born 12-29-173)

Hip Hop (Rap Music/Electro): This year in Hip Hop **the LA Dream Team** released their debut album *Kings of the West Coast* on **Dream Team Records**. Their most noted single, *The Dream Team Is In The House* was a cult classic that lit up the club scene and airways coast to coast and also peaked at #138 on the *Billboard 200*.

Members: Rudy Pardee & Chris Wilson **City**: Los Angeles, California

Producers: Rudy Pardee, Snake Puppy, The Real Richie Rich, Courtney Branch & Tracy Kendrick

- ⇒ **Magazine News: This year Magic Johnson** of the LA Lakers lands cover of *Sports Illustrated*.
- ⇒ **San Francisco News**: **On December 6, 1985, the S.F Chronicle** described a "Super Cocaine" known on the streets as crack, rock, or base and explained how it was being smoked in a pipe to produce intense euphoria.
- ⇒ **World News**: **On December 13, 1985, France** sues the United States over the discovery of an AIDS serum.
- ⇒ **New York News**: On December 16, 1985, organized crime Boss Paul Castellano was shot to death outside of a New York City restaurant on orders from John Gotti who later seized power.

1985 – Urban American
Grammy Award Recipients – 27th Annual

Awards, 1985: Prince wins Record of the Year. (When Doves Cry)

Awards, 1985: Prince wins Album of the Year. (Purple Rain)

Awards, 1985: Prince wins Song of the Year. (Purple Rain)

Awards, 1985: Prince & Ray Charles win Best Arrangement on an Instrumental *(Every Breath You Take)*

Awards, 1985: Prince wins Best Vocal Arrangement for Two or More Voices *(Purple Rain)*.

Awards, 1985: Shirley Caesar wins Best Soul Gospel Performance, Female *(Sailin)*.

Awards, 1985: Andrae Crouch wins Best Soul Gospel Performance, Male *(Always Remember)*.

Awards, 1985: Shirley Caesar & Al Green win Best Gospel Performance by a Duo or Group *(Sailin on the Sea of Your Love)*.

Awards, 1985: Donna Summer wins Best Inspirational Performance *(Forgive Me)*.

Awards, 1985: Wynton Marsalis wins Best Jazz Instrumental, Soloist *(Hot House Flowers)*.

Awards, 1985: Count Basie wins Best Jazz Instrumental Performance, Big Band *(88 Basie Street)*.

Awards, 1985: Joe Williams wins Best Jazz Vocal Performance *(Nothin' but the Blues)*.

Awards, 1985: Tina Turner wins Best Pop Vocal Performance, Female *(What's Love Got to With It)*.

Awards, 1985: Prince wins Best Pop Performance by a Duo or Group with Vocal *(Let's Go Crazy)*.

Awards, 1985: Ray Parker, Jr. wins Best Pop Instrumental Performance *(Ghostbusters)*.

Awards, 1985: Chaka Khan wins Best R&B Vocal Performance, Female *(I Feel for You)*.

Awards, 1985: Prince wins Best R&B Vocal Performance, Male *(When Doves Cry)*.

Awards, 1985: James Ingram & Michael McDonald win Best R&B Performance by a Duo or Group with Vocal *(Yah Mo b There)*.

Awards, 1985: Herbie Hancock wins Best R&B Instrumental Performance *(Sound System)*.

Awards, 1985: Prince, Songwriter wins Best Rhythm & Blues Song *(I Feel for You Performed by Chaka Khan)*.

Awards, 1985: Black Uhuru wins Best Reggae Recording *(Anthem)*

1985

MTV Video Music Awards – 2nd Annual

Video of the Year: *Don Henley* – "The Boys of Summer"

Best Male Video: *Bruce Springsteen* – "I'm on Fire"

Best Female Video: *Tina Turner* – "What's Love Got to Do With It"

Best Group Video: *USA for Africa* – "We Are the World"

Best New Artist Video: *Til Tuesday* – "Voices Carry"

Best Concept Video: *Glenn Frey* – "Smuggler's Blues"

Most Experimental Video: *Art of Noise* – "Close (To the Edit)"

Best Stage Performance in a Video: *Bruce Springsteen* – "Dancing in the Dark"

Best Overall Performance in a Video: *Philip Bailey & Phil Collins* – "Easy Lover"

Viewer's Choice: *USA for Africa* – "We Are the World"

1985 – Billboards Year End – Hot 100 Singles

1985	Urban Music 27% of Billboard's Year End Hot 100	27%
5	**Chaka Khan** – *I Feel for You*	Warner Bros.
17	**Kool and the Gang** - *Cherish*	De-Lite
22	**Stevie Wonder** – *Part Time Lover*	Tamla
23	**Whitney Houston** – *Saving All My Love*	Arista
26	**New Edition** – *Cool It Now*	MCA
29	**Teena Marie** - *Lovergirl*	Epic
31	**Ready for the World** – *Oh Sheila*	MCA
32	**DeBarge** – *Rhythm of the Night*	Motown
38	**The Pointer Sisters** – *Neutron Dance*	Planet
40	**Commodores** – *Nightshift*	Motown
43	**Aretha Franklin** – *Freeway of Love*	Arista
47	**Whitney Houston** – *You Give Good Love*	Arista
49	**Diana Ross** – *Missing You*	RCA
51	**Prince and the Revolution** – *Raspberry Beret*	Paisley Park
52	**Billy Ocean** - *Suddenly*	Jive
57	**Tina Turner** – *We Don't Need Another Hero*	Capitol
62	**Sade** – *Smooth Operator*	Epic
63	**Mary Jane Girls** – *In My House*	Gordy
69	**Kool and the Gang** - *Misled*	De-Lite
80	**Ashford & Simpson** - *Solid*	Capitol
85	**DeBarge** - *Who's Holding Donna Now*	Gordy
89	**Kool and the Gang** - *Freah*	De-Lite
90	**Jermaine Jackson** – *Do What You Do*	Arista
91	**The Time** – *Jungle Love*	Warner Bros.
93	**Tina Turner** – *Private Dancer*	Capitol
94	**Aretha Franklin** – *Who's Zoomin' Who*	Arista
96	**Lionel Richie** – *Penny Lover*	Motown

1985 – Record Labels in Hip Hop Music

Profile Records: With the release of RUN D.M.C's sophomore album the label was standing on the top of the hill. The Rap group had quickly risen to the top of the Rap game and they were taking no prisoners.

Elektra Records: After the split of Grandmaster Flash and The Furious Five, Elektra signed the legendary DJ *Grandmaster Flash* and released a new group that continued to produce some Hip Hop classics.

Sutra Records: The label again found success with the Fat Boys as their sophomore album topped the charts. It seemed the combination of lyrics from the *Disco 3* and production from *Kurtis Blow* was the winning recipe.

Kru-Cut Records: Founded in 1984 by *Alonzo Williams*, the L.A based label got it's 1st taste of success with the release of the *World Class Wreckin' Cru*, which would be the catalyst to something far greater.

Select Records: Founded in 1981 by Fred Munao, the label made its mark this year with the release of *UTFO*. The Rap group made waves with a hot track called *Roxxane, Roxanne*, which went on to be one of the best Hip Hop records ever made.

Sleeping Bag Records: Founded in 1981 by Arthur Russell, William Socolov, and Juggy Gales. The New York based label released *Mantronix* and their self-titled album this year, and found themselves at #16 on the Billboard Hot Dance charts.

Schoolly D Records: Founded in Philadelphia by rapper Schoolly D. The MC released his self-titled debut album this year under his own label that produced a few great Hip Hop classics.

Def Jam Records: Founded by *Rick Rubin* in 1983 while attending N.Y.U, the label released its first single in the Punk Rock genre by Hose. Rubin and *Russell Simmons* would meet soon after to begin the formation of a Hip Hop Dynasty. Their first Hip Hop singles, *It's Yours* by *T La Rock & Jazzy Jay*, *I Need a Beat* by LL Cool J, and *Rock Hard* by the *Beastie Boys* released in 1984 planted the **Def Jam** flag and garnered a distribution deal with **CBS Records**, while also launching subsidiary labels **OBR Records** and **Rush Associated Labels**. Def Jam won big this year with LL Cool J's gold selling album *Radio*, which eventually went platinum.

In 1985, Hip Hop began to stand on its own two feet after riding into the spotlight on the backs of many R&B, Blues, and Jazz legends. The culture was built on a *"We'll take whatever we want, and you can't do a damn thing about it!"* attitude. This same energy derived from the poverty-stricken ghettos, showed the onlookers that the Hip Hop Culture had nothing to lose and everything to gain. We were tired of being hungry, broke, and just damn poor; Hip Hop to us was our collective consciousness and still is. The music industry became our platform and Hip-Hop would use this outlet to spread our neighborhood news, good or bad, throughout the world.

"Broken glass everywhere

People pissin' on the stairs, you know they just don't care

I can't take the smell, can't take the noise

Got no money to move out, I guess I got no choice

Rats in the front room, roaches in the back

Junkies in the alley with a baseball bat

I tried to get away but I couldn't get far

'cuz a man with a tow truck repossessed my car"

- Grandmaster Melle Mel (The Message)

Circa 1986

The Show

- ⇒ **TV News—Music Videos: This year BET** premiered *Video LP*, a show where viewers called in live during a half-hour period to give their opinions on featured music videos.
- ⇒ **TV News—Music Videos: On February 17, 1986,** *Dial MTV* premiered on **MTV**. The show featured the top 5 to 10 videos requested by fans who dialed in their favorite videos.
- ⇒ **TV News—Soul Train: On March 22, 1986, LL Cool J** was a featured guest.

Hip-Hop (Rap Music): April 29, 1986, **Whodini** released their 3rd album *Back in Black* on **Jive Records**. The album featured classic hits, *One Love, Funky Beat,* and *Growing Up* which pushed it to platinum status.

Producer: Larry Smith

- ⇒ **Film News—Semi-Autobiography: On May 2, 1986, Columbia Pictures** released "*Jo Jo Dancer, Your Life is Calling,*" a semi-autobiography about **Richard Pryor** who starred in and directed the film as well. Produced by *Richard Pryor,* distributed by **Indigo Productions** and written by *Paul Mooney, Rocco Urbisci* and *Richard Pryor* the film earned $18,034,150.00 at the box office.

Hip-Hop (Rap Music): May 6, 1986, **The Fat Boys** released their 3rd and final album *Big & Beautiful* for **Sutra Records**. The album reached #10 on the R&B charts and pinned two hit singles with *In the House* and *Sex Machine*.

Producers: Mark Morales, Damon Wimbley, Dave Ogrin, Fresh Gordon, Darren Robinson, Tony Moran and Albert Cabrera

"Well I had it worse, as you can see

My clothes ripped off of my body

Then things went bad, when I wasn't lookin'

Someone yelled out, soft, soft Brooklyn

They thought I said it and would you believe

Everybody in the party cold chased after me."

- Cool Rock Ski (In the House)

⇒ **Magazine News: This year** after winning Super Bowl XX, **Chicago Bears' Walter Payton and William "Refrigerator" Perry** land the cover of *TIME*.

⇒ **Magazine News: In May of 1986, Whitney Houston** lands the cover of *People*.

Hip-Hop (Rap Music): May 15, 1986, **RUN-D.M.C** released their 3rd album *Raising Hell* on *Profile Records*. The album peaked at #1 on the Hip Hop and R&B charts, while going triple platinum. RUN-D.M.C. broke the mold and proved to the industry that (*Hip Hop*) Rap Music was a viable form as they topped the charts in several countries. The 1st single released from the album, *My Adidas*, would show the true power of Hip Hop fans when Adidas sales sky rocketed.

Producers: Russell Simmons & Rick Rubin

⇒ **Sports News—NCAA/NBA: On June 19, 1986 University of Maryland college basketball star and 1st round draft pick of the Boston Celtics, Len Bias** dies of a cocaine overdose just hours after he was selected in the 1986 NBA Draft by the Celtics.

Hip-Hop (Rap Music): July 7, 1986, **Doug E. Fresh & the Get Fresh Crew** released their debut album *Oh, My God!* on ***Reality Records***. The album reached #21 on the R&B charts, and its most noted single, *The Show* went on to be a cult classic.

Members: Doug E. Fresh, MC Ricky D, aka (*Slick Rick*), Barry Bee & Chill Will

City: Harlem, New York   **Producers**: Dennis Bell & Ollie Cotton

⇒ **Film News—Comedy/Horror: On July 18, 1986, New World Pictures** released "*Vamp*" starring **Grace Jones**, directed by *Richard Wenk*, produced by *Donald P. Borchers*. The film earned $4.9 Million at the box office.

⇒ **Magazine News: In July of 1986, Prince** lands the cover of *SPIN*.

Hip Hop (Rap Music): July 25, 1986, **Philadelphia Rapper, Steady B** released his debut album *Bring the Beat Back* on ***Jive Records***. Steady B reached #44 on the R&B/Hip Hop charts with hot singles, *Get Physical*, *Stupid Fresh*, and *Bring the Beat Back* leading the way.

City: Philadelphia, Pennsylvania   **Producers**: Lawrence Goodman, Marley Marl

"To write rhymes like these, intelligence is needed

Just stating the facts, don't mean to sound conceited

Practice every day, write rhyme after rhyme

The way I murder my suckers might as well be a crime

Cause the name's Steady B, Stupid Fresh is the title

Some say it's true, I'm a sucker MC's idol."

-Steady B (Stupid Fresh)

Hip-Hop (Rap/Miami Bass/Porn Rap): July 25, 1986, Miami, Florida Rap Group **the 2 Live Crew** released their debut album *2 Live Crew is What We Are* on **Skyywalker Records**. 2 Live Crew was mostly noted for their sexually explicit rap songs like *We Want Some P*****, *Throw the D****, and *Cuttin' it Up*. Like the old saying goes, "Sex sells," and in this case, it pushed the Miami group's debut album to gold status with no air play!

City: Miami, Florida **Members**: Luke, Fresh Kid Ice, Brother Marquis, Mr. Mixx, Amazing Vee & Verb.

⇒ **Film New – Comedy/Drama: On August 8, 1986, Spike Lee** released his 1st feature film "*She's Gotta Have It*" produced by *Spike Lee* for **40 Acres & A Mule Filmworks**, distributed by **Island Pictures**. Stars included, ***Tracy Camilla Johns, John Canada Terrell, Redmond Hicks, Raye Dowell** and **Spike Lee*** himself. The film earned $7,137,502.00 at the box office.

Hip-Hop (Rap/Pop/Dance): August 13, 1986, Oakland rapper, **MC Hammer** independently released his debut album *Feel My Power* on **Bustin' Track Records**. His most noted track *Get It Started* created a street buzz that would change history.

City: Oakland, CA. **Producer**: Felton Pilate of Con Funk Shun

Hip-Hop (Rap Music): This year *Egyptian Lover* released his sophomore album *One Track Mind* on *Egyptian Empire Records*. Egyptian Lover scored again peaking at #37 on the R&B charts further building his legacy as a hit record producer.

Producer: Egyptian Lover

Hip-Hop (Breakin/Pop Lockin): Every dance crew that was about their business would have a routine to rock with the Egyptian Lover tracks.

Hip-Hop (Rap Music): This year, New York rapper, **Just-Ice,** released his debut album *Back to the Old School* on **Sleeping Bag Records**.

City: Castle Hill, Bronx, New York   **Producers**: Kurtis Mantronik & Just-Ice

"I'll wax and maim, rappers who proclaim

To be the epitome of this game

Fronting like you hard, rugged and rough

Soft like butter, creamy like a puff

On the mic no sense, head very dense

Just listen to the gangster and I will convince."

-Just-Ice (Going Way Back)

Hip-Hop (Rap Music): This year New York emcee, **Kool Moe Dee** released his debut self-titled solo album on *Jive records*. Kool Moe Dee's solo project sold over 300,000 units out the gate and peaked at #23 on the R&B/Hip Hop charts.

Producers: Moe Dewese, Robert Wells, Teddy Riley, Pete Harris, LaVaba Mallison & Bryan New

"I rocked her to the left, rocked her to the right

She felt so good, hugged me so tight

I said, "Good night"

Three days later...

Woke up fussing, yelling and cussing

Drip drip dripping and puss puss pussing

I went to the bathroom and said "Mama mia!"

I'm a kill that girl next time I see her"

-Kool Moe Dee (Go See the Doctor)

Hip-Hop (Rap/Electro/Funk): This year **Mantronix** released their sophomore album *Music Madness* on **Sleeping Bag Records**.

Producer: Kurtis Mantronik

◊ **Hip-Hop (Fashion):** The culture did everything its way, even down to the eye wear, below are photos of some cultural icons sporting *Cazal* eye glasses.

Hip-Hop (Rap Music): This year **The Skinny Boys** released their debut album *Weightless* on **Warlock Records**. The group was influenced by the Fat Boys.

City: Bridgeport, Connecticut **Members**: Superman Jay, Shockin' Shawn & The Human Jock Box **Producers**: Chuck Chillout & Mark Bush

⇒ **TV News — Talk Show:** *On September 8, 1986 The Oprah Winfrey Show* debuts on daytime television, created and hosted by *Oprah Winfrey*, and produced by **Harpo Productions** located in Chicago, Illinois.

◊ **Hip-Hop (Fashion):** While some rocked the Shell Toe Adidas, others preferred the suede Puma's. Both shoes, however, became must haves for any Hip Hop head. (*With the fat strongs in 'em…*)

Hip-Hop (Rap/Jazz): This year Brooklyn rap group, **Stetsasonic** released their debut album *On Fire* on **Tommy Boy Records**. The debut album peaked at #32 on the R&B charts.

City: Brooklyn, New York   **Members**: Daddy O, Wise, Frukwan, Prince Paul, MC Delite, Bobby Simmons & DBC   **Producers**: Stetsasonic

◊ **Film News—Comedy: On October 10, 1986, 20th Century Fox** released "*Jumpin' Jack Flash*" starring *Whoopi Goldberg*, directed by *Penny Marshal*, story by *David H. Franzoni*.

◊ **TV News—Soul Train: On October 25, 1986, RUN-D.M.C.** were featured guests.

◊ **Magazine News: In October of 1986, RUN-D.M.C.,** lands cover of *Right On*!

Hip-Hop (Rap Music): This year **Schoolly D** released his debut album *Saturday Night! – The Album* on **Schoolly D records**. The album peaked at #59 on the Black Albums chart and reached #4 on the UK indie charts.

Producer: Schoolly D

⇒ **Politics — Drug Act: On October 27, 1986, President Ronald Regan** signed into law the *Ant-Drug Abuse Act of 1986*. The act changed the system of federal supervised release from a *rehabilitative* system into a *punitive* system. Most noted of the changes was a mandated minimum 5-year sentence without parole for possession of 5 grams of crack cocaine and also mandated the same sentence for 500 grams of powder cocaine.

Hip-Hop (Rap Music/Sexplicit): November 5, 1986, **Too Short** released *Raw, Uncut and X-Rated* on **75 Girls Records**. The EP featured signature Too Short tracks that he would trade mark in the Rap game with cult classics like, *She's A B***h, Blow Job Betty*, and *Oakland, California*.

Producer: Dean Hodges

"Too $hort baby, I'm so hard / Pimpin' these h***s on the boulevard

But I'm not here to tell ya 'bout me / I got a little story 'bout a nasty freak

She's the kind of girl you think about in bed / Blow job Betty givin' real good head

Bust a left nut, right nut in her jaw / Sperm on her cheeks is all ya saw."

-Too $hort (Blow Job Betty)

⇒ **TV News — Soul Train: On November 8, 1986, Whodini** were featured guests.
⇒ **Miami News — Drug War: On November 18, 1986, The U.S.** indicts the Medellin Drug Cartel leaders, Pablo Escobar, Carlos Lehder, and Jose Gonzalo Rodriguez Gacha under the RICO Act. The cartel was named the largest cocaine smuggling organization in the world.

Hip-Hop (Rap Music/Rock): November 11, 1986, **the Beastie Boys** released their album *Licensed to Ill* on **Def Jam Records**. The Rap-Rock album topped the Billboard 200 at #1, while holding #2 on the R&B/Hip Hop charts, fueled by hot tracks, *Paul Revere, Brass Monkey, Hold it Now, Hit it, No Sleep till Brooklyn, Girls,* and the *New Style*.

Producers: Rick Rubin, Beastie Boys

"Now here's a little story I've got to tell

About three bad brothers you know so well

It started way back in history

With Adrock, M.C.A., and me – Mike D."

-Mike D (Paul Revere)

Hip-Hop (Rap Music/Electro Funk): December 1, 1986, **Afrika Bambaata & Soulsonic Force** released *Planet Rock* on **Tommy Boy Records** as a collection of previous hot singles.

Producers: Fats Comet Productions, Arthur Baker, Keith LeBlanc, Doug Wimbush, Skip McDonald, and John Robie.

Hip-Hop (Breakin): Dance crews often traveled with cardboard squares and boom boxes to different neighborhoods to battle other dance crews. It's often said that many chose breakin' over gang bangin' during this era, and Bambaata played a big part in it.

Hip-Hop (Rap Music): December 8, 1986, **Queens, New York** rap group, **Salt-N-Pepa** released their debut album *Hot, Cool & Vicious* on **Next Plateau Records**. The all-female rap group became one of the first to go certified gold & platinum in the U.S. with hot legendary tracks, *My Mic Sound Nice, Tramp, I'll Take Your Man,* and *The Showstopper* setting the Hip Hop Culture on fire.

City: Queens, New York   **Members**: Salt, Spinderella, & Pepa

Producer: Hurby "Luv Bug" Azor

"I'm the queen on the mic, and it's true when I say

That the Pepa MC is here to stay

And you know if I was a book I would sell

Cuz every curve on my body got a story to tell."

-Pepa (My Mic Sounds Nice)

Hip-Hop (Rap Music/Dance): This year **Joeski Love** released *Pee Wee's Dance* on **Elektra Records**. The single went platinum and started a dance craze throughout the Hip Hop Culture.

Producer: Vince Davis

◊ **Hip-Hop (Fashion):** Many major brands experienced a huge boost in sales as the Hip Hop culture began to promote their products. If your favorite MC sported the brand in their video or just wore it every day, we were going to buy it and sport it as well. Below LL Cool J sports the bucket Kangol hat.

Hip-Hop (Rap Music): This year Queens, New York rap group, **Kool G Rap & DJ Polo** released their single *It's a Demo* on **Cold Chillin Records**. When Marley Marl dropped the single, it was intended to be just as the name indicated "a demo," but the streets liked what they heard and Kool G Rap & Polo was born.

City: Corona, Queens, New York   **Members**: Dj Polo & Kool G Rap

Producer: Marley Marl

(Juice Crew)

"People in the audience, Kool G Rap is my name

I write rhymes and insert them inside your brain

And DJ Polo, the man I'm behind

He operates turntables when I'm rocking my rhymes, see...

Psychopath on the phonograph, nut of the cuts

You heard the boy slice, is he nice or what?"

-Kool G Rap (It's a Demo)

Hip-Hop (Rap Music/Gangsta): This year California rapper, **ICE-T** released his classic single *6' N the Mornin* on **Techno Hop records**. The single was one of the 1st Gangsta Rap tracks to get national notoriety and also inspired several up-and-coming gangsta rap groups.

City: Los Angeles (Crenshaw), California **Producer:** The Unknown DJ.

"6' N the morning' police at my door / Fresh Adidas squeak across the bathroom floor

Out the back window I make an escape

Don't even get a chance to grab my old school tape

Mad with no music but happy' cause I'm free

And these streets to a player is the place to be

Gotta knot in my pocket weighin' at least a grand

Gold on my neck, my pistols close at hand."

-ICE-T (6'n the Mornin')

1986 – Urban American
Grammy Award Recipients – 28th Annual

Awards, 1986: Quincy Jones (producer) wins Record of the Year *(We Are the World)*.

Awards, 1986: Michael Jackson & Lionel Richie (songwriters) win Song of the Year *(We Are the World)*.

Awards, 1986: Sade wins Best New Artist.

Awards, 1986: B.B. King wins Best Traditional Blues Recording *(My Guitar Sings the Blues)*.

Awards, 1986: Whoopi Goldberg wins Best Comedy Recording *(Whoopi Goldberg – Original Broadway Show Recording)*.

Awards, 1986: Shirley Caesar wins Best Soul Gospel Performance, Female *(Martin)*.

Awards, 1986: Marvin Winans wins Best Soul Gospel Performance, Male *(Bring Back the Days of Yea and Nay)*.

Awards, 1986: The Winans win Best Soul Gospel Performance by a Duo or Group *(Tomorrow)*.

Awards, 1986: Jennifer Holliday wins Best Inspirational Performance *(Come Sunday)*.

Awards, 1986: Bobby McFerrin & Jon Hendricks win Best Jazz Vocal Performance, Male *(Another Night in Tunisia)*.

Awards, 1986: Wynton Marsalis wins Best Jazz Instrumental Performance, Group *(Black Codes from the Underground)*.

Awards, 1986: Whitney Houston wins Best Pop Vocal Performance, Female *(Saving All My Love for You)*.

Awards, 1986: Quincy Jones (producer) wins Best Pop Performance by a Duo or Group. *(We Are the World; Performed by USA for Africa)*.

Awards, 1986: Aretha Franklin wins Best R&B Vocal Performance, Female *(Freeway of Love)*.

Awards, 1986: Stevie Wonder wins Best R&B Vocal Performance, Male *(In Square Circle)*.

Awards, 1986: Commodores win Best R&B Performance by a Duo or Group with Vocal *(Nightshift)*.

Awards, 1986: Jimmy Cliff wins Best Reggae Recording *(Cliff Hanger)*.

1986

MTV Video Music Awards – 3rd Annual

Video of the Year: *Dire Straits* - "Money for Nothing"

Best Male Video: *Robert Palmer* – "Addicted to Love"

Best Female Video: *Whitney Houston* - "How Will I Know"

Best Group Video: *Dire Straits* – "Money for Nothing"

Best New Artist in a Video: *A-Ha* – "Take on Me"

Viewer's Choice Award: *A-Ha* – "Take on Me"

Best Direction in a Video: Steven Barron, *A-Ha* – "Take on Me"

Best Choreography in a Video: *Prince and the Revolution* – "Raspberry Beret"

1986 – Billboards Year End – Hot 100 Singles

1986	Urban Music 34% of Billboard's Year-End Hot 100	34%
1	Dionne Warwick, Gladys Knight, Elton John & Stevie Wonder – *That's What Friends are For*	Warner Bros.
2	Lionel Richie – *Say You, Say Me*	Motown
3	Klymaxx – *I Miss You*	MCA
4	Patti LaBelle & Michael McDonald – *On My Own*	MCA
6	Whitney Houston – *How Will I Know*	Arista
7	Eddie Murphy – *Party All the Time*	Columbia
11	Whitney Houston – *Greatest Love of All*	Arista
12	Atlantic Starr - *Secret Lovers*	A&M
16	Billy Ocean – *There'll Be Sad Songs (To Make You Cry)*	Jive
19	Prince and the Revolution - *Kiss*	Paisley Park
31	Billy Ocean – *When the Going gets Tough, the Tough get Going*	Jive
32	Janet Jackson – *When I Think of You*	A&M
39	Lionel Richie – *Dancing on the Ceiling*	Motown
40	Miami Sound Machine - *Conga*	Epic
43	Janet Jackson – *What Have You Done For Me Lately*	A&M
47	Miami Sound Machine – *Words Get in the Way*	Epic
52	The Jets – *Crush on You*	MCA
55	Sade – *The Sweetest Taboo*	Epic
58	Janet Jackson - *Nasty*	A&M
60	Jermaine Stewart – *We Don't Have to Take Our Clothes Off*	Arista
61	Lisa Lisa & Cult Jam – *All Cried Out*	Columbia
65	James Brown – *Living in America*	Scotti Bros.
67	El DeBarge – *Who's Johnny*	Gordy
68	Cameo – *Word Up!*	Atlanta Artists
71	Tina Turner – *Typical Male*	Capitol
77	Time Social Club - *Rumors*	Jay
79	Miami Sound Machine – *Bad Boy*	Epic
83	Shelia E – *A Love Bizarre*	Warner Bros.
89	RUN-D.M.C. – *Walk This Way*	Profile
90	Anita Baker – *Sweet Love*	Elektra
93	Starpoint – *Object of My Desire*	Elektra
95	Force MDs – *Tender Love*	Tommy Boy
97	Lionel Richie – *Love Will Conquer All*	Motown
100	Stevie Wonder – *Go Home*	Tamla

1986 – Record Labels in Hip Hop Music

Jive: Initially finding its major success in Hip Hop with the release of *Whodini*, the label claimed a larger stake of the game with the addition of *Kool Moe Dee* and *Steady B,* as both new rap artists experienced success with their 1986 releases along with *Whodini*.

Sutra: 1986 proved to be bittersweet for the label as their top selling Hip Hop group, the *Fat Boys*, recorded their 3rd and final album with the label. The album reached #10 on the charts.

Profile: Proud to be the home of the Kings of Hip Hop, *RUN-D.M.C.* Profile continued to ride the Hip Hop wave as *RUN-D.M.C.'s* latest album continued to set Hip Hop records and gold and platinum status.

Reality: Released as the Hip Hop subsidiary of **Fantasy Records**, the San Francisco, California based label which was originally founded in 1949 by Max and Sol Weiss was proof that Hip Hop was now a reputable brand and industry heads wanted a piece. Reality would score big by signing and releasing *Doug E Fresh & The Get Fresh Crew's* classic album, *Oh, My God*.

SkyyWalker: Originally founded in 1985 by *Luther Campbell* (Luke) and *David Chackler*. The Miami based label and its founder, who was also a member of its infamous rap group the *2Live Crew*, brought a new X-rated style of Hip Hop to the genre that would sell out arenas, pack dance floors, and get banned from radio and several other places. The label name would eventually change to **Luke Records** due to a suit between Luther Campbell and George Lucas over the Star Wars name, Skywalker.

Egyptian Empire: With his heavy bass and electric riffs, the Egyptian Lover continued to bless the culture with classic break dance tracks.

Sleeping Bag: With the addition of rapper *Just-Ice*, Sleeping Bag and its top act *Mantronix* was beginning to build its brand.

Warlock: The New York based label originally founded in 1985 by Adam Levy with a focus on Hip Hop released the *Skinny Boys* this year. The rap act was inspired by the rap trio the *Fat Boys*.

Tommy Boy: Already establishing itself as a reputable Hip Hop label, Tommy Boy signed the politically-based rap group *Stetsasonic*. The group's debut album reached #32 on the charts, increasing the label's current value.

Schoolly D: *Schoolly D* pushed his album and career to the top of the charts as he released cult classics under his own label.

75 Girls: *Too $hort* continued to build onto his pimpin, hustler style persona by releasing a hit EP containing sexually explicit tracks.

Def Jam: Still riding on the success of *LL Cool J's* previous hit album, Def Jam released the first ever, all white rap group, the *Beastie Boys*. The album produced several Hip Hop classics and cemented the group into Hip Hop history.

Next Plateau: Originally founded in 1984 by Eddie O'Loughlin, the New York based label released the female trio *Salt N Pepa* this year. The group smashed the charts with Gold and Platinum sales while cementing their place in the culture as icons.

Elektrta: No stranger to hits, the label found a diamond in the ruff when it signed *Joeski Love* and released his 1st hit single, *Pee Wee's Dance*. The dance was based on the then popular Pee Wee Herman's Playhouse as the host Pee Wee himself would do a dance that *Joeski Love* would eventually turn into a Hip Hop culture dance that garnered platinum sales.

Cold Chillin: Founded in 1986 by Tyrone Williams, run by Len Fichtelberg and Queens (Queensbridge), New York, DJ/Producer *Marley Marl*, the label got a taste of success this year with the release of *Kool G Rap & DJ Polo's* single, *It's a Demo*. Marley Marl, in his own right, was a force in the Hip Hop Culture and he would soon impose his will by releasing a group of Hip Hop assassins known as the *Juice Crew*.

Techno Hop: Founded in 1984 by the *Uknown DJ*, the California based label released a Hip Hop Gangsta classic that would inspire a generation of West Coast rappers; *6'N the Mornin* by Crenshaw area rapper, *ICE-T* resonated with the playas, hustlers, and gangsters of the day.

Many doors opened for the Hip Hop culture in 1986; several female MC's showed that they could go toe-to-toe with the braggadocios male MC's, while the art form expanded its content attracting even more fans. It also became obvious that Hip Hop was a powerful vehicle for promoting brands, from Adidas to Puma's, Cazals to Kangol's, Turntables to Boomboxes, Hip Hop brought in the dough! It would be this same leverage, the power of the consumer dollar, that made believers out of chumps. Some of those chumps (*buddy hustlers*) would eventually overlook the culture's authenticity and find themselves in a bad position.

"But see ah, ah, that's the life, ah, that I lead

And you sucker MC's is who I please

So take that and move back, catch a heart attack

Because there's nothin' in the world, that Run'll ever lack

I cold chill at a party in a b-boy stance

And rock on the mic and make the girls wanna dance

Fly like a dove, that come from up above

I'm rockin' on the mic and you can call me Run-Love."

-Run (Sucker MC's)

Circa 1987

Iconic

⇒ **Music Industry News: On January 3, 1987,** *Aretha Franklin, Marvin Gaye, Bo Diddley, Smokey Robinson,* **and** *Jackie Wilson* get inducted into the *Rock and Roll Hall of Fame*.

Hip-Hop (Rap Music/Politics/Consciousness): February 10, 1987, **Def Jam** released a political consciousness onto the nation in the form of Super Rap Group, *Public Enemy*. Lead MC, *Chuck D*, hype man and MC, *Flava Flav, Terminator X*, and the platoon of S1W's (Combat Ready Soldiers) led by *Professor Griff*. The politically charged group took on the media and all bull**** they tried to feed us. P.E wore the logo of a man in the cross hairs of a rifle, a symbol we gladly took on and resonated with. To the Hip Hop Culture, P.E was the Black Panthers with turntables and a microphone. Rappers prior to Public Enemy did speak about what was going on in their hoods, but P.E. gave us a stage to stand on to fight the power. Their debut album *Yo! Bum Rush the Show* reached #25 on the Black Albums charts, but was #1 in the streets.

City: Long Island, New York   **Members**: Chuck D, Flava Flav, Professor Griff, Terminator X, Khari Wynn, DJ Lord, Sister Souljah, and The S1W's.
Producers: The Bomb Squad

Hip-Hop (Rap Music/Gangsta): *March 3, 1987,* **Boogie Down Productions** released their debut album *Criminal Minded* on ***B-Boy Records***. The album was filled with Hip Hop classics, with flows by ***MC, KRS-1***. Most popular *South Bronx, The Bridge is Over*, and *Elementary*, would go down as iconic records in the culture along with the rest of the album. KRS-1's delivery and content would set him apart from many other MC's.

City: South Bronx, New York   **Members**: Scott La Rock, KRS-1

Producers: Scott La Rock, KRS-1 & Ced-Dee

⇒ **Film News—Comedy: On March 20, 1987,** *The Samuel Goldwyn Company* released *Hollywood Shuffle* starring **The Hollywood Shuffle Players** directed & produced by *Robert Townsend*. The film earned $5,228,617.00 at the box office.

⇒ **Magazine News: In March of 1987, Anita Baker** lands cover of *JET*.

⇒ **Magazine News: This year RUN-DMC** lands cover of *Record Mirror*.

Hip-Hop (Rap Music): April 7, 1987, **DJ Jazzy Jeff & The Fresh Prince** released their debut album *Rock the House* on *Jive records*. The albums most noted track, *Girls Ain't Nothing but Trouble*, showed off the skills of new Philadelphia MC, **The Fresh Prince**, while **DJ Jazzy Jeff** proved to be brutal on the 1s and 2s.

City: West Philadelphia, Pennsylvania **Members**: DJ Jazzy Jeff, The Fresh Prince, and Ready Rock C **Producers**: Dana Goodman, Lawrence Goodman

"Listen homeboys don't mean to bust your bubble

But girls of the world ain't nothing but trouble

So next time a girl gives you the play

Just remember my rhyme and get the hell away"

-Fresh Prince (Girls aint Nothin but Trouble)

Hip-Hop (Rap Music): May 20, 1987, **Whodini** released *Open Sesame* on *Jive records*. The 4th album by the group did reach gold status, but failed to pin any iconic hits like in prior years.

Producers: Whodini, Sinister, & Larry Smith

"The words love and life both have four letters

But they're two, different things all together

'Cuz I've liked many ladies in my day

But just like the wind, they've all blown away

You see, to love someone is atmosphere

But to both they'll share, when one's not there"

-Ecstasy (One Love)

⇒ **Film News – Comedy: On May 20, 1987, Paramount Pictures** released *"Beverly Hills Cop II"* starring **Eddie Murphy**, directed by *Tony Scott*, produced by *Don Simpson* and *Jerry Buckheimer*. The film earned $300 million at the box office.

Hip-Hop (Rap Music): May 22, 1987, **Dana Dane** released his debut album *"Dana Dane with Fame"* on **Profile Records**. Dana Dane was a big hit with the fans with his melodic story-telling and English rap accent. It's most noted singles, *Nightmares, Delancey Street*, and *Cinderfella Dana Dane*, help push it to #2 on the Hip Hop/R&B charts.

City: Fort Green, Brooklyn, New York   **Producer**: Hurby "Luv Bug"

"Once upon a time, Brooklyn was the scene

In the project that they called Fort Greene

There lived a young man, Cinderfella's his name

To make it interesting it's me, Dana Dane"

-Dana Dane (Cinderfella Dana Dane)

Hip-Hop (Rap Music): May 29, 1987, **LL Cool J** released his sophomore album *Bigger and Deffer* on **Def Jam Records**. LL dropped the 1st ever rap ballad, *I Need Love* on this album and sent the culture to the moon; there was no stopping us now. The Hip Hop Culture could conquer all, and LL Cool J's 3 million album sales proved it.

Producers: DJ Pooh, L.A. Posse, and LL Cool J

"When I'm alone in my room

Sometimes I stare at the wall

And in the back of my mind

I hear my conscious call

Telling me I need a girl who's as sweet as a dove

For the first time in my life, I see I need love"

-LL Cool J (I Need Love)

Hip-Hop (Rap Music): July 7, 1987, Hip Hop duo **Eric B. & Rakim** released their debut album *Paid in Full* on *4th & B'way Records*. The razor-sharp lyrics of Rakim and precise DJ skills of Eric B. laced the streets with a melodic flavor that left Hip Hop junkies in awe. The album reached #58 on the Billboard 200 and #1 in the streets, with hits, *I Ain't No Joke*, *Eric B. for President*, *Paid in Full*, I *Know I Got Soul*, *My Melody*, and *Move the Crowd*. This proved two things: **1) Rakim** had moved to the top of the MC chain, and any MC worth their weight had to see him, **2) Eric B. & Rakim** were ahead of their time; the fact that the album didn't peak at #1 on several charts proved that industry heads responsible for spins and chart ratings didn't really understand Hip Hop after all.

City: New York, New York   **Members**: Eric B. & Rakim

Producers: Eric B. & Rakim

⇒ **Government – Iran-Contra: On July 7, 1987, Oliver North, Jr.** tells Congress that higher officials approved his secret Iran-Contra Operations.

⇒ **Government – Iran-Contra: On July 15 -22, 1987, Admiral John M. Poindexter,** then National Security Adviser, testifies and states that he authorized use of Iran arms sale profits to aid contras.

Hip Hop (Rap/Sexplicit): July 20, 1987, **Too $hort** released *Born to Mack* on ***Dangerous Music records***. Its most noted track, *Freaky Tales*, went on to be a cult classic and pushed the album to #50 on the Top R&B/Hip Hop charts.

Producers: Too $hort & T. Bohanon

"I met this girl, her name was Joan

She loved the way I rocked on the microphone

When I met Joan, I took her home

She was just like a doggy all on my bone"

-Too $hort (Freaky Tales)

Hip-Hop (Rap /Gangsta): July 28, 1987, **ICE-T** released his debut album *Rhyme Pays* on *Sire records*. The album hit the streets after the success of the previously released *6'N the Mornin*, and peaked at #26 on the R&B/Hip Hop charts.

Producer: Afrika Islam

"Deuce, deuce revolver was my problem solver

Had a def girl, really didn't wanna involve her

In the life of a gangster, used to rob bankster

But now I'm locked up, I'm just a punk low rankster

Jail cells know me too damn well

Seems like I've built on earth my own personal hell"

-ICE-T (Pain)

⇒ **Magazines: In 1987 Prince** lands the cover of *SPIN*.

Hip-Hop (Rap Music): August 8, 1987, Queensbridge, New York rapper, **MC Shan** released his debut album *Down By Law* on **Cold Chillin Records**. Shan and KRS-1, prior to both their album releases went round for round with *The Bridge* and *The Bridge is Over* dis records, which created a ton of momentum and anticipation for the MC's album releases. Shan's album reached #40 on the Top R&B Album charts.

City: Queens, Queensbridge, New York   **Producer**: Marley Marl

(Juice Crew)

"You love to hear the story again and again

Of how it all got started way back when

The monument is right in your face

Sit and listen for a while to the name of the place"

-MC Shan (The Bridge)

⇒ **Government — Iran Contra: President Ronald Regan** states that Iran arms-Contra policy went astray and accepts responsibility.

Hip-Hop (Rap Music): August 14, 1987, **The Fat Boys** released *Crushin'* on *Tin Pan Apple Records*. This would be the group's 4th album and the first on a new label; it peaked at #10 on the R&B charts proving that the *Fat Boys* were still relevant. Their most noted hit, *Wipe Out*, was a cover version of the **Beach Boys'** hit, who also sung background on the Fat Boys version.

Producers: The Fat Boys, Gary Rottger, The Latin Rascals. Van Gibbs & Eddison Electrik

⇒ **Drugs — Legal: This year** the legal, but lethal drug Prozac was released in the U.S. by Eli Lilly & Company.

⇒ **Drugs — Legal: This year** the FDA approves the drug AZT to be used in the treatment of AIDS.

Hip-Hop (Rap Music): August 21, 1987, **Steady B** released his sophomore album *What's My Name* on *Jive Records*. The album reached #49 on the R&B/Hip Hop album charts.

Producer: Lawrence Goodman

⇒ **Hip Hop News: On August 27, 1987, *DJ Scott La Roc*** of *BDP* died of complication from a gun-shot wound he received outside of the Highbridge Homes projects in the South Bronx. *Scott La Roc* died on the operating table at Lincoln Hospital — *He was only 25.*

⇒ **Music Industry News: On September 11, 1987, Reggae Legend Peter Tosh** is murdered during a home invasion.

⇒ **Magazine News: Bill Cosby** lands cover of the 1987 September edition of *TIME*.

⇒ **Magazine News: In September of 1987, Lisa Bonet** lands cover of *HARPERS BAZAAR.*

⇒ **Music Industry News: On October 8, 1987, Rock & Roll legend Chuck Berry** receives a star on the *Hollywood Walk of Fame*.

Hip-Hop (Rap Music): October 17, 1987, **the** *Skinny Boys* released their sophomore album *Skinny & Proud* on **Jive Records**.

Producers: Mark Bush & Chuck Chillout

⇒ **Magazine News**: **In October of 1987, LL Cool J and RUN-D.M.C** appear on the 2nd cover of an all new Teen and Music magazine known as *Word Up!* The magazine was operated by *Scott Mitchell Figman* and *Kate Ferguson*.

⇒ **Hip Hop—Slang**: *Whack* – Meaning silly, dumb or stupid, not appealing.

Hip-Hop (Rap /New Jack Swing): October 27, 1987; Mt. Vernon, New York rap group, **Heavy D & the Boyz** released their debut album *Living Large* on **Uptown Records**. Heavy D brought a feel good, dance swag to the culture while still delivering sharp lyrical content, and he was one of the first to put his dance crew in the spotlight with him. Heavy D's hot tracks, *Mr. Big Stuff* and *The Overweight Lover's in the House* help push the debut album to #10 on the Top Soul Album charts.

City: Mount Vernon, New York   **Members**: Heavy D, Eddie F, Trouble T Roy & G-Whiz   **Producers**: DJ Eddie F, Marley Marl & Teddy Riley

"Sittin in my room with my smoking jacket on

The fireplace is burning and the girlie is WARM

Time to make my move, so gently I kiss her

Whisper in her ear, and tell her that I miss her

She might try to pop that boyfriend junk

But I don't really care because I know he's a punk"

-Heavy D (The Overweight Lover's in the House)

Hip-Hop (Rap/New Jack Swing): November 3, 1987, **Kool Moe Dee** released his sophomore album *How Ya Like Me Now* on ***Jive Records***. The title track along with *Wild Wild West* pushed the album to platinum status.

Producers: Teddy Riley, M. Dewese, Lavaba Mallison, Bryan "Chuck" New & Pete Q. Harris.

"How you think I feel to see another MC

Gettin' paid usin' my rap style

And I'm playin' in the background meanwhile

I aint with that

You can forget that

You took my style

I'm takin it back"

-Kool Moe Dee (How Ya like me Now)

Hip-Hop (Rap Music/Gangsta): November 6, 1987, Compton, California rap group, **N.W.A (N***** With Attitudes)** released their debut album *N.W.A. and the Posse* on *Ruthless Records*. Its most noted track, *Boyz-N-the-Hood* became a Hip Hop classic and pushed the album to #39 on the R&B/Hip Hop charts and went certified gold.

City: Compton, California   **Members**: Ice Cube, Dr. Dre, Eazy E, DJ Yella & MC Ren.

Producer: Dr. Dre

⇒ **Music Industry News: On November 18, 1987, CBS Records** is purchased by the *Sony Corporation* in a deal estimated to be worth $2 billion.

⇒ **Film News—Comedy: On December 8, 1987, Paramount Pictures** releases *Eddie Murphy's* stand up classic *RAW*, produced by *Eddie Murphy Productions*. The film earned $50,504,655.00 at the box office.

⇒ **TV News—Soul Train: On November 14, 1987, Whodini** were featured guests.

⇒ **TV News—Soul Train: On November 21, 1987, LL Cool J** was a featured guest.

Hip-Hop (Rap Music/Hardcore): This year, **Just-Ice** released his sophomore album *Kool & Deadly* on **Sleeping Bag Records**. The album is slated as one of the first hardcore classics of our culture, most noted track, *Going Way Back* featuring *KRS-1*.

Producers: Just-Ice and KRS-1

⇒ **TV News — Soul Train: On November 28, 1987,** *Eric B & Rakim,* were featured guests.
⇒ **TV News — Soul Train: On December 5, 1987,** *Public Enemy* were featured guests.
⇒ **Magazine News: In December of 1987, Lisa Bonet** lands the cover of *EBONY*.

Hip-Hop (Rap Music): In 1987, Bronx, New York rapper, *T La Rock* released his debut album *Lyrical King (From the Boogie Down Bronx)* on **Sleeping Bag Records**.

City: Bronx, New York **Producers**: T La Rock, Kurtis Mantronik, Louie Lou

"Sound plus rhythm done up with finesse

Is equivalent to the adjective "best"

Now it's time to introduce

Neo-rhymes combined with a group with juice

Dance – to the musical tune

On the microphone, gonna make you swoon"

-T La Rock (It's Yours)

Hip-Hop (Fashion/Dapper Dan): **In Harlem, New York** the culture even had its own tailor who would customize most anything to make you *Fresh*! **Dapper Dan** would become synonymous with Hip Hop as the artists and fans alike sport his tailor-made gear.

Jam Master Jay Sports *The Louie,* ***Dapper Dan's*** custom fit.

Rakim sports *The Gucci*, **Dapper Dan's** custom fit.

Salt N Pepa sports their famous custom made *Dapper Dan's*.

Hip-Hop (Rap Music): In 1987, Philadelphia rap artist, **Tuff Crew & Krown Rulers** released *Phanjam* on **Soo Def Records**. (*Not to be confused with So So Def Recordings & Jermaine Dupri.*)

Region: Philadelphia, Pennsylvania **Producers**: Ced Gee, Kool Keith, Tuff Crew

Hip-Hop (Rap Music/Electro/Miami Bass): In 1987, Florida Rap Crew, **MC A.D.E. and Posse** released *Just Sumthin to Do* on **4 Sight Records**. The crew wrecked the streets with their high-powered bass tracks, which was the way to go in Miami at the time.

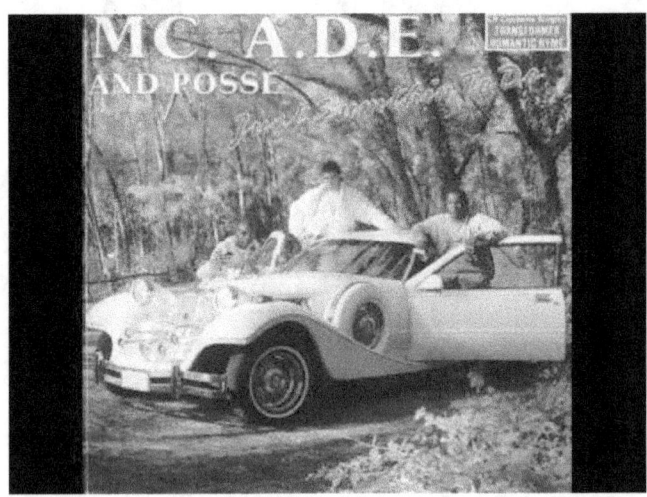

City: Miami, Ft. Lauderdale, Florida   **Producer**: Adrian Hines

Hip-Hop (Rap Music/Electro/Miami Bass): In 1987; Florida rapper, **Gigolo Tony** released *Ice Cold* on **4 Sight Records**. The 305 had made a reputation in the 80's for bass music; anyone with a sound system would have at least three Miami bass tapes in their collection. With the flux of underground radio stations and bass music, Miami had created an identity in Hip Hop.

City: Miami, Florida   **Producer**: Gigolo Tony

Hip Hop (Rap Music/Electro Bass): In 1987; Bronx, New York rapper, *MC Shy D* released *Gotta be Tough* on **Luke Records**. Although he was born in the Bronx, Shy-D was one of the first MC's to make his mark both in Atlanta and Miami, and rocked the clubs and sound systems with his unique voice and electro bass hooks and samples.

City: Atlanta, GA by way of The Bronx, New York

Hip-Hop (Rap Music): In 1987, Harlem, New York rapper, **Spoonie G** released *The Godfather of Rap* on **Tuff City Records**.

City: Harlem, New York   **Producers**: Aaron Fuchs, Marley Marl, and Teddy Riley

Hip-Hop (Rap Music): In 1987, rap crew **Kaos** released *Court's in Session* on **Bad Boy Records**. (*Not to be confused with Bad Boy Entertainment & Sean Combs.*)

Members: King Grand, Russell D. Cole   **Producer**: Kaze Productions, Inc.

Hip-Hop (Rap Music/Miami Bass): Florida gave birth to one of the first DJ crews, known as **the Jam Pony Express**, originally founded in 1981 by Ft. Lauderdale *DJ's Slic Vic, Hot Rod, Diamond Dick,* and *Mr. M.B.* The crew dropped mix tapes of the hottest tracks that featured them "regulating" or inserting their own lyrics in between verses, while turning down the track. This DJ style caught on big in the south and was a favorite among car clubs, shake joints and Southern Bass heads; several DJ's would join the J.P.E. going forward.

City: Ft. Lauderdale, Florida

ANTWAN BANK$

1987 – Urban American

Grammy Award Recipients – 29th Annual

Awards 1987: Bill Cosby wins Best Comedy Recording *(Those of You With or Without Children, You'll Understand)*.

Awards 1987: Philip Bailey wins Best Gospel Performance, Male *(Triumph)*.

Awards 1987: Deniece Williams & Sandi Patti win Best Gospel Performance by a Duo or Group, Choir or Chorus *(They Say)*.

Awards 1987: Deniece Williams win Best Soul Gospel Performance, Female *(I Surrender All)*.

Awards 1987: Al Green wins Best Soul Gospel Performance, Male *(Going Away)*

Awards 1987: The Winans, win Best Soul Gospel Performance by a Duo or Group, Choir or Chorus *(Let My People Go)*.

Awards 1987: Bobby McFerrin wins Best Jazz Vocal Performance, Male *(Round Midnight)*.

Awards 1987: Miles Davis wins Best Jazz Instrumental Performance, Soloist *(TuTu)*.

Awards 1987: Wynton Marsalis wins Best Jazz Instrumental Performance, Group *(J Mood)*.

Awards 1987: Dionne Warwick, Gladys Knight, Elton John & Stevie Wonder win Best Pop Performance by a Duo or Group with Vocal *(That's What Friends Are For)*.

Awards 1987: Anita Baker wins Best R&B Vocal Performance, Female *(Rapture)*.

Awards 1987: James Brown wins Best R&B Vocal Performance, Male *(Living In America)*.

Awards 1987: Prince and The Revolution win Best R&B Performance by a Duo or Group with Vocal *(Kiss)*.

Awards 1987: Anita Baker, Gary Bias & Louis A. Johnson (Songwriters) win Best Rhythm & Blues Song *(Sweet love performed by Anita Baker)*.

Awards 1987: Tina Turner wins Best Rock Vocal Performance, Female *(Back Where You Started)*.

1987

MTV Video Music Awards – 4th Annual

Video of the Year: *Peter Gabriel* – "Sledgehammer"

Best Male Video: *Peter Gabriel* – "Sledgehammer"

Best Female Video: *Madonna* – "Papa Don't Preach"

Best Group Video: *Talking Heads* – "Wild Wild Life"

Best New Artist in a Video: *Crowded House* – "Don't Dream It's Over"

Best Concept Video: *Peter Gabriel* – "Sledgehammer"

Best Choreography in a Video: *Janet Jackson* – "Nasty"

Viewer's Choice Award: *U2*.

Video Vanguard Award: *Peter Gabriel and Julien Temple*.

1987

Soul Train Music Awards – 1st Annual.

Award, Gregory Abbott wins Best New Artist.

Award, Janet Jackson wins Best Music Video *(What Have You Done for Me lately)*

Award, Cameo wins Album of the Year – Group or Band *(Word Up)*

Award, Janet Jackson wins Album of the Year – Female *(Control)*

Award, Luther Vandross wins Album of the Year – Male *(Give Me the Reason)*

Album, Anita Baker wins Best Single, Female *(Sweet Love)*

Award, Gregory Abbott wins Best Single, Male *(Shake You Down)*

Award, Cameo wins Best Single by Group or Band *(Word Up)*

Award, Al Green wins Best Gospel Album by a Solo Artist *(He is the Light)*

Award, The Winans win Best Gospel Album by a Group or Choir *(Let My People Go)*

Award, George Howard wins Best Jazz Album by a Solo Artist *(Love Will Follow)*

Award, Bob James and **David Sanborn** Best Jazz Album by a Group or Band *(Double Vision)*

Award, RUN-DMC wins Best Rap Single *(Walk This Way)*

Award, RUN-DMC wins Best Rap Album *(Raising Hell)*

1987 – Billboards Year End – Hot 100 Singles

1987	Urban Music 27% of Billboard's Year-End Hot 100	27%
3	**Gregory Abbott** – *Shake You Down*	Columbia
4	**Whitney Houston** – *I Wanna Dance With Somebody (Who Loves Me)*	Arista
14	**Atlantic Starr** – *Always*	Warner Bros.
16	**Jody Watley** – *Looking for a New Love*	MCA
17	Lisa Lisa and Cult Jam – *Head to Toe*	Columbia
22	**Whitney Houston** – *Didn't We Almost Have It All*	Arista
29	**Club Nouveau** – *Lean On Me*	Warner Bros.
31	**Lisa Lisa and Cult Jam** – *Lost In Emotion*	Columbia
36	**Aretha Franklin & George Michael** – *I Knew You Were Waiting (For Me)*	Arista
37	**Janet Jackson** – *Control*	A&M
38	**Prince** – *U Got the Look*	Paisley Park
43	**The Jets** – *You Got It All*	MCA
45	**Michael Jackson & Siedah Garret** – *I Just Can't Stop Loving You*	Epic
48	**Janet Jackson** – *Let's Wait Awhile*	A&M
57	**The System** – *Don't Disturb This Groove*	Atlantic
59	**Michael Jackson** – *Bad*	Epic/CBS
60	**Prince** – *Sign O' the Times*	Paisley Park
67	**Ben E. King** – *Stand by Me*	Atco
71	**LeVert** – *Casanova*	Atlantic
72	**Gloria Estefan and Miami Sound Machine** – *Rhythm is Gonna Get You*	Epic
73	**The Whispers** – *Rock Steady*	Solar/Capitol
87	**Smokey Robinson** – *Just to See Her*	Motown
90	**The Jets** – *Cross My Broken Heart*	MCA
91	*Kool and The Gang* – *Victory*	De-Lite
95	**Lionel Richie** – *Ballerina Girl*	Motown
98	**Beastie Boys** – *(You Gotta) Fight for Your Right (To Party!)*	Def Jam
100	**Ready for the World** – *Love You Down*	MCA

1987 – Record Labels in Hip Hop Music

Def Jam: With the release of *Public Enemy's* debut album breaking ground on the conscious side of Hip Hop and *LL Cool J* dropping the first Rap ballad, Def Jam securely planted its flag in this iconic year of Hip Hop.

B-Boy Records: Originally founded in the Bronx, New York, 1987 by Jack Allen and William Kamarra, the label tasted its first bit of Hip Hop success with the debut release of BDP's *Criminal Minded* and its first singles, *South Bronx* and *The Bridge Over* which dropped in 1986 and 1987 respectively before the album. BDP would soon leave the label due to monitory reasons.

Jive: No stranger to Hip Hop success the A&R team struck gold again with the debut release of *Jazzy Jeff & The Fresh Prince*, new releases from *Kool Moe Dee*, *Whodini*, *Steady B*, and the *Skinny Boys*; Jive was playing for keeps and their roster and charts proved it.

Profile: It would be a Fort Greene MC by the name of *Dana Dane* from the Kangol Crew outside of *RUN-DMC* that kept the label relevant. The classic album *Dana Dane with Fame* garnered several hits in this iconic year of Hip Hop.

4th & B' Way: Originally formed in 1984 by Chris Blackwell as a subsidiary of *Island Records* to specialize mostly in Hip Hop music, the label would be the lucky one to drop the debut album of *Eric B* and *Rakim, Paid in Full*, which not only featured the iconic lyrics of Rakim, but the transcending DJ and sample style of Eric B, a style that changed the platform of the culture instantly.

Dangerous Music Records: Now seasoned in the Hip Hop Culture, Oakland, California rapper, *Too $hort* upped his game and released *Born to Mack* under his own imprint; *Dangerous Music*.

Sire: Originally founded in 1966 by Seymour Stein and Richard Gottehrer as Sire Productions, it released mostly progressive rock music. Fast forward to the 80's, the label signed Ice-T as one of its only rap acts.

Cold Chillin: In their 2nd year of business the label released Queensbridge rapper, MC Shan debut album *Down by Law* and experienced great success which helped lay the platform to an iconic run.

Tin Pan Apple: Originally created in 1987, in New York by *Fat Boys* manager, Charles Stettler. After leaving **Sutra Records,** the *Fat Boys* released their new album *Crushin'* on *Tin Apple* which went platinum with a big push from their hit single, *Wipeout*, a remake of the Beach Boys' classic.

Uptown: Originally founded 1986 in New York City by Andre Harrell, one half of the rap duo *Dr. Jeckyll* and *Mr. Hide*. Uptown inked a distribution deal with **MCA Records** and went on to release a Hip Hop classic album *Living Large* by *Heavy D* and *The Boy,* and Uptown was well on its way to success.

Ruthless: Originally founded by California rapper, *Eric "Eazy-E" Wright*, 1987 in Compton, California. The label released a compilation album this year, *N.W.A. and the Posse*. The albums most noted single, *Boyz-n-the Hood* caught fire and lit flame to the culture, ushering in *Gangsta Rap Music*. This iconic run would change the rap game from here on out and conservative America's worse nightmare, *"N***** With Attitude"* would come from Compton, California.

Sleeping Bag: The label continued to stay relevant with releases from *T La Rock* and *Just-Ice*.

Soo Def: Founded in Philadelphia, Pennsylvania in 1986 by Sandy Drummond the label released *Phanjam* by *Tuff Crew/ Krown Rulers*. Phila continued to plant flags in Hip Hop.

4 Sight: Founded in 1984, Ft. Lauderdale, Florida by William Hines. Down South, Florida had its own flavor of Hip Hop known as Miami Bass. The success of the Bass music brought a different element to the culture. 4 Sight would add to the culture with the release of *MC. A.D.E.* and *Gigolo Tony*.

Luke: Originally **Luke Skyywalker Records,** the label underwent a name change after legal disputes with Star Wars execs. Keeping true to form, Luke released another Miami Bass album to feed the culture, but this time the artist was a New York born artist who laid claim to the South. *MC Shy D* firmly planted his seed in the South and dropped an iconic album to boot.

Tuff City: Originally founded in 1981 by journalist Aaron Fuchs in New York. The label released *Spoonie G's* (former member of the *Treacherous Three*) debut solo album, *The Godfather of Rap*. The album received moderate success amongst the other rap albums dropped this year.

Bad Boy: The Original **Bad Boy Records** released a classic album this year, *Court's in Session* by Brooklyn rap crew, *Kaos*. The album contained some record samples that would go on to be used over and over again in the culture as well as a rap style. The producers *Kenny 'Dope" Gonzalez, Russell D. Cole,* and *Todd Terry* would become synonymous among Hip Hop producers.

As a Hip Hop head, I believe that 1987 was the year that culminated the Authenticity of Hip Hop. Several monumental MC's debuted their styles this year along with trend setting tracks like LL's *I Need Love*, the Fat Boy's *Wipeout*, Kool Moe Dee's, *Wild Wild West* with the New Jack swing track. Mega producer *Teddy Riley* along with *Marley Marl* created pathways, 4-way stops, 2-way lanes, and opened doors for the culture that were unimaginable years prior. *Heavy D* made being overweight, sexy and featured two dancers in his crew, front and center. *Jazzy Jeff* & the *Fresh Prince* brought a transparent style to the culture.

MC Shan and *KRS-1* brought the Rap battle to the forefront and launched successful careers from that battle. *KRS-1,* aside from the battle, delivered a rap style that would test any MC. *Public Enemy* said the hell with the b******** and placed black consciousness center stage with *Yo! Bum rush the Show,* while *N.W.A.* ushered in a biopic of everyday life in Compton, California that became to be known as Gangsta Rap.

Then just when you thought you heard it all this year, *Dana Dane* dropped some story telling jewels on his album *Dana Dane with Fame* & my favorite, *Cinderfella Dana Dane*. I was hyped in '87 at the state of Hip Hop, but nothing can compare to that moment when I was sitting in homeroom and my cousin gave me this mix tape he got from New York; I popped it in the Walkman and when I pressed play, all I heard was, "*I ain't no Joke, I used to let the mic smoke!*" Damn! I just dropped the Walkman on the floor.

I knew at that moment that Hip Hop as we knew it was going to change, and *Eric B & Rakim* were going to be the reason. I mean deadly lyrics over precise cuts, scratches, mixes, and samples. *Dope!*

Eric B. & Rakim

"I aint no joke, I used to let the mic smoke

Now I slam it when I'm done and make sure it's broke

When I'm gone no one gets on 'cause I won't let

Nobody press up and mess up the scene I set

I like to stand in the crowd and watch the people wonder damn

But think about it then you'll understand

I'm just an addict addicted to music

Maybe it's a habit, I gotta use it."

-Rakim (I Ain't No Joke)

Circa 1988

Our Thing!

Hip Hop (Rap Music): After two prior hit singles, one in 1986, (*It's My Beat*) and the other in 1987 (*I Got Da Feelin'*/*It's like That Y'all*), Queens, New York MC, *Sweet Tee* released her debut album, *It's Tee Time* on **Profile Records**. The album produced 4 hit tracks, *On the Smooth Tip, I Got da Feelin', It's Like That Y'All,* and *Why Did it Have to Be Me*, which pushed the album to #31 on the R&B charts. *Sweet Tee*, aka *Suga,* one of the first female MC's to hit the charts with her rap style and swag, inspired many female rappers to get into Hip Hop.

City: Queens, New York **Producers**: Hurby Luv Bug & The Invincibles, Jazzy Joyce

"Testin my mic, one-two, one-two

I'm here to entertain, yes, this means you

Don't need no help, all by myself

I proceed cos you need to enjoy yourself

Try to compare? Oh, don't you dare"

-Sweet Tee (On the Smooth Tip)

⇒ **Music Industry News:** On January 20, 1988, *The Supremes* are inducted into the Rock & Roll Hall of Fame.

Hip-Hop (Rap Music/Gangsta/Southern/Hardcore): February 17, 1988; Houston, Texas rap group, **Geto Boys** released their debut album on ***Rap-A-Lot Records***. The album didn't make much noise but did establish the *Geto Boys* and Houston, Texas in the Hip Hop culture along with a Hardcore and Southern rap style.

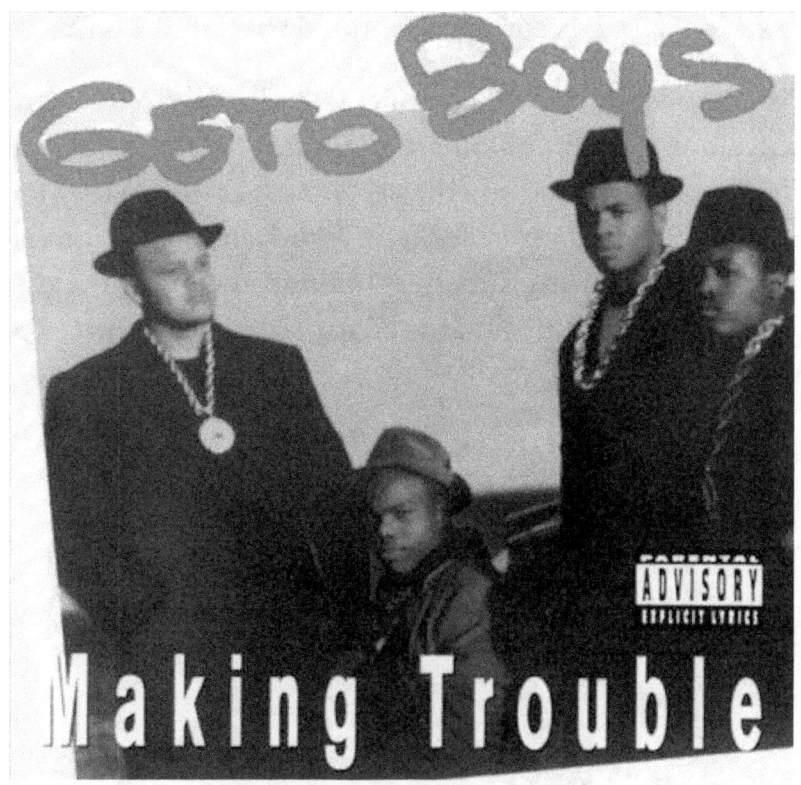

City: Houston, Texas **Members**: Bushwick Bill, DJ Ready Red, Prince Johnny C & Sire Jukebox **Producers**: Cliff Blodget, Karl Stephenson & Geto Boys

⇒ **Politics—Iran-Contra Scandal: On January 25, 1988, CBS News Anchor, Dan Rather and Vice President, George H. W. Bush** clash over the VP's role in the Iran-Contra Scandal which involved the illegal sale of weapons and drugs to help support the Nicaraguan Contra's during a continuous TV interview.

⇒ **New Jersey News: February 1, 1988, School Principal Joe Clark** appears on cover of *TIME*.

⇒ **Politics—Iran-Contra Scandal: On February 3, 1988, The Democratic-controlled U.S. House of Representatives** rejects President Ronald Regan's bid for $36.25 million to support the Contras.

⇒ **Film News—Action**: February 12, 1988, **Lorimer Film Entertainment** released *"Action Jackson: It's Time for Action"* starring **Carl Weathers** and **Vanity**. The film was directed by *Craig R. Baxley*, produced by *Joel Silver* and earned $20,256,975 at the box office.

⇒ **Film News—Musical Comedy Drama**: February 12, 1988, **40 Acres and a Mule Filmworks and Columbia Pictures** released *School Daze* starring **Larry Fishburne, Tisha Campbell, Ossie Davis, Giancarlo Esposito** and **Art Evans**; directed, written and produced by *Spike Lee*, earing $14,545, 844 at the box office.

Hip-Hop (Rap Music): March 1, 1988, Long Island, New York rapper, *Biz Markie* released his debut album *Goin' Off* on **Cold Chillin Records**. The album brought a different feel to Hip Hop with Biz's comedic yet serious at times story tellin' classic tracks like, *Vapors, Nobody Beats the Biz, Make the Music with Your Mouth, Biz,* and *Pickin' Boogers*, made the album number #1 in the streets. Although the culture gave the album high praise, the industry heads over radio and the charts failed yet again to recognize Hip Hop at its truest form.

City: Long Island, New York **Producer**: Marley Marl

(Juice Crew)

- ⇒ **Politics—Iran-Contra Scandal: On March 16, 1988, Vice Admiral John Poindexter and Lt. Colonel Oliver North** are both indicted on conspiracy charges for defrauding the United States with illegal acts used to finance the Contras.
- ⇒ **TV News—Soul Train: On March 5, 12 & 26, 1988, Kool Moe Dee, Heavy D & The Boyz, and Salt N Pepa** were featured guests.
- ⇒ **Politics—Presidential Race: On March 26, 1988, United States Presidential Candidate Jesse Jackson** defeats candidate Michael Dukakis in the Michigan Democratic caucuses.

Hip-Hop (Rap Music): March 29, 1988, **DJ Jazzy Jeff & The Fresh Prince** released their sophomore album, *He's the DJ, I'm the Rapper* on *Jive Records*. The album penned a few hits, most noted, *Parents Just Don't Understand*, which won the rap group the first ever Grammy Award in Hip Hop for Best Rap Performance. **Jazzy Jeff & The Fresh Prince** reached #12 on the charts, while their vinyl eventually went double platinum. The group's rap style resonated with main stream America opening yet another door for the culture.

Producers: The Fresh Prince, Jazzy Jeff, & Pete Harris

- ⇒ **Magazine News: This year Naomi Campbell** lands the cover of *Paris Vogue* & *Vogue Italia*.

- ⇒ **Film News—Crime Drama: April 15, 1988. Orion Pictures Corporation** released *Colors* starring, *Don Cheadle, Leon Robinson, Damon Wayans,* and *Glen Plummer*. The movie is based on the street life of L.A Crip's and Blood's gang activity, screenplay by *Michael Schiffer*, directed by *Dennis Hopper* and earned $46,616,067 at the box office.
- ⇒ **TV News—Soul Train: On April 16, 1988, Dana D**ane was a featured guest.
- ⇒ **Magazine News: April 25, 1988, Muhammad Ali** appears on cover of *Sports Illustrated.*
- ⇒ **Magazine News: April 1988, Boxer Evander Holyfield** appears on cover of *RING*.

Hip-Hop (Rap Music): In April of 1988, **Grandmaster Flash and the Furious Five** released their sophomore album *On the Strength*, which was also a reunion album due to an early break up after the success of their debut album. This one however was released on *Elektra* and not *Sugar Hill records*.

Producers: Grandmaster Flash and the Furious Five

- ⇒ **Politics: April 11, 1988, presidential candidate Jesse Jackson** lands cover of *TIME*.
- ⇒ **Magazine News: In April of 1988, Iman** lands cover, German magazine *Madame*.

⇒ **World News: On May 16, 1988, The U.S. Surgeon General C. Everett Koop** announced that the addictive properties in nicotine are similar to those of heroin and cocaine.

⇒ **U.S. Law: On May 16, 1988, The Supreme Court** rules that police officers do not need a search warrant to search through discarded garbage (*California v. Greenwood*).

⇒ **Magazine News: May 16, 1988, Michael Jackson** appears on cover of *JET*.

⇒ **Magazine News: May 19, 1988, Lisa Bonet** appears on cover of *Rolling Stone*.

Hip-Hop (Rap Music): May 17, 1988, **RUN-DMC** released their 4th album *Tougher than Leather* on **Profile Records**. The album garnered a few hit singles and went on to earn platinum status while peaking at #2 on charts.

Producers: Russell Simmons, Rick Rubin, RUN-D.M.C., & Davy DMX.

Hip-Hop (Rap Music): May 31, 1988, **BDP** released sophomore album *By All Means Necessary* on ***Jive Records***. The album released after the death of founding member *DJ Scott La Rock,* moved away from the violent content that embodied the first album *Criminal Minded*. KRS-1, from this moment on vowed to uplift, empower, inform, and only release Hip Hop conscious music, taking on the moniker *The Teacher,* and he peaked at #18 on the R&B/Hip Hop charts (***R.I.P. Scott La Roc***).

Producer: KRS-One

"Let's begin

What where why or when / Will all be explained

Like instructions to a game / See I'm not insane

In fact I'm kind of rational / When I be asking

Yo who is more dramatical / This one or that one

The white one or the black one / Pick the punk

And I'll jump up to attack one"

-KRS-One (My Philosophy)

Hip-Hop (Rap Music): May 31, 1988, **Doug E. Fresh** released *The World's Greatest Entertainer* on **Reality Records**. The album peaked at #7 on the R&B/Hip Hop charts pushed by most noted single, *Keep Risin' to the Top*.

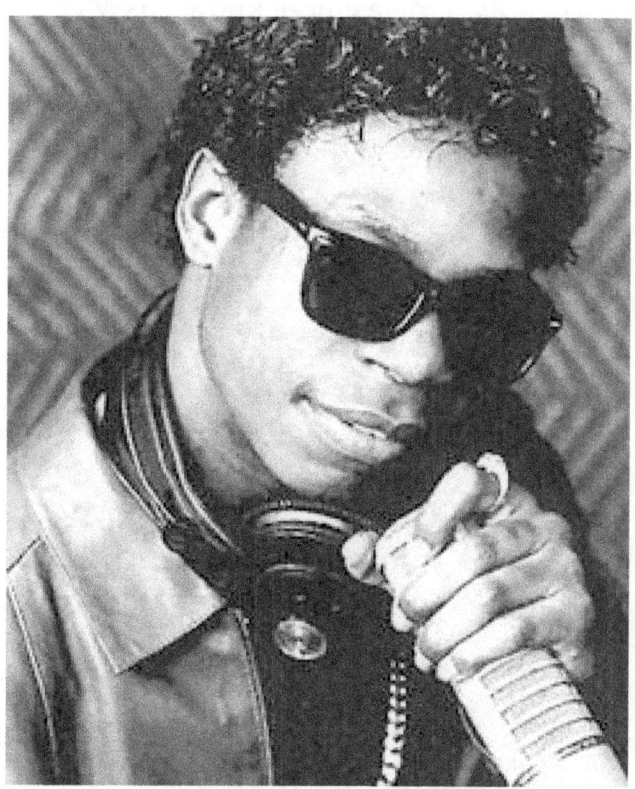

Producers: Doug E. Fresh, Eric "Vietnam" Sadler, Carl Ryder, Ollie Cotton.

⇒ **Magazine News: May 1988, Boxer George Forman** appears on the cover of *RING*.
⇒ **Magazine News: May 1988, Kim Fields** lands cover of *JET*.

Hip-Hop (Rap Music): June 7, 1988, **Audio Two** released their debut album *What More Can I Say?* on **First Priority Records**. *Audio Two's* debut album caught a street buzz from the single *Top Billin'* which helped push it to #45 on the R&B/Hip Hop charts. This single also featured lyrics from a deadly female emcee known as *MC Lyte*.

City: Brooklyn, New York   **Members**: Kirk "Milk Dee" Robinson, Nat "Gizmo" Robinson   **Producers**: Milk D, DJ Gizmo & Daddy O.

"MC am I people call me Milk

When I'm bustin' up a party I feel no guilt

Gizmo's 432utting', up for the

Suckers that's, down with me

The One of us, that's how I feel

To be down you must appeal"

-Milk D (Top Billin)

Hip-Hop (Rap Music): June 7, 1988, **EPMD** released their debut album *Strictly Business* on *Fresh/Sleeping Bag Records*. EPMD introduced yet another style to the genre, Eric's slow, but precise lyrics along with Parrish's insolent delivery, made the duo instant legends while reaching gold status.

City: Brentwood, New York   **Members**: Erick Sermon, PMD, DJ Scratch

Producers: EPMD

"Relax your mind, let your conscience be free

And get down to the sounds of EPMD

Well you should keep quiet while the MC rap

But if you tired- then go take a nap

Or stay awake and watch the show I take

Because right now – I'm bout to shake' n 'bake"

-Erick Sermon (You Gots to Chill)

⇒ **Magazine News**: **June 16, 1988, Terence Trent D'Arby** appears on the cover of *Rolling Stone*.

Hip-Hop (Rap Music): June 21, 1988, **Big Daddy Kane** released his debut album *Long Live the Kane* on **Cold Chillin' Records**. Kane brought a smooth, bad boy rap style to the genre, while his content included conscious, playboy, and braggadocios lyrics. The emcee also featured two dancers known as *Scoop* and *Scrap Lover*, the three often performed dance routines during stage shows and in music videos adding yet another layer to *Big Daddy Kane* whose lyrics were also deadly.

City: Bedford-Stuyvesant, Brooklyn, New York   **Members**: Big Daddy Kane, Scoop & Scrap Lover, DJ Mister Cee   **Producer**: Marley Marl

(Juice Crew)

"Rappers stepping to me, they want to get some

But I'm the Kane, so yo, you know the outcome

Another victory

They can't get with me

So pick a BC date cause you're history"

-Big Daddy Kane (Ain't No Half Steppin)

⇒ **Music Industry News: On June 27, 1988, Motown Records** is sold to *MCA Records* for $61 Million.

⇒ **Magazine News**: **June 27, 1988, Boxing Champ Mike Tyson** appears on cover of *TIME*.

Hip-Hop (Rap Music/Political/Conscious): June 28, 1988, **Public Enemy** released their sophomore album *It Takes a Nation of Millions to Hold Us Back* on *Def Jam Records*. The album became a cult classic, while peaking at #1 on the Black Album charts, and reached platinum status behind the success of hit tracks, *Don't Believe the Hype, Bring the Noise, Night of the Living Baseheads, and Rebel without a Pause*.

Producers: Chuck D, Hank Shocklee, Rick Rubin

"Back

Caught you lookin' for the same thing

It's a new thing, check out this I bring

Uh Oh the roll below the level

'Cause I'm livin' low next to the bass, c'mon

Turn up the radio"

-Chuck D (Don't Believe the Hype)

⇒ **Film News—Comedy: June 29, 1988, Paramount Pictures** released *Coming to America* starring **Eddie Murphy, James Earl Jones, Arsenio Hall** and **James Amos**. The movie was directed by *John Landis*, story by *Eddie Murphy*, and earned $288,752,301 at the box office.

Hip-Hop (Rap Music): July 26, 1988, **Eric B. & Rakim** released their sophomore album *Follow the Leader* on **Uni Records**. The duo had made their presence known with the previous release and by the time this one dropped, everyone was checking for them. Rakim delivered yet again with mind bending lyrics over Eric's DJ delivery; hot singles, *Follow the Leader*, *The R*, and *Microphone Fiend*, pushed the album to #22 on the charts while earning gold status.

Producers: Eric B. & Rakim

Hip-Hop (Rap Music): July 26, 1988, **Salt-N-Pepa** released their sophomore album *A Salt with a Deadly Pepa* on **Next Plateau Records**. The album peaked at #8 on the R&B/Hip Hop charts, while its most noted single, *Shake Your Thing*, helped it reach gold status. Salt-N-Pepa's fan base grew in large proportions as the groups style and format appealed to a diverse group of women, while at the same time spitting lyrics that caught the attention of males alike.

Producer: Hurby Luv Bug

⇒ **Magazine News: July 25, 1988, Track star Florence Griffith-Joyner** appears on the cover of *Sports Illustrated*.
⇒ **Magazine News: July 1988, Eddie Murphy** lands cover of *Vanity Fair*.
⇒ **Magazine New: July 1988, Michael Spinks and Mike Tyson** appear on cover of *RING*.
⇒ **Magazine News: July 1988, married couple Mike Tyson and Robin Givens** land cover of *LIFE*.

Hip-Hop (Rap Music/Gangsta/Political): August 8, 1988, **N.W.A** released their sophomore album (1st as a group), *Straight Outta Compton* on **Ruthless Records**. The album struck a chord with conservative America due to its authentic street content; Government Officials, Law Enforcement and the FBI especially took offense. But *N***** With Attitude* was just what the country needed; the Compton, California group spoke about the violence that went on in their hood every day. It was so compelling that many thought it to be fiction, but it was all too damn real. The most noted tracks, *Straight Outta Compton, Gangsta Gangsta, Express Yourself,* and *F*** the Police,* put the controversial rap group and Compton on the Hip Hop map. *NWA* was to the West Coast what *PE* was to the East Coast, and it was all Hip Hop. America got smacked in the face with its ugly truth. *Police Brutality and Racism were alive and in effect.*

Producers: Dr. Dre, DJ Yella, Eazy-E

*"F*** the Police coming straight from the underground*

*A young n**** got it bad cause I'm brown*

And not the other color so police think

They have the authority to kill a minority"

*-Ice Cube (F*** the Police)*

⇒ **Magazine News: August 8, 1988, Eddie Murphy** lands cover of *People.*

⇒ **Music News: On August 12, 1988, Public Enemy** performs a concert at Riker's Island Prison for 250 inmates and 100 journalists.

Hip-Hop (Rap Music/Miami Bass/Sexplicit): August 17, 1988, *2 Live Crew* released their sophomore album *Move Somethin'* on **Luke Records**. Its hottest singles, the title track *Move Somethin'* and *Do Wah Diddy*, pushed it to gold status while peaking at #20 on the R&B/Hip Hop charts.

Producers: Luke Skyywalker, Mr. Mixx

⇒ **Magazine News: In August of 1988, Naomi Campbell** appears on cover of *L.A. Style.*

Hip Hop (Rap Music): In 1988 California rappers, **J.J Fad** released their debut album *Supersonic* on **Ruthless/Atco Records**. They're most noted for the title track, *Supersonic*, which became a Hip Hop classic and displayed a rapid rap style with comedic word play.

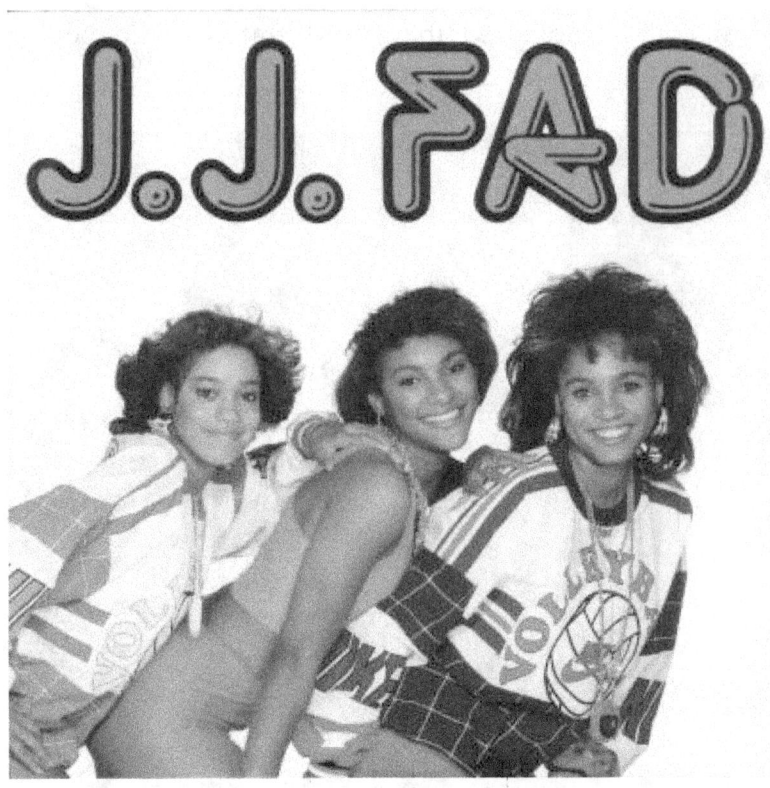

City: Rialto, California. **Members**: Juana "MC J.B" Burns, Dania "Baby D" Birks, Michelle "Sassy C" Franklin-Ferrens **Producers**: Arabian Prince, DJ Yella, Dr. Dre

⇒ **Magazine News:** This year **Robin Givens** lands cover of *People*.

Hip-Hop (Rap Music): September 1, 1988, **Seattle rapper, Sir Mix-A-Lot** released his debut album "*Swass*" on his own label, ***Nastymix Records***. *Sir Mix-A-Lot* first claimed Hip Hop notoriety in 1987 with his hit single *Posse on Broadway*; to his credit the emcee introduced a different style and sound to our culture and we loved it! The success of the hit single which was also included on this album led to a recording contract with **Def Jam *Records*** who re-released the album on CD. The album would go on to garner platinum status. *Posse Up!*

City: Seattle, Washington **Producer**: Sir Mix-A-Lot

"Me and Kid Sensation and that home away from home

In the Black Benz Limo with the cellular phone

I'm callin' up the posse it's time to get rippin'

The freaks a need a sunroof to keep you sucka's trippin

Everybody's lookin if your jealous turn around

The AMG kick keeps us closer to the ground"

-Sir Mix-A-Lot (Posse on Broadway)

⇒ **TV News: September 6, 1988, MTV** debuts *Yo! MTV Raps*, a Hip Hop Music show which was hosted by *Fab 5 Freddy*, *Ed Lov*er, and *Doctor Dre'*.

Hip-Hop (Rap Music/Gangsta): September 13, 1988, ***ICE-T*** released his sophomore album *Power* on ***Sire Records***. His most noted single, *I'm Your Pusher*, would be one of the first Gangsta rap video tracks to get major air play on *MTV*.

Producers: Afrika Islam, Ice-T   **Crew**: *Rhyme $yndicate*

⇒ **Magazine News: This year 1988, two Harvard University (Cambridge, Massachusetts) students, David Mays & Jonathan Shecter** founded a rap newsletter that focused on Hip Hop music, its culture, and politics. This newsletter eventually evolved into a full color magazine known as ***The Source***, which also became a staple in Hip Hop Culture.

Hip-Hop (Rap Music): September 13, 1988, **MC Lyte** released her debut album *Lyte as a Rock* on **First Priority Records**. The album peaked at #50 on the charts, but became iconic in the streets. Lyte, a female emcee brought more heat to the already competitive male dominated rap game. Her braggadocios, confident, cocky, and battle rap style along with a precise delivery made all emcees take notice. Her most noted singles, *10% Dis, Paper Thin, I Cram to Understand U (Sam), Lyte as a Rock,* and *Kickin' 4 Brooklyn* certified this album as a cult classic.

City: Brooklyn, New York   **Members**: MC Lyte, DJ K Rock, **Dancers**: Leg 1 & Leg 2

Producers: Audio Two, Alliance, King of Chill, Prince Paul

"When you say you love me, it doesn't matter

It goes to my head as just chit chatter

You may take this egotistical or just worry free

But what you say I take none of it seriously"

-MC Lyte (Paper Thin)

Hip-Hop (Rap Music/Gangsta): September 13, 1988, **Eazy-E** released his debut album on *Ruthless records*. The most noted tracks, *Eazy-Duz-it*, *We Want Eazy*, and *Eazyer Said Than Dunn* topped the charts placing the album at #12 on the R&B/Hip Hop charts.

City: Compton, California   **Producers**: Dr. Dre, DJ Yella

"A miracle of modern creation

Eazy E's on the set

Hyped up with the bass

And a little bit of what ya love

From a brother who's smooth like a criminal

I mean subliminal

Otherwise known as a villain"

-Eazy E (We Want Eazy)

Hip-Hop (Rap Music): September 13, 1988, **Steady B** released *Let The Hustlers Play* on *Jive Records*. The Phila emcee continued to represent and peaked at #56 on the Soul album charts.

Producers: KRS-One, Steady B, Chuck Nice, Lawrence Goodman

Crew: *Hilltop Hustlers*

⇒ **Fashion:** Any MC worth their weight sported a few, fat gold chains, aka dookie ropes, and fat gold rings to embellish their persona among the culture. *Slick Rick* and *Big Daddy Kane* sport their jewels below.

Hip-Hop (Rap Music): September 20, 1988, **Rob Base & DJ E-Z Rock** released their debut album *It Takes Two* on **Profile Records**. The title track created a dance craze throughout the culture and shot to platinum status.

City: Harlem, New York   **Members**: Rob Base & DJ E-Z Rock

Producers: William Hamilton, Rob Base, DJ E-Z Rock

Hip-Hop (Rap Music/Pop/Dance): September of 1988, **MC Hammer** released his sophomore album *Let's Get It Started* on **Capitol Records**. Hammer introduced a rap style that was more focused on entertainment than hardcore. His choreographed dance moves, flashy attire & fast paced music appealed more commercially than any other Hip Hop records. This, however, caused controversy with the culture, most even said that "Hammer aint Hip Hop." But, the numbers told a different story as the record spawned several hits, *Turn This Mutha Out*, *Pump it Up*, *Let's Get it Started*, and *They Put Me in the Mix*, pushed the so-called Not-Hip Hop artist to #1 with double platinum record sales.

Hip-Hop (Rap Music): September 20, 1988, **Marley Marl** released *In Control, Volume 1*, a compilation of emcees from the *Juice Crew* on **Cold Chillin' Records**. The album featured Juice Crew members: *Biz Markie, Roxanne Shante', Big Daddy Kane, Kool G Rap, Craig G, MC Shan, Masta Ace, Percy Tragedy,* and a guest appearance by *Heavy D & the Boyz*. Its most noted tracks, that kept the entire next 12 months rockin', were *Droppin' Science* and *The Symphony*; these two hits brought enough fire to push the album to #25 on the R&B/Hip Hop charts and from #1 to iconic in the streets.

Producer: Marley Marl

(*Juice Crew*)

"When I get stupid to the point that I'm mentally mad

My rhymes start to flow, so I simply must brag

About my style that makes you vibrant, I keep drivin

Until the song turns me to a hip-hop giant

Me and Marley Marl, were goin one on one

For any sucker rapper that chooses to come"

-Craig G (*Droppin' Science*)

⇒ **Magazine News: September 22, 1988, Tracy Chapman** appears on cover *Rolling Stone.*

⇒ **Music News: On September 24, 1988, The God Father of Soul, James Brown** faces charges due to an interstate police chase in Augusta, Georgia, which took place after he waved a gun during a seminar in one of his buildings demanding to know who used his bathroom.

Hip-Hop (Rap Music): October 4, 1988, **Ultramagnetic MC's** released their debut album *Critical Beatdown* on *Next Plateau Records*. The album reached #57 on the charts, its most noted track, *Ego Trippin*, brought another funky beat to the list of cult favorites and cemented the emcees place in Hip Hop.

City: Bronx, New York   **Members**: Kool Keith, Ced-Gee, TR Love, Moe Love, DJ Jaycee

Producers: Paul C, Ced-Gee, Ultramagnetic MC's

⇒ **Magazine News: October 10, 1988, Track stars Florence Griffith-Joyner & Jackie Joyner-Kersee** appear on the cover of *Sports Illustrated*.

Hip-Hop (Rap Music): October 21, 1988, **Kid 'N Play** released their debut album *2 Hype* on **Select Records**. The duo's most noted tracks, *2 Hype, Gittin Funky*, and *Rollin' with Kid 'n Play*, pushed the album to #9 on the charts, while earning gold status. *Kid N' Play* embodied dance routines with most all of their songs making the two must-see TV. Kid sported a signature high top fade with a good guy image, while Play sported the low top with a bad boy image which worked well for the duo and cemented them with legendary status.

City: Queens, New York **Members**: Kid, Play, DJ Whiz

Producers: Hurby Luv Bug, The Invincibles

Hip-Hop (Rap Music): October 25, 1988, **MC Shan** released his sophomore album *Born to Be Wild* on **Cold Chillin' Records**. This album included the answer dis record to KRS-One and *BDP* with *Juice Crew Law*.

Producer: Marley Marl

(*Juice Crew*)

⇒ **Business News: On October 30, 1988, Tobacco giant Philip Morris** buys *Kraft Foods* for $13.1 billion.

Hip-Hop (Rap Music): This year Kingston, Jamaica born MC, **Chubb Rock** released his debut album *Chubb Rock feat Howie Tee* on **Select Records**. The album reached #54 on the E&B charts.

City: Kingston, Jamaica by way Brooklyn, New York **Producer**: Hitman Howie Tee

Hip-Hop (Rap Music): November 1, 1988, **Slick Rick** released his debut album *The Great Adventures of Slick Rick* on **Def Jam Records**. The album topped the charts at #1 and featured hot tracks, *Teenage Love, Children's Story*, and *Hey Young World*. Slick Rick proved to be a master at the art of Story-telling; his vivid rhymes took you on a trip created by his word flow, which ironically turned out to be the perfect story line for the now popular music videos. The chap from London was instantly a Hip Hop legend.

City: Bronx, New York by way of Mitcham, London, England

Producers: The Bomb Squad, Jam Master Jay, Slick Rick

"Aye sport, here's a thought from the old school crew

A serious situation we all go threw

It deals wit your feelins, so hear what I say

It's like a dyke, but nothing seems to go your way

Bust this, two people, they really like each other/ He says there's no one else

And she claims there is no other"

-Slick Rick (Teenage Love)

Hip-Hop (Rap Music/Conscious/House): November 8, 1988, **the Jungle Brothers** released their debut album *Straight Out the Jungle* on **Warlock Records**. The album peaked at #39 on the R&B charts and a classic *Hip-House* hit single, *I'll House You*. The JB's promoted conscious and original content in their music, and also spawned the *Native Tongues* movement, a collective of artists with the same focus.

City: New York City, New York **Members**: Mike G, Afrika Baby Bam, Sammy B

Producers: Todd Terry, Jungle Brothers **Crew**: *Native Tongue*

Hip-Hop (Rap Music/Gangsta/Southern): This year Houston rapper, **Raheem** released his debut album *The Vigilante* on **Rap-A-Lot Records**.

City: Houston, TX. **Producers**: James Smith, Karl Stephenson

Hip-Hop (Rap Music/Gangsta): November 15, 1988, **King-Tee** released his debut album *Act a Fool* on **Capitol Records**. The album reached #35 on the charts due to the success of the title track and *Bass*.

City: Compton, California   **Producers**: DJ Pooh, King Tee

⇒ **U.S. Law—War on Drugs:** On November 18, 1988, President Ronald Regan signs a bill that will provide the death penalty for murderous drug traffickers.
⇒ **Sports News: On November 21, 1988, media mogul Ted Turner** buys Jim Crockett Promotions, aka NWA Crocket, and turns it into WCW (*World Championship Wrestling*).
⇒ **Hip Hop—Slang:** *On the Strength* – This is for real, no b**********!

Hip-Hop (Rap Music/Miami Bass): This year in Hip Hop, **MC Cool Rock & MC Chaszy Chess** released *Boot the Booty* on **Vision Records**. The album featured the popular Miami Bass-laced tracks adding more flavor to the Florida Bass Culture.

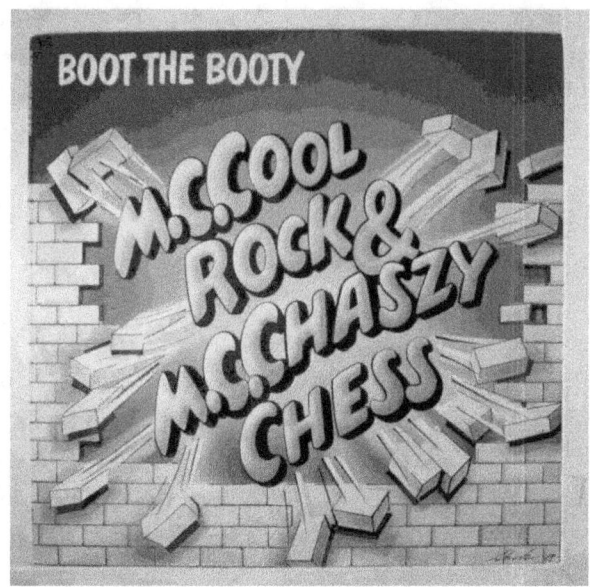

Producer: Clay Dixon

Hip-Hop (Rap Music/Electro Bass): This year in Hip Hop, **MC Shy-D** released *Comin' Correct in 88* on **Luke Skyywalker Records**. The album was a hit on the bass scene and kept the clubs jumpin. Its most noted track, *Shake It*, became a Hip Hop classic.

Producers: DJ Toomp, DJ Mike Fresh, MC Shy D

Hip-Hop (Rap Music): This year in Hip Hop, **The 7A3** released their debut album *Coolin' in Cali* on *Geffen Records*. The title track caught a buzz and the album peaked at #47 on the R&B/Hip Hop charts.

City: Los Angeles, California by way of Brooklyn & Queens, New York

Members: DJ Muggs, Brett & Sean Bouldin

Hip-Hop (Rap Music): This year **Tuff Crew** released *Danger Zone* on *Warlock Records;* this would the first album for Warlock after leaving *So Def Records*.

⇒ **TV News — Soul Train**: On December 3, 1988, **EPMD** were featured guests.

Hip-Hop (Rap Music): This year **J.V.C. F.O.R.C.E.** released *Doin' Damage* on **B-Boy Records**. The groups hottest track, *Strong Island*, caught the ears of the Hip Hop junkies and became a cult favorite.

City: Long Island, New York   **Members**: DJ Curt Cazal, AJ Rok, B-Luv

Hip-Hop (Rap Music): This year **Masters of Ceremony** released *Dynamite* on **Strong City Records**. The group experienced earlier success with singles, *Crime* in '85, and *Sexy* and *Cracked Out* in '86. This album became a classic among the culture, but failed to chart.

City: New Rochelle, New York   **Members**: Grand Puba Maxwell, Dr. Who, DJ Shabazz

Producers: Grand Puba, Jazzy Jay

Hip-Hop (Rap Music): This year in Hip Hop, **Super Lover Cee and Casanova Rud** released their debut album *Girls I Got 'Em Locked* on **Elektra/DNA International records**. The duo first claimed success with the release of their 1987 single *Do the James*, sent hot street vibes through the culture. *Girls I Got 'Em Locked* became a Hip Hop favorite credited to the rap flow of Super and Rud, who also filmed their video at home in Astoria Projects.

City: Astoria Projects, New York **Members**: Caliente Fredrick, Erik Rudnicki

Producers: Super Lover Cee & Casanova Rud

Hip-Hop (Rap Music): This year **Stetsasonic** released *In Full Gear* on **Tommy Boy Records**. The album pinned a few classic singles, *Talkin' All that Jazz*, *Sally*, and *Float On*, which helped the album reach #20 on the R&B charts.

Producer: Ced Gee

Hip-Hop (Rap Music): This year **K-9 Posse** released their debut self-titled album on *Arista Records*.

City: Formed in Teaneck, New Jersey   **Members**: Wardell Mahone, Vernon Lynch, Terrence Sheppard

Hip-Hop (Rap Music/Electro Bass): This year **Rodney O & Joe Cooley** released *Me and Joe* on *Egyptian Empire Records*. The duo pinned success with hit singles, *Everlasting Bass, Colley High*, and *This is For The Homies*; the duo implemented the classic rap style delivery over electro funk beats and classic DJ cuts with scratch blends, and placed #187 on the charts, but remained a cult classic.

City: Compton, California   **Members**: Rodney O, Joe Cooley, General Jeff

Producers: Rodney O, Joe Cooley, General Jeff

Hip-Hop (Rap Music): This year **Def IV** released *Nice & Hard* on **Rap-A-Lot Records**.

City: Houston, Texas   **Members**: Prince E-Z-Cee, Vicious Lee, Lonnie Mac & Jon B

Producers: Doug King, James A Smith

Hip-Hop (Rap Music): This year **the Krown Rulers** released *Paper Chase* on **Warlock Records**.

Producers: The Krown Rulers, Dave from the Tuff Crew

Hip-Hop (Rap Music/Electro/Miami Bass): This year *Bass Patrol* released *"Rock This Planet"* on **Joey Boy records**.

Producers: Calvin Mills II, Carlton Mills

Hip-Hop (Rap Music): This year **The Skinny Boys** released *Skinny (They Can't Get Enough)* on **Jive Records**. The album reached #71 on the R&B/Hip Hop charts.

Producer: Mark Bush

Hip-Hop (Rap Music/Gangsta): This year **Schoolly D** released *Smoke Some Kill* on **Jive Records**. *Schoolly D* reached #50 on the R&B/Hip Hop charts with his 3rd album.

Producer: Schoolly D

Hip-Hop (Rap Music): This year **Tall Dark and Handsome** released their self-titled album *Tall Dark and Handsome* on **B-Boy Records**.

City: Bronx, New York   **Members**: Boo Love, MC KD, Money Ray the DJ

Hip-Hop (Rap Music): This year **Cash Money & Marvelous** released their debut album *Where's the Party At?* on **Sleeping Bag Records**.

City: Philadelphia, Pennsylvania   **Members:** DJ Cash Money, Marvelous

⇒ **Film News—Comedy:** December 14, 1988, MGM/UA Communications Company release "*I'm Gonna Git You Sucka*" starring **Keenen Ivory Wayans, Jim Brown, Antonio Fargas, Isaac Hayes** and **Ja'net Dubois**, directed and written by *Keenen Ivory Wayans*, earning $13,030,057 at the box office.

⇒ **Magazine News: December 26, 1988, Track star Florence Griffith-Joyner** appears on cover of *Sports Illustrated*.

⇒ **TV News—New Year's Eve Special: On December 31, 1988, DJ Jazzy Jeff & The Fresh Prince** appeared on *ABC's*, 17th annual *New Year's Rockin' Eve* special.

1988

Soul Train Music Awards – 2nd Annual.

Award, Gladys Knight and the Pips is honored with the Heritage Award.

Award, Miki Howard wins Best New Artist.

Award, Janet Jackson wins Best Music Video (*Control*).

Award, Michael Jackson wins Best Single by a Male (*Bad*).

Award, Michael Jackson wins Album of the Year (*Bad*).

Award, LeVert wins Album of the Year – Group (*The Big Throwdown*).

Award, Natalie Cole wins Best Single, Female (*I Live for your Love*).

Award, Whitney Houston wins Album of the Year – Female (*Whitney*).

Award, LeVert wins Best Single – Group, Band (*Casanova*).

Award, LL Cool J wins Best Rap Single (*I Need Love*).

Award, LL Cool J wins Best Rap Album (*Bigger and Deffer*).

Award, The Winans wins Best Gospel Album, Group or Choir (*Decisions*).

Award, Vanessa Bell Armstrong wins Best Gospel Album, Solo (*Following Jesus*).

Award, Najee wins Best Jazz Album for (*Najee's Theme*).

Award, Hiroshima wins Best Jazz Album, Group or Band for (*Go*).

1988

MTV Video Music Awards – 5th Annual

Video of the Year: *INXS – "Need You Tonight/Mediate"*

Best Male Video: *Prince feat Sheena Easton – "U Got the Look"*

Best Female Video: *Suzanne Vega – "Luka"*

Best Group Video: *INXS - "Need You Tonight/Mediate"*

Best New Artist in a Video: *Guns N' Roses – "Welcome to the Jungle"*

Best Concept Video: *Pink Floyd - "Learning to Fly"*

Best Video from a Film: *Los Lobos - "La Bamba"*

Breakthrough Video: *INXS - "Need You Tonight/Mediate"*

Best Stage Performance in a Video: *Prince feat Sheena Easton – "U Got the Look"*

Best Choreography in a Video: *Janet Jackson – "The Pleasure Principle"*

Viewer's Choice: *INXS - "Need You Tonight/Mediate"*

Video Vanguard Award: *Michael Jackson.*

1988 – Urban American
Grammy Award Recipients – 30th Annual

Award, 1988: Jody Watley wins Best New Artist.

Award, 1988: Deniece Williams wins Best Gospel Performance, Female *(I Believe In You)*.

Award, 1988: CeCe Winans wins Best Soul Gospel Performance, Female *(For Always)*.

Award, 1988: Al Green, wins Best Soul Gospel Performance, Male *(Everything's Gonna Be Alright)*.

Award, 1988: The Winans & Anita Baker win Best Soul Gospel Performance by a Duo or Group, Choir or Chorus *(Ain't No Need to Worry)*.

Award, 1988: Bobby McFerrin wins Best Jazz Vocal Performance, Male *(What is This Thing Called Love)*.

Award, 1988: Wynton Marsalis wins Best Jazz Instrumental Performance, Group *(Marsalis Standard Time – Volume 1)*.

Award, 1988: Mercer Ellington wins Best Jazz Instrumental Performance, Big Band *(Digital Duke)*.

Award, 1988: Whitney Houston wins Best Pop Vocal Performance, Female *(I Wanna Dance With Somebody, Who Loves Me)*.

Award, 1988: Aretha Franklin wins Best R&B Vocal Performance, Female *(Aretha)*.

Award, 1988: Smokey Robinson wins Best R&B Vocal Performance, Male *(Just to See Her)*.

Award, 1988: Aretha Franklin & George Michael win Best R&B Performance by a Duo or Group with Vocal *(I Knew You Were Waiting, For Me)*.

Award, 1988: Bill Withers (Songwriter) wins Best Rhythm & Blues Song *(Lean on Me performed by Club Nouveau)*.

Award, 1988: Peter Tosh wins Best Reggae Recording *(No Nuclear War)*.

1988 – Billboards Year End – Hot 100 Singles

1988	Urban Music 25% of Billboard's Year-End Hot 100	25%
6	Whitney Houston – *So Emotional*	Arista
12	Terence Trent D'Arby – *Wishing Well*	CBS
13	Gloria Estefan & Miami Sound Machine – *Anything for You*	Epic
15	Billy Ocean – *Get Outta My Dreams, Get into My Car*	Jive
21	Michael Jackson – *Man In the Mirror*	Epic
33	Whitney Houston – *Where Do broken Hearts Go*	Arista
36	Michael Jackson – *The Way You Make Me Feel*	Epic
37	Bobby McFerrin – *Don't Worry, Be Happy*	EMI
51	The Jets – *Make it Real*	MCA
55	Jody Watley – *Don't You Want Me*	MCA
58	Terence Trent D'Arby – *Sign Your Name*	Columbia
59	Roger Troutman – *I Want to Be Your Man*	Reprise
60	Pebbles - *Girlfriend*	MCA
61	Michael Jackson – *Dirty Diana*	Epic
62	Gloria Estefan & Miami Sound Machine – *1-2-3*	Epic
63	Pebbles – *Mercedes Boy*	MCA
67	New Edition – *If It Isn't Love*	MCA
68	The Jets – *Rocket 2 U*	MCA
74	Keith Sweat – *I Want Her*	Elektra
75	Natalie Cole – *Pink Cadillac*	Columbia
76	Tracy Chapman – *Fast Car*	Elektra
79	Bobby Brown – *Don't Be Cruel*	MCA
87	Al B. Sure! – *Nite and Day*	Warner Bros.
89	Whitney Houston – *One Moment in Time*	Arista
90	Gloria Estefan & Miami Sound Machine – *Can't Stay Away from You*	Epic

1988 – Record Labels in Hip Hop Music

Profile: Cemented from the success of RUN-D.M.C, the label used its weight and nose for a hit record to sign Rob Base and DJ EZ Rock, and released Sweet Tee's debut album as well. These three albums carved out a nice piece of the charts in '88, securing a huge flow of revenue for the label.

Rap-A-Lot: Founded in 1986 by James Prince, the Houston, Texas based label specialized in Gangsta and Southern Hip Hop. This year, Rap-A-Lot made its imprint on the culture with the release of Raheem, Def IV, and the Geto Boys.

Cold Chillin: Home of the Juice Crew, Marley Marl and his counter parts dropped several hit albums this year as the label planted its Hip Hop flag with classic albums from Biz Markie, Big Daddy Kane, MC Shan, and Marley's hit, *Juice Crew Compilation*.

Jive: Still riding high from the spoils of Whodini's early success, the label capitalized on market share with the release of Jazzy Jeff & The Fresh Prince, BDP, Steady B, Skinny Boys, and Schoolly D, claiming a firm piece of Hip Hop in '88.

Elektra: Eager to claim a piece of the Hip Hop pie, Elektra released a reunion album from Grandmaster Flash & the Furious Five, along with two cult classics from Super Lover Cee and Casanova Rud.

Reality: The label followed up the success from Doug E Fresh's last hit with more from the Beat Box, MC keeping the brand relevant.

First Priority Music: Founded by Nat Robinson, the father of Audio Two member Kirk, aka Milk D. Robinson originally launched the label to release Audio Two's music. He struck gold with hit album's, *Top Billin'* by Audio Two, and MC Lyte's debut classic, *Lyte as a Rock*.

Fresh/Sleeping Bag: Known for their nose for new talent, Sleeping Bag dropped the smash debut album by EPMD and also sparked flames with new group, Cash Money & Marvelous.

Def Jam: No longer one of the few, but one of many, Def Jam forged on with timeless classics and this year, P.E. took the culture by storm once again while Slick Rick laced the game with his art of story-telling.

Uni: Originally founded in 1966 as Universal City records, the label emerged again this year with the release of Eric B & Rakim's sophomore hit album. Just like any other label in the industry, MCA wanted their piece of the Hip Hop pie and Uni was the vehicle they devised to make it happen.

Next Plateau: With the success of Salt N Pepa's hit record along with a hot street buzz for the new Ultramagnetic MC's album, the label carved out a nice niche in the market.

Sire: The label released another gangsta classic from California MC, ICE-T keeping the label relevant to the culture.

B-Boy: After losing BDP to Jive, the label tried to maintain relevancy in the game, but only produced sub-par music compared to that of the *Criminal Minded* album, which set the standard for their brand.

Warlock: Originally founded in 1985 by Adam Levy, the New York based label released two albums this year, one of which went on to be a Hip Hop classic, the Jungle Brothers and Krown Rulers. This would only be the beginning of a fledging corporation.

Ruthless: The Compton based label coined Gangsta rap with classic releases from NWA, Eazy-E, and J.J., Fad leaving a mark on the culture that would usher in a new era in Hip Hop.

Luke: Miami Bass music created a whole new line within the culture with the explicit content of the 2 Live Crew and a unique voice from MC Shy D that added to the catalog of the Florida and Atlanta scenes.

Nastymix: The Seattle based label originally founded by Sir Mix-A-lot and Nasty Nes, gained national attention this year with the release of *Posse on Broadway*. This pioneered the Northwest Hip Hop sound that coincided with Seattle Hip Hop dance crews known as Boppers.

Capitol: Trying to cash in on a slice of Compton, the label signed gangsta rapper King Tee as an attempt to be relevant in the Hip Hop game.

So Def: The indie label released another album from one of its veteran groups, Tuff Crew; although the playing field had become crowded with more talent, they remained somewhat competitive.

Egyptian Empire: Egyptian Lover struck pay dirt with the release of Rodney O & Joe Cooley, and released some Hip Hop classics.

Arista: With the release of their new rap group K9, Arista didn't fare well within the culture; it didn't feel authentic to the true Hip Hop heads.

Vision: MC Cool Rock & MC Chaszy Chess produced a Miami Bass cult classic with *Boot the Booty* that created a hot buzz for the Vision label.

Select: After the success of U.T.F.O, the label would strike gold once more with the release of Kid n' Play, creating an entirely new lane within the culture.

Tommy Boy: Stetsasonic, one of the first multi-MC groups, kept their label relevant this year among the talented rap scene.

Strong City: Founded by Jazzy Jay and Rocky Bucano in New Rochelle, NY. After success with a few singles starting in 1985 the indie label released *The Masters of Ceremony*, which featured a young Grand Puba Maxwell and some early production by a young Teddy Riley.

Geffen: Not to be out done by the competition, Geffen released The 7A3, but only garnered moderate success.

Joey Boy: The Florida based label dropped the Southern Miami bass album by Bass Patrol adding to the popular Miami Bass sound.

In 1988 over 50 Hip Hop albums were released and several featured new rap artists from different cities across America. The culture was not only growing, but adding more sectors to its already successful make-up. *Kid N' Play* introduced authentic Hip Hop, but laced with entertaining dance moves and personality, *N.W.A* cemented the Gangsta rap style, *MC Lyte* took female rappers to another level, *Biz Markie* created a lane all his own with a comedic rap style, *Slick Rick* became the culture's ultimate story teller, EPMD's gold selling lyrics and production added another successful layer to the rap game, The *Jungle Brothers* introduced the House music style to Hip Hop with the release of *I'll House You*, *Sir Mix-A-Lot* dropped a funky production and rap style on us with *Posse on Broadway* representing Seattle, Washington; Marley Marl killed the game with the release of one of the first ever rap compilation's featuring over 7 emcees called *The Symphony*. The biggest surprise would come from an Oakland, California MC, whom I prefer to call an entertainer, by the name of *MC Hammer*. By the 80's standards Hammer didn't fit any Hip Hop mold and the culture gave him tons of slack for it. His rap cadence was unheard of and his clothes weren't culture-based at all. He created a persona that won over the masses and crashed commercial media, becoming more popular than any Hip Hop artist at the time. I witnessed one of the best stage performances in my life when I saw Hammer in concert. This guy was a diehard entertainer and his crew didn't slack off either, needless to say while the haters did not approve, he sold over 2 million records and he was just getting started. I'm sure most of us O.G. Hip Hop heads said at least once that *"Hammer ain't Hip Hop,"* but we know the lyrics to at least three of his songs.

I recall thinking back then, *"If the culture continues growing at this alarming rate, pretty soon it will take over the music industry."* The way I saw it was simple; rap appeals to everyone because of its authentic content and where it comes from, more people can relate to being poor and misunderstood than they can to being rich. Hip-Hop, because of its foundation will touch all music genres, Country, Rock & Roll, Gospel, Jazz, Blues, R&B, Disco, and so on. *Why? Because they all can relate to our stories!*

I can remember back in '88 when we were in the hood, bored as hell, so we brought out the huge card board box that we used to spin on, went in the house and put on our Puma wind breakers and got my homeboy named Baby Bro from the block to bring out his boom box so we could break dance.

> He said, *"Yo, check out this tape I stole from my cousin, it's that female rapper, Roxanne Shante!"*
> I said, *"Bro, we already heard that joint... put on something else!"*

He replied, *"Man just listen, this sh** is fresh."* And it went like this....

(*Juice Crew*)

"Let me tell you a story yes

How I got to be so fresh

It happened one day you know

While I was sitting upstairs

Listenin' to the radio – huh

They said that it's a contest

We'll give the most money to the rapper who's the best

I said yo let me enter / Cuz I know I'm down

And everybody knows / it was all around town"

-Roxxane Shante (Queen of Rox)

Circa 1989

The Evolution

- **TV News — Variety/Talk Show: On January 3, 1989, the Arsenio Hall Show** debuted in syndication. Hall was a staple in the Hip Hop culture as he allowed performances and appearances from several Hip-Hop Artists through the show's tenure. The show was produced by *Arsenio Hall Communications* and distributed by *Paramount Domestic Television*.

Hip Hop (Rap Music/Rock/Pop): January 23, 1989; Los Angeles MC *Tone Loc* released *Loc-ed After Dark* on *Delicious Vinyl Records*. Loc's debut album pinned three chart toppers and reached #1 on the Billboard charts. *Wild Thing, Funky Cold Medina*, and *I Got it Goin On* went on to be cult classics and pushed the album to double platinum status.

City: Los Angeles, California   **Producers**: The Dust Brothers, Matt Dike & Michael Ross.

- **Politics: On January 20, 1989, George H.W. Bush** becomes United States president.
- **Music News — Georgia: On January 23, 1989, The Godfather of Soul, James Brown** is sentenced to 6 years in jail for charges relating to a high-speed chase through two States.

⇒ **Movie News — Dance/Drama:** On February 10, 1989, *TriStar Pictures* released *"Tap"* starring **Gregory Hines**, **Suzanne Douglas** and **Sammy Davis, Jr.**, directed & written by *Nick Castle*, the film earned $9.1 million at the box office.

Hip-Hop (Rap Music/Gangsta/Sexplicit): This year, Oakland MC, **Too Short** pinned double platinum sales with his album *Life Is... Too Short* released on **Dangerous Music/Jive/RCA Records**. The title track along with *CussWords*, *Oakland*, and *Don't Fight the Feelin'*, added yet another chapter to the legend of *Too Short*.

Producers: Too Short, R. Austin, Al Eaton, T. Bohanon

⇒ **Politics — Iran Contra Scandal: On March 3, 1989, Robert McFarlane,** the former National Security Advisor, is only fined $20,000 and sentenced to 2 year's probation for misleading congress about the Iran Contra Affair. (*Ricky Ross is doing hard time.*)

Hip-Hop (Rap Music/Southern/Gangsta): March 12, 1989, **the Geto Boys** released their sophomore album with two new members, *Grip it! On That Other Level* on **Rap-A-Lot Records**. The most noted track, *Do It Like a G.O*, pushed it to #19 on the R&B/Hip Hop charts.

City: Houston, Texas **Members**: Willie D, Bushwick Bill, Dj Ready Red, Scarface
Producers: Dj Ready Red, James Smith, Doug King, Johnny C, John Bido

⇒ **Movie News—Biography: In March of this year Warner Bros.** released *"Lean on Me,"* a film inspired by Patterson, New Jersey High School Principal, *Joe Clark;* directed by *John G. Avildsen,* starring **Morgan Freeman** and **Robert Guillaume**. *"Lean on Me"* earned $31,906 million at the box office.

Hip-Hop (Rap Music/Alternative/Psychedelic/Conscious): March 14, 1989, New York rap trio **De La Soul** released their debut album *3 Feet High and Rising* on **Tommy Boy/Warner Bros. Records**. The album peaked at #1 on the Hip Hop/R&B charts with a push from new era tracks, *Potholes in My Lawn, Buddy, and Me Myself and I.* De La introduced yet another style to our culture that resonated with a core audience.

City: Long Island, New York   **Producers**: Prince Paul & De La Soul

Members: Posdnous, Maseo, Dave   **Crew**: *Native Tongue*

⇒ **TV News—Miniseries: On March 19-20, 1989, Oprah Winfrey** and *Harpo Productions* released *The Women of Brewster Place* on **ABC**. The series was based on *Gloria Naylor's* novel of the same name. Brewster Place starred, **Oprah Winfrey, Shari Belafonte, Moses Gunn, Robin Givens, Jackee' Harry, Cicely Tyson, Larenz Tate, Paul Winfield, Leon, Lynn Whitfield, Mary Alice,** and **Lonette Mckee.**

⇒ **Magazine News**: **In March of 1989, La Toya Jackson** appears in *Playboy Magazine (Spain).*

Hip-Hop (Rap Music): March 14, 1989, **Kool G Rap & DJ Polo** released *Road to the Riches* on *Cold Chillin Records*. After the success of their previous single, *It's A Demo*, the title track added more weight to the rap crew making them contenders in the rap game.

Producer: Marley Marl   (*Juice crew*)

TV News — Soul Train: On April 22, 29, 1989, Rob Base & DJ E-Z Rock, Tone Loc were featured guests.

Hip-Hop (Rap Music): May 12, 1989, rap duo **Nice & Smooth** released their self-titled debut album on *Fresh/Sleeping Bag Records*. The duo's most noted track *Funky for You* coined their trade mark, tag team rap style which sometimes included comedic content.

City: Bronx, NYC, N.Y. **Producers**: Nice & Smooth **Members**: Greg Nice, Smooth B

⇒ **Protest News — Los Angeles, California: On May 15-25, 1989, LA School teachers** go on strike and win 24% pay increase and more administrative control.
⇒ **TV News — Soul Train: In May of 1989, E.U and Doug E. Fresh** were featured guests.

Hip-Hop (Rap Music/Jazz/Conscious): June 6, 1989, rap duo **Gang Starr** released *No More Mr. Nice Guy* on **Wild Pitch Records**. *Guru's* razor-sharp delivery over *DJ Premier's* beats made heads bob and feet tap. The debut album peaked at #83 on Billboard, while it's most popular single, *Positivity* reached #19 on the rap charts, while *Manifest* became a cult classic.

City: Brooklyn, New York by way of Boston, Massachusetts & Houston, Texas

Members: DJ Premier, Guru **Producers**: The 45 King, Guru, DJ Premier

"I go for glory, I take an inventory

Countin all the tough luck ducks while I narrate

Relate and equate, dictate and debate

My fate is to be, cold makin history

I use sincerity, but I'm so very deep"

-Guru (Manifest)

Hip-Hop (Rap Music): June 9, 1989, **LL Cool J** released his junior album *Walking with a Panther* on **Def Jam records**. LL once again proved that he had the Midas touch pinning several hit singles *Jingling Baby, Going Back to Cali, Big Ole Butt, One Shot at Love,* and *I'm That Type of Guy*, which pushed the album to platinum status.

Producers: LL Cool J, Rick Rubin, The Bomb Squad, Dwayne Simon, DJ Cut Creator

⇒ **Magazine News: On June 12, 1989, NBA star and Chicago Bull, Michael Jordan** lands cover of *JET*.
⇒ **Politics: On June 13, 1989, president George H.W. Bush** stopped the minimum wage bill that was passed by Congress earlier on May 17, 1989. If passed, the bill would have increased the minimum wage to $4.55.
⇒ **TV News—Soul Train: On June 17, 1989, MC Hammer** was a featured guest.
⇒ **Magazine News: On July 17, 1989, Heavyweight Boxer, George Foreman** lands cover of *Sports Illustrated*.

Hip-Hop (Rap Music/Edutainment/Political): July 4, 1989, **BDP** released *Ghetto Music: The Blueprint of Hip Hop* on *Jive records*. Boogie Down Productions peaked at #7 on the R&B/Hip Hop charts and garnered several hot tracks, *Why is That, The Blueprint, Jack of Spades, You Must Learn, Ghetto Music,* and *World Peace* earning gold status.

Producer: KRS-One

"Why isn't young black kids taught black?

They're only taught how to read, write, and act

It's like teaching a dog to be a cat

You don't teach white kids to be black

Why is that? Is it because we're the minority?

Well black kids follow me"

-KRS-One (Why is That?)

⇒ **Politics—Iran Contra Scandal: On July 5, 1989, Oliver North** is given two years' probation, ordered to perform 1200 hours in community service, and fined $150,000 for the crimes he committed in the Iran Contra Affair. (*Ricky Ross is doing hard time.*)

⇒ **Movie News—Comedy/Drama: On July 21, 1989 Spike Lee** released "*Do The Right Thing*" which was produced by his company **40 Acres and a Mule Filmworks** and distributed by **Universal Pictures**. The film directed by Spike, starred himself, **Ruby Dee, Giancarlo Esposito** and several others, and earned $37.3 Million at the box office.

Hip-Hop (Rap Music/Rock): July 25, 1989, **the Beastie Boys** released *Paul's Boutique* on *Capitol Records*. Unlike their previous release with *Def Jam*, this album didn't have the break out success like *Licensed to Ill*. Once it gained momentum, it would eventually reach double platinum status.

Producers: Beastie Boys, Dust Brothers, Marlo Caldato, Jr.

Hip Hop (Rap Music/Hardcore/Gangsta): July 27, 1989, **Schoolly D** released *Am I Black Enough for You??* on *Jive Records*.

Producers: Schoolly D, Dj Code Money

Hip-Hop (Rap Music): August 1, 1989, **The D.O.C** released his debut album *No One Can Do It Better* on **Ruthless Records**. Doc's debut album peaked at #1 on the R&B/Hip Hop charts fueled by hot tracks, *It's Funky Enough*, and *The Formula*, which pushed the album to Platinum status. *In November of this year, The D.O.C. was involved in a fatal car crash that crushed his larynx, putting an end to his solo artist career. But he continued to ghost write hits!*

City: Los Angeles, California by way of Dallas Texas   **Producers**: Dr. Dre, Eazy-E

Hip-Hop (Rap Music): August 1, 1989, **EPMD** released their sophomore album *Unfinished Business* on **Fresh/Sleeping Bag Records**. Its most noted single, *So Wat Cha Sayin'* became a cult classic, pushing the album to #1 on the R&B/Hip Hop charts.

Producers: EPMD

⇒ **TV News — BET: On August 11, 1989, Black Entertainment Television** debuted *Rap City*, a 1-hour time block dedicated to Hip Hop. The show featured rap music videos, guest DJ's, and MC interview's, all centered on the show's host. Rap City hosts consisted of **1.** *Chris "The Mayor" Thomas,* **2.** *Hans "Prime" Dobson,* **3.** *Prince Dejour,* **4.** *Joe Clair,* **5.** *Leslie "Big Lez" Segar,* **6.** *Big Tigger,* **7.** *J-Nicks,* and **8.** *Q45*. The show was created by BET unseen VJ *Alvin Jones* along with *Keith Paschell*.

Hip-Hop (Rap Music): September 19, 1989, **Big Daddy Kane** released his sophomore album *It's a Big Daddy Thing* on **Cold Chillin Records**. Kane's authentic rap style continued to put all competition on notice, while separating himself from the pack. His diverse content touched on politics, conscious awareness, dance music, romance, and battle rap with tracks like, *Calling Mr. Welfare, Children R the Future, Young Gifted and Black, Smooth Operator, Rap Summary, Wrath of Kane, I Get the Job Done,* and *Another Victory* that should have garnered platinum sales in the main stream. Kane perhaps was ahead of his time or the music outlets obviously still had a problem identifying authentic Hip Hop. The album eventually reached gold status.

Producers: Big Daddy Kane, Mister Cee, Marley Marl, Easy Mo Bee, Prince Paul & Teddy Riley. (*Juice Crew*)

"Rappers I replace, rub out, and erase

Competition you must be on freebase, Smokin' or chokin', bound to be broken

Man, get your damn hands off the mic that I'm choking"

-Big Daddy Kane (Young Gifted and Black)

Hip-Hop (Rap Music): October 3, 1989, **MC Lyte** released her sophomore album *Eyes on This* on **First Priority/Atlantic Records**. Lyte pinned several hot tracks, *Cha Cha Cha, Cappuccino, Stop, Look, Listen, and I Am the Lyte*, which pushed the album to #6 on the R&B/Hip Hop charts further cementing the MC's place in Hip Hop history.

Producers: PMD, The King of Chill, Grand Puba, Audio Two, Marley Marl, and Nat Robinson

Hip-Hop (Rap Music/Gangsta): This year Los Angeles rap duo **Low Profile** released their debut album, *We're in This Together* on **Priority Records**. The album reached #66 on the R&B/Hip Hop charts, while penning a few rap classics, *Funky Song, That's Y They Do It, and Pay Ya Dues*.

City: Los Angeles, California **Members**: DJ Aladdin, WC **Producers**: DJ Aladdin, Doug Young (Exec)

Hip-Hop (Rap Music): October 10, 1989, **Biz Markie** released his sophomore album *The Biz Never Sleeps* on **Cold Chillin Records**. Biz won over the culture with his Rap Ballad, *Just A Friend*, with his off key singing and vivid story telling. The hit single peaked at #5 on Billboard and helped push the album to #9 on the R&B/Hip Hop charts, while earning gold status as he continued to create his own lane.

Producers: Cool C, Biz Markie

(Juice Crew)

⇒ **Hip Hop (Fashion): In the 80's** the ladies rocked the fitted Jordache jeans and drove all of us men crazy.

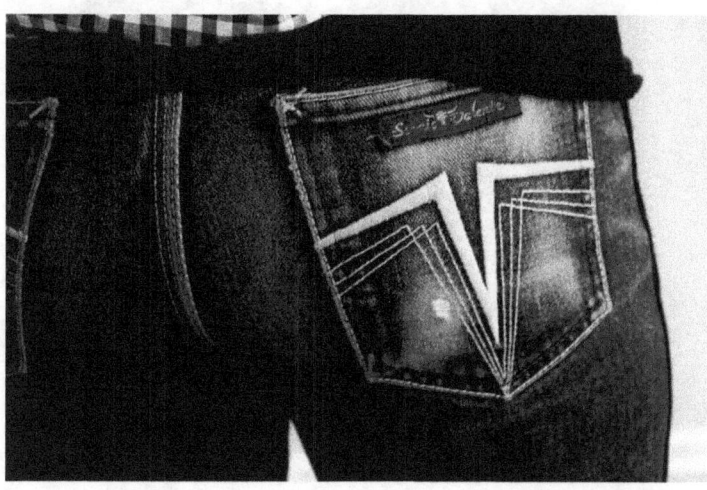

⇒ **Hip Hop — Slang:** *Skins* – Used by males to describe sex, *"What's up baby, when can I get them skins?"*

Hip-Hop (Rap Music/Gangsta): October 10, 1989, **Ice-T** released *The Iceberg/Freedom of Speech… Just Watch What You Say!* on **Sire Records**.

Producers: Ice – T, Afrika Islam   **Crew**: Rhyme $yndicate

⇒ **TV News — Soul Train: On October 21, 1989, Young MC** was a featured guest.

Hip-Hop (Rap Music): October 24, 1989, **Craig G** released his debut album *The Kingpin* on **Atlantic Records**. The album didn't hit the charts, but Craig G's rap style would gain respect among his peers and the culture as he evolved.

City: Queensbridge, New York   **Producer**: Marley Marl (*Juice Crew*)

Hip Hop (Rap Music): October 31, 1989, **DJ Jazzy Jeff & The Fresh Prince** released *And in This Corner* on *Jive Records*. The album peaked at #39 on the Billboard charts and was certified gold.

Producers: DJ Jazzy Jeff, The Fresh Prince

Hip-Hop (Rap Music): October 31, 1989, **Roxanne Shante'** released *Bad Sister* on *Cold Chillin Records*. Not as successful as her previous hits, the album did reach #52 on the R&B/Hip Hop charts.

Producer: Marley Marl, Q Neighbor

⇒ **Magazine News: On October 2, 1989, Bill and Camille Cosby** lands cover of *JET*.

Hip-Hop (Rap Music/Jazz/Conscious): November 7, 1989, **The Jungle Brothers** released their sophomore album *Done By the Forces of Nature* on **Warner Bros. Records**. The JB's second album reached #46 on the R&B/Hip Hop charts.

Producers: Kool DJ Red Alert, Jungle Brothers

(*Native Tongue crew*)

Hip-Hop (Rap Music): This year Miami rap duo **Young and Restless** released their debut album *Something to Get You Hyped* on **Pandisc Records**. The groups most noted singles, *Poison Ivy*, and *B Girls*, received heavy air play along with a music video in rotation on MTV as the album reached #104 on the Billboard 200.

City: Miami, Florida **Members**: Leonerist Lamar Johnson, Charles Trahan

Hip-Hop (Rap Music/Conscious): November 7, 1989, New Jersey MC, **Queen Latifah** released her debut album *All Hail the Queen* on *Tommy Boy Records*. The Queen carved out a lane for herself right from the start with lyrics demanding respect for all women, her classic hit single, *Ladies First,* which featured UK MC, ***Monie Love*** cemented her place in Hip Hop immediately. *All Hail the Queen* reached #6 on the Hip Hop/R&B charts while earning gold status.

City: Newark, New Jersey **Producers**: KRS-One, Daddy-O, DJ Mark the 45 King, Prince Paul and Louis 'Louie, Louie' Vega (*Native Tongue Crew*)

"The ladies will kick it, the rhyme that is wicked

Those that don't know how to be pros get evicted

A woman can bear you, break you, take you

Now it's time to rhyme, can you relate to"

-Queen Latifah (Ladies First)

Hip-Hop (Rap Music): November 14, 1989, New York, MC's, **3rd Bass** released their debut album *The Cactus Album* on **Def Jam Records**. 3rd Bass quickly resonated with the culture because of their rap skills. The hottest tracks on the album, *The Gas Face, Brooklyn Queens*, and *Steppin' to the A.M* became cult classics while pushing the album to #5 on the R&B/Hip Hop charts, earning gold status.

City: Queens/Brooklyn/ New York, New York **Members**: MC Search, Pete Nice, DJ Richie Rich **Producers**: The Bomb Squad, Sam Sever, MC Search, Pete Nice, Prince Paul

⇒ **Magazine News: On November 15, 1989, Muhamad Ali** lands cover of *Sports Illustrated.*

Hip-Hop (Rap Music): November 17, 1989, **Rob Base** released *The Incredible Base* on *Profile Records*. Unlike the previous hit album, the sophomore release didn't create such a buzz, but did however make it to #20 on the R&B/Hip Hop charts.

Producers: DJ E-Z Rock, William Hamilton, Rob Base

Hip-Hop (Rap Music): This year Connecticut MC, **Stezo** released his debut album *Crazy Noise* on **Sleeping Bag Records**. *Crazy Noise* quickly became a cult classic with the success of *It's My Turn*, and *Freak the Funk* pushing it to #37 on the R&B/Hip Hop charts.

City: New Haven, Connecticut **Producer**: Stezo

Hip-Hop (Rap Music): This year Queens MC, **Kwame'** released his debut album *Kwame the Boy Genius featuring a New Beginning* on **Atlantic Records**. *Kwame'*, only 16 at the time of this release, brought a different swag to the Hip Hop genre. He featured a band along with a unique fashion sense, mainly polka dots along with a high top fade with instinctive dye designs. Two classics stand out from the album, *The Rhythm*, and *The Man We All and Love*, which separated Kwame' from the traditional MC's.

City: Queens, New York **Producers**: Kwame', Hurby "Luv Bug" Azor

⇒ **Movie News—Comedy/Crime: On November 17, 1989, Eddie Murphy** directed *"Harlem Nights"* starring himself, **Redd Foxx, Della Reese & Richard Pryor** & several others. The film was distributed by *Paramount Pictures* and produced by *Eddie Murphy Productions*. It earned $90 Million at the Box office.

Hip-Hop (Rap Music): This year Kingston, Jamaica born MC, **Chubb Rock** released his sophomore album *And the Winner is with Howie Tee* on **Select Records**. This album would fare better than the previous peaking at #28 on the R&B charts. Chubb Rock contributed yet another swag to the culture with his rap style and Jamaican accent over energetic tracks.

Producer: Hitman Howie Tee

⇒ **Magazine News: In November of this year, late night talk show host, Arsenio Hall** and **Jay Leno** land cover of *Rolling Stone*.

⇒ **Hip Hop (Slang)**: *Chill* – Calm down, be cool, quit acting stupid!

Hip-Hop (Rap Music): This year Brookyln MC, **Special Ed** released his debut album *Youngest in Charge* on **Profile Records**. Special Ed hit the scene with precise rhymes over hard hitting beats and spawned several classics, selling over 500, 000 copies; *I Got it Made*, *I'm the Magnificent*, and *Think about It*, are considered some of the best rap songs ever made.

City: Brooklyn, N.Y. **Producer**: Hitman Howie Tee

"I'm your idol, the highest title, numero uno

I'm not a Puerto Rican, but I'm speakin so that you know

And understand I got the gift of speech and it's a blessin

So listen to the lesson I preach

I talk sense condensed into the form of a poem

Full of knowledge from my toes to the top of my dome"

-Special Ed (I Got It Made)

Hip Hop (Rap Music): This year Phila MC, **Cool C** released his debut album, *"I Gotta Habit"* on **Atlantic Records**. The album peaked at #51 and penned a cult classic with his single *Glamorous Life*.

City: Philadelphia, Penn. **Producers**: Lawrence Goodman, Warren McGlone

(*Crew: Hilltop Hustlers*)

Hip-Hop (Rap Music/Hardcore): This year New Jersey MC, **Chill Rob G** dropped his debut album *Ride the Rhythm* on **Wild Pitch Records**. Chill Rob created buzz with *Bad Dreams & Court is Now Session*.

City: Jersey City; New Jersey **Producer**: The 45 King

Hip-Hop (Rap Music/Gangsta): This year Oakland rap crew, **415** released their debut album *41Fivin* on ***Big League Records***.

City: Oakland, California   **Members**: Richie Rich & D-Loc **Producers**: DJ DRYL, J.E.D., Digital D, Kirk Crumpler

Hip-Hop (Rap Music/Instrumentals): This year Bronx DJ and producers, **45 King and Louie Louie** released *"Rhythmical Madness."* This album is considered to be one the first rap instrumentals to ever be released.

City: Bronx, New York

Hip-Hop (Rap Music/Gangsta): Before Houston, Texas MC, **Willie D** joined the *Geto Boys*, he released his 1st solo album *Controversy* on **Rap-A-Lot Records**. The album featured the gangsta track *Do It Like a G.O.* with former Geto Boys member's *Prince Johnny C & Jukebox Slim*. That track would later be added to the newly formed *Geto Boys* album featuring *Scarface & Bushwick Bill*, replacing the former members on the single.

City: Houston, Texas **Producers**: DJ Ready Red, Doug King, Johnny C, Lil J

Hip-Hop (Rap Music): This year in Phila, rap trio, **Three Times Dope** releases their debut album *Original Stylin'* on **Arista Records**. The group won over the culture with original slang over funky beats with tracks like *Greatest Man Alive* and *Funky Dividends*, which pushed the album to #122 on the Billboard 200.

City: Philadelphia, Penn. **Members**: EST, Chuck Nice, Woody Wood **Producers**: Chuck Nice, Steady B, Lawrence Goodman (*Crew: Hilltop Hustlers*)

Hip-Hop (Rap Music): This year, New Jersey rap crew **The New Style** released their debut album *Independent Leaders* on **Bon Ami/MCA Records**. The group would undergo an image and name change later and become *Naughty by Nature*.

City: East Orange, N.J **Members**: Treach, Kay Gee, Vinnie **Producer**: The New Style

Hip-Hop (Rap Music/Pop): This year London born rapper, **Young MC** released his debut album *Stone Cold Rhymin'* on **Delicious Vinyl Records**. Young pinned commercial success with his hot single *Bust a Move*, which peaked at #7 on the charts and is considered to be one of the first pop rap singles.

City: Queens, N.Y. **Producers**: Quincy Jones, Dust Brothers

Hip-Hop (Rap Music): This year Canadian MC, **Maestro Fresh Wes** released his debut album *Symphony in Effect* on **Attic/LMR Records**. Wes was proof that the culture was reaching uncharted ground; his style resonated with fans and placed Canada on the Hip Hop map. His most noted single *Let Your Backbone Slide* peaked at #1 on the charts and earned gold status, a first for a Canadian MC.

City: Toronto, Ontario, Canada   **Producers**: Peter & Anthony Davis

⇒ **HipHop — Slang:** *Buggin, Illin or Trippin* – Doing crazy, irregular or insane sh**.

Hip-Hop (Rap Music): This year Oakland, California rap duo **Oaktown 3.5.7**, released their debut album *Wild & Loose* on MC Hammer's **Bust It Records**.

City: Oakland, California   **Members**: Sweet L.D., Trouble T

Hip-Hop (Rap Music): This year California MC, **Breeze** released his debut album *The Young Son of No One* on **Atlantic Records**. The album peaked at #60 on the charts.

City: Los Angeles, California   **Producers**: L.A Posse

Hip-Hop (Rap Music/Afro-Centric): This year New York rapper, **Divine Styler** released his debut album *Word Power* on **Epic Records**. The album resonated with the culture and created a buzz for Divine's style of offbeat rap, his most noted tracks were, *Ain't Sayin' Nothin, and Free Styler*.

City: Brooklyn, N.Y. **Producers**: Bilar Bishar, Divine Styler **Crew**: Rhyme $yndicate

Hip-Hop (Rap Music/Miami Bass): This year Florida producer, **DJ Magic Mike** released *DJ Magic Mike & The Roayl Posse* on **Cheetah Records**.

City: Orlando, FL. **Producer**: DJ Magic Mike

Hip-Hop (Rap Music/Conscious/Political): This year Harlem born MC, **Def Jef** released his debut album *Just a Poet with Soul* on **Delicious Vinyl Records**. Jef created his own lane as one of the 1st sociopolitical rappers to emerge in the culture.

City: Harlem, N.Y **Producer**: Def Jef, Dust Brothers

Hip-Hop (Rap Music): This year **Donald D** former member of the Bronx rap crew, *The B-Boys*, released his solo album *Notorious* on **Rhyme $yndicate Records**.

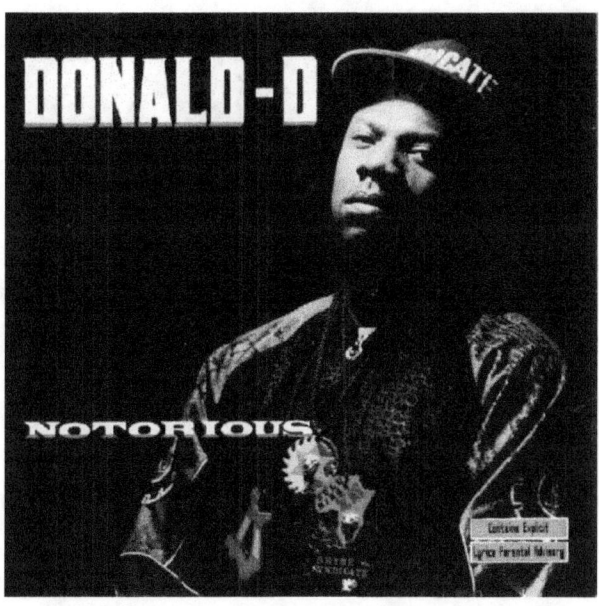

City: Bronx, New York   **Producers**: Afrika Islam, Donald D **Crew**: Rhyme $yndicate

Hip-Hop (Rap Music): This year **Bronx MC, Antoinette** released her debut album *Who's the Boss?* on **Next Plateau Records**. The album peaked at #47 on the charts, but she was most known for her battles with *MC Lyte*, which are classics all on their own.

City: Bronx, N.Y. **Producers**: I.G. Off, Ultramagnetic MC's, Jay Ellis

Hip-Hop (Rap Music/Conscious): This year Long Island MC, **Freddie Foxxx** released his debut solo album, *Freddie Foxxx is Here* on **MCA Records**.

City: Long, Island, N.Y.

Hip Hop (Rap Music/Hardcore): This year **Just-Ice** released his album *Desolate One* on **Fresh/Sleeping Bag Records**. The album peaked at #19 on the R&B/Hip Hop charts.

Producers: Just-Ice, KRS-One

⇒ **Hip-Hop News—Compton, California: On December 23, 1989, Ice Cube** leaves *N.W.A* after financial issues and several conflicts with manager Jerry Heller and *Eazy-E*.

Hip-Hop (Rap Music/Electro): This year, Inglewood, rapper, producer & DJ, **Arabian Prince** released his debut album *Brother Arab* on **Orpheus Records**.

City: Inglewood, California **Producer**: That Guy

Hip-Hop (Rap Music/Latin): This year Cuban born MC, **Mellow Man Ace** released his debut album *Escape from Havana* on **Capitol Records**. Mellow introduced the Latin rap style to the culture and pinned three hit singles, *Mentirosa, Rhyme Fighter*, & *If You Were Mine*, which pushed the album to #69 on the Billboard charts.

Mellow Man Ace
Capitol Records

City: Pinar Del Rio, Cuba **Producers**: Dj Muggs, Johny Rivers, Def Jef, Dust Bros, Tony G

⇒ **TV News—Music Television: This year MTV** debuted *MTV Unplugged*. The show featured musical artists performing their music on stage live with an acoustic band.

⇒ **Magazine News: This year Word Up!** featured several Hip Hop artists on their covers: *Big Daddy Kane, Flava Flav, EPMD, Salt N Pepa, DJ Jazzy Jeff & The Fresh Prince, LL Cool J, Special Ed, Heavy D & The Boyz, Kwame, De La Soul, Kool Moe Dee, D Nice, Kid N Play, Sir-Mix-A lot, J.J Fad, Rob Base & DJ E-Z Rock, Sweet Tee* making *Word Up!* an official platform for the culture. The publication also came with several pull-out posters of your favorite artist that many of us collected and hung on our bedroom walls.

Hip-Hop (Tradition? Marketing? or Bad habit?): Olde English aka 8 ball, a 40-oz of *malt liquor* was used to *self-medicate* many lost souls in the hood. It seemed that everywhere you looked we had a liquor store on every other corner. The gold 40oz of beer always ended up in someone's lyrics or in the latest video; hell, we even poured a few shots out on the pavement in memory of our lost ones or for the homies locked away. Makes you wonder why the higher content of beer, this one made of malt liquor, was so heavily marketed in the hood. *Rap your minds around that!*

Malt Liquor – Beer having a relatively high alcohol content, usually 5 to 8 percent.
Regular beer alcohol content ranges from 3.9% - 5.9%

1989

Soul Train Music Awards – 3rd Annual

Award, Anita Baker wins Best R&B/Urban Contemporary Song of The Year (*Giving You The Best That I got*)

Award, AL B. Sure wins Best Contemporary New Artist.

Award, Michael Jackson wins Best R&B/Urban Contemporary Music Video (*Man in the Mirror*)

Award, Michael Jackson wins Best R&B/Urban Contemporary Single, Male (*Man in the Mirror*)

Award, Bobby Brown wins Best R&B/Urban Contemporary Album of The Year, Male (*Don't Be Cruel*)

Award, New Edition wins Best R&B/Urban Contemporary Album of The Year, Group Band or Duo (*Heart Break*)

Award, Anita Baker wins Best R&B/Urban Contemporary Single, Female (*Giving You the Best That I Got*)

Award, Anita Baker wins Best R&B/Urban Contemporary Album of The Year (*Giving You the Best That I Got*)

Award, E.U. wins Best R&B/Urban Contemporary Single, Group or Duo (*Da Butt*)

Award, DJ Jazzy Jeff & The Fresh Prince wins Best Rap Album (*He's the DJ, I'm the Rapper*)

1989

MTV Video Music Awards – 6th Annual

Video of the Year: *Neil Young*– "This Note's for You"

Best Male Video: *Elvis Costello*– "Veronica"

Best Female Video: *Paula Abdul*– "Straight Up"

Best Group Video: *Living Colour*– "Cult of Personality"

Best New Artist in a Video: *Living Colour*– "Cult of Personality"

Best Rap Video: *DJ Jazzy Jeff & The Fresh Prince*– "Parents Just Don't Understand"

Best Dance Video: *Paula Abdul*– "Straight Up"

Video from a Film: *U2 & B.B. King Best*– "When Love Comes to Town"

Best Breakthrough Video: *Art of Noise & Tom Jones*– "Kiss"

Best Stage Performance in a Video: *Living Colour*– "Cult of Personality"

Best Direction in a Video: *Madonna*– "Express Yourself," Directed by David Fincher

Best Choreography in a Video: *Paula Abdul*– "Straight Up"

Best Special Effects in a Video: *Michael Jackson*– "Leave Me Alone," Special Effects by Jim Blashfield

Viewer's Choice: *Madonna*– "Like a Prayer"

1989 Urban American Grammy Award Recipients – 31st Annual

Award, 1989: Bobby McFerrin wins Record of the Year *(Don't Worry, Be Happy)*.

Award, 1989: Bobby McFerrin wins Song of the Year *(Don't Worry, Be Happy)*.

Award, 1989: Tracy Chapman wins Best New Artist.

Award, 1989: The Winans win Best Gospel Performance by a Duo or Group, Choir or Chorus *(The Winans Live at Carnegie Hall)*.

Award, 1989: Aretha Franklin wins Best Soul Gospel Performance, Female *(One Lord, One Faith, One Baptism)*.

Award, 1989: BeBe Winans wins Best Soul Gospel Performance, Male *(Abundant Life)*.

Award, 1989: Take 6 wins Best Soul Gospel Performance by a Duo or Group, Choir or Chorus *(Take 6)*.

Award, 1989: Betty Carter wins Best Jazz Performance, Female *(Look What I Got!)*.

Award, 1989: Bobby McFerrin wins Best Jazz Vocal Performance, Male *(Brothers)*.

Award, 1989: Take 6 wins Best Jazz Performance, Duo or Group, *(Spread Love)*.

Award, 1989: Roberto Carlos wins Best Latin Pop Performance, *(Roberto Carlos)*.

Award, 1989: Ruben Blades wins Best Tropical Latin Performance, *(Antecedente)*.

Award, 1989: Linda Ronstadt wins Best Mexican-American Performance, *(Canciones de Mi Padre)*.

Award, 1989: Tracy Chapman wins Best Pop Vocal Performance, Female, *(Fast Car)*.

Award, 1989: Bobby Mcferrin wins Best Pop Vocal Performance, Male *(Don't Worry, Be Happy)*.

Award, 1989: Anita Baker wins Best R&B Vocal Performance, Female *(Giving You the Best That I Got)*.

Award, 1989: Terence Trent D'Arby wins Best R&B Vocal Performance, Male *(Introducing the Hardline According to Terence Trent D'arby)*

Award, 1989: Gladys Knight & The Pips win Best R&B Performance by a Duo or Group with Vocal *(Love Overbroad)*.

Award, 1989: Chick Corea wins Best R&B Instrumental Performance, Orchestra, Group or Soloist *(Light Years)*.

Award, 1989: Jazzy Jeff & The Fresh Prince win Best Rap Performance *(Parents Just Don't Understand)* **Would be the first for a Rap Group to win a Grammy, and this marked the 1st year that the Rap category was added to the Grammy Awards.*

Award, 1989: Ziggy Marley & the Melody Makers win Best Reggae Recording *(Conscious Party)*.

Award, 1989: Carlos Santana win Best Rock Instrumental Performance, Orchestra, Group or Soloist *(Blues for Salvador)*.

Award, 1989: Tina Turner win Best Rock Vocal Performance, Female *(Tina Live in Europe)*.

Award, 1989: Jesse Jackson wins Best Spoken Word or Non-Musical Recording *(Speech by Rev. Jesse Jackson)*.

*Winning the Grammy was bittersweet for the Phila rap duo and the culture, the industry showed us all what they thought of Hip Hop when they didn't even broadcast Jazzy Jeff's and The Fresh Prince's award acceptance live like they did the other recipients. The rap duo would spark a boycott against the Grammy's soon after.

1989 – Billboards Year End – Hot 100 Singles

1989	Urban Music 31% of Billboard's Year-End Hot 100	31%
2	Bobby Brown – *My Prerogative*	MCA
4	Paula Abdul – *Straight Up*	Virgin
5	Janet Jackson – *Miss You Much*	A&M
6	Paula Abdul – *Cold Hearted*	Virgin
8	Milli Vanilli – *Girl You Know It's True*	Arista
10	Anita Baker – *Giving You the Best That I Got*	Elektra
14	Gloria Estefan – *Don't Wanna Lose You*	Epic
16	Milli Vanilli – *Girl I'm Gonna Miss You*	Arista
19	Bobby Brown – *On Our Own*	MCA
21	Milli Vanilli – *Blame It on the Rain*	Arista
28	Milli Vanilli – *Baby Don't Forget My Number*	Arista
30	Paula Abdul – *Forever Your Girl*	Virgin
33	Tone Loc – *Wild Thing*	Delicious Vinyl
36	Neneh Cherry – *Buffalo Stance*	Virgin
42	Young MC – *Bust A Move*	Delicious Vinyl
44	Prince - *Batdance*	Warner Bros.
46	Jody Watley – *Real Love*	MCA
48	Bobby Brown – *Every Little Step*	MCA
64	Karyn White – *The Way You Love Me*	Warner Bros.
65	Tone Loc – *Funky Cold Medina*	Delicious Vinyl
67	Natalie Cole – *Miss You Like Crazy*	EMI
69	Karyn White – *Secret Rendezvous*	Warner Bros.
75	Surface – *Shower Me With Your Love*	Columbia
80	Bobby Brown - *Roni*	MCA
89	Vanessa Williams – *Dreamin'*	Wing
90	Babyface – *It's No Crime*	Solar
92	Donna Summer – *This Time I Know It's Real*	Warner Bros.
93	Michael Jackson – *Smooth Criminal*	Epic
95	Bobby Brown – *Rock Wit'cha*	MCA
96	Sa-Fire – *Thinking of You*	Cutting
100	Soul II Soul – *Keep on Movin*	Virgin

1989 – Record Labels in Hip Hop Music

Delicious Vinyl: Founded 1987 in the city of LA by DJ's, Matt Dike and Michael Ross, the two-approach production by blending rock and rap beats to deliver a sound that spawned platinum hits. 1989 was a chart-topping year for the label, with triple platinum selling, *Tone Loc's* #1 break out pop hits, *Wild Thang* & *Funky Cold Madina* along with chart topping platinum hit, *Bust a Move* by *Young MC,* and the emergence of *Def Jef*. Delicious Vinyl had a foothold on what came to be known as Rock/Pop Rap and raked in plenty of coin.

Dangerous Music: Oakland rapper, *Too Short* continued to reel in fans with the release of his 1989 album. A few complained about the content, but the true Hip Hop heads that lived the stories he told, gave Short their full support and so did those who were mesmerized by his explicit lyrics.

Rap-A-Lot: The Houston label found its niche with their most successful act, *The Geto Boys*. Rap-A-Lot was quickly picking up momentum, and the culture noticed and started checking for Texas MC's.

Tommy Boy: Further establishing itself as a force in Hip Hop, Tommy Boy gained more notoriety with the album release of Native Tongue members, *Queen Latifah* and *De La Soul*. It should also be noted that the labels founder, Tom Silverman, was also VP of ***Warner Bros. Records*** during this time and it was no coincidence that Warner Bros. was the distributor for Tommy Boy music during his time as VP of Warner Bros. *(1985-2002)*.

Cold Chillin: Marley Marl and the Juice Crew stood tall among men with rapid hits and a growing catalog to boot. Big Daddy Kane held the title of God MC and backed it with deadly content and a smooth persona. Roxanne Shante, Biz Markie, Kool G Rap & Polo held their own as the legend of Cold Chillin continued to blossom. Now in their 2nd year of a ***Warner Bros.*** 5-year distribution deal, the label was set for the big stage.

Sleeping Bag: With the release of four projects this year, its subsidiary ***Fresh*** showed they really weren't sleeping at all. EPMD, Nice & Smooth, Just-Ice, and Stezo all smashed the airwaves with cult classics making the label a force in the industry.

Wild Pitch: The label released their new artists, Chill Rob G and Gang Starr this year, and placed in the Top 20 on the Billboard charts with Gang Starr's *Positivity*. Guru's rap style displayed a word play on diction that kept the fans intrigue.

Def Jam: The King of Rap labels didn't let the culture down with the release of LL Cool J's new album, along with another classic from the Beastie Boys and the success of 3rd Bass' gold selling album, *The Cactus Album*. The rap styles of 3rd Bass members, MC Search and Pete Nice, added yet another cool layer to the Hip Hop genre.

Jive: Out of all the labels, Jive had found itself as the vehicle that carried the first ever Grammy Award winning Rap group. When Jazzy Jeff and The Fresh Prince walked across that stage to receive the Grammy Award for *Parents Just Don't Understand*, it was a major step in history for Hip Hop.

Ruthless: Riding high from the success of N.W.A., Eazy-E continued to ride the wave with the release of *No One Can Do it Better* by the vivid story teller, The D.O.C. His hottest tracks, *It's Funky Enough* and *The D.O.C. & The Doctor* peeked at #1 on the charts for two weeks straight.

First Priority: The Queen MC known as MC Lyte continued to cement her status as one of the top lyricists in the game. Her most noted track, *Cha Cha Cha* rocked the air waves, but it would be the lyrical assault displayed in *Slave 2 the Rhythm* that kept the competition on guard, while *I Am the Lyte, Shut the Eff Up! (H**), Stop, Look, Listen,* & *Cappuccino* became cult jewels and pushed the album to #6 on the charts.

Priority: Usually playing the background as the distribution channel in the partnership. Priority released the debut album *We're in This Together* by California based group, Low Profile, whose members included DJ Aladdin and a young WC.

Sire: With the release of ICE-T's newest album the label played it's roll of supporting and pushing content that many other labels would not touch. This same label also was home to acts like Madonna and Depeche Mode.

Atlantic: The label had a great year with the success of new era artist, Kwame, Cool C, Craig G, and Breeze. With cult classics, *I Gotta Habit* & *Glamorous Life* by Cool C, along with *The Rhythm* by Kwame; Atlantic label Hip Hop execs actually looked like geniuses.

Warner Bros: The Jungle Brothers, aka JB's, released their sophomore album under the industry giant, but only reached moderate success commercially. It would be their Afrocentric persona and jazz infused sound that paved the way for the crew of the Native Tongue collective.

Pandisc: The Miami Bass label found commercial success with the release of Young & Restless, whose hottest singles, *Poison Ivy* and *B Girls*, reached #104 on the Billboard 200, while their music video gained massive airplay on MTV.

Profile: A new kid was on the block and he went by the name of Special Ed. His lyrics and confident persona rocked the culture and kept the competition on their feet. Ed's debut album *Youngest in Charge* spawned some classic hits that pushed sales over 500 thousand copies in his debut.

Select: The combination of Chubb Rock and hot producer Hitman Howie Tee, who is also Chubb's cousin, kept Select in the game. The Chubbster had a swag all his own and it resonated well with the culture.

Big League: The Oakland, California label made traction this year with the release of 415, the groups most noted MC's, Richie Rich and D-Loc, would add to the Bay area Hip Hop scene laid by Too-Short.

Arista: With a hot classic on their hands by 3 X Dope, Arista remained relevant in the rap game for the time being. But it would be a joint venture between Arista, Baby Face, and L.A. Reid this year creating LaFace Records who would introduce an entirely new revenue stream to the industry, which would rise from the New South; LaFace's home would be the ATL.

Bon Ami: Founded by *Sylvia Robinson* after her **Sugar Hill Records** folded in 1985, the Godmother of Hip Hop took another shot at the game by signing and releasing New Jersey rap group, The New Style who would eventually change their name to *Naughty by Nature*.

Attic: Originally founded in 1974 by Tom Williams, and Alexander Mair in Canada. The Canadian indie label hit pay dirt with the release of Toronto, Ontario MC, Maestro Fresh-Wes' Top 40 hit *Let Your Backbone Slide*. Wes' rap skills delivered on every point, so much so that his music crossed borders during a time when few outsiders got any respect in the American founded Hip Hop Genre.

Epic: Known for its diversity, the label stayed true to form by releasing the debut album *Word Power* by Divine Styler. His most noted track, *Ain't Sayin' Nothin* resonated with the culture during a time when Hip Hop also displayed a conscious.

Cheetah: Originally founded in Orlando, Florida, 1988 by Tom Reich the label was mostly known for Miami Bass music. Cheetah would make its bones this year off the success of DJ Magic Mike, a Dj known across the country for his Miami Bass mix tapes.

Rhyme Syndicate: From the camp of ICE-T, the label released the debut album *Notorious* by Donald D. This would be the 2nd artist of ICE-T's Rhyme Syndicate to release a debut album this year (*Divine Styler*).

Next Plateau: Riding high from the success of Salt N Pepa, the label dropped the debut album of female rapper, MC Antoinette. Her album *Who's the Boss?* peaked at #47 on the charts. Antoinette received most of her buzz from the underground battles she had with MC Lyte. Although the album made the charts, she didn't receive the same fire as her competitor, MC Lyte.

MCA: After saving the label from bankruptcy the label's head, Irving Azoff would leave this year to form **Giant Records**. MCA would create a new holding company this year called MCA Music Entertainment Group which was headed by Al Teller, who was also former President of United Artist Records. After the formation of the new holding company, its parent company, MCA, Inc. was purchased this year by the Matasushita group—(*Now who owns the catalog?*). Amongst all the change, the label released the debut album of Freddie Foxxx.

Orpheus: Releasing the debut album of Arabian Prince, *Brother Arab* placed the label in uncharted waters, but as time would tell, change is good.

Capitol: The Grandfather record label made history again this year by releasing Cuban MC, Mellow Man Ace's debut album *Escape from Havana*, which reached #69 on the charts and resonated with the culture.

As the 80's came to an end, Hip Hop had grown from a small culture raised in the New York ghettos to an international business. Most of the independent rap labels found themselves partnering with major labels to take advantage of their distribution channels. This made the music available to the masses across the globe, but it came at a cost. Many artists found themselves giving up creative control of their content as well as the freedom to release their music when and where they chose. It all came to a head when N.W.A along with ICE-T, and several other artists released tracks expressing how they felt about law enforcement and the way they treated minorities in the hood.

Hip Hop at its core is authentic and un-apologetic, so it should have been no surprise to anyone when *F*** the Police* by N.W.A and *Cop Killer* by ICE-T (*Body Count*), found its way to the masses. The culture embraced the tracks because we understood 100 percent why the artists made them. It would be those same major labels that backed the Hip-Hop labels with distribution who started crying like a bunch of babies. The government, along with politicians and law enforcement applied pressure on the labels that distributed the material, forcing them to either reject many upcoming projects with similar content or end the distribution deals all together. This thing we call Hip-Hop had evolved into a conscious platform and major labels found themselves in a dilemma — *to remain a player in this billion-dollar machine or give way to the crybabies*. While the culture was yelling FREE SPEECH!, the major labels ran for the hills, and it would only get worse before it got better… or did it? This my friends began the regulation of Hip-Hop, and it all started to change once those majors returned from those hills.

"Self-destruction, bro, you're goin low

How can you kill a person you don't really-even know?

In jail, you played hard until one slapped you silly

Turned you over like girlie and rode you like a sissy"

-WC *(How Ya Livin')*

Most Influential MC's, Producers, and DJ's of the Decade (80's)

A Crown is awarded to DJ's and Producers. **5 being the max.**

A Mic is awarded to the MC's. **5 being the max.**

Kurtis Blow

Beginning in 1980 to 1985, since the release of his first single, Kurtis Blow remained relevant to the culture with several hit tracks such as, "The Breaks", "If I ruled the World," "Basketball," and many more hits. He increased his contribution in 1984 when he produced several hit records for **The Fat Boys,** *all while producing hits for himself as well. For this I salute Kurtis Blow with 5 Mics and 5 Crowns as one of the most influential Hip Hop legends. His contribution was pivotal in setting the format for how the talented MC slash producer could leverage their talents in the Hip Hop industry.*

Too Short

Since the release of his first album in 1983, the Bay Area MC continued to drop music for the entire decade. When the majority of Hip Hop was coming from New York, Too Short represented Oakland, California and the Bay with his own original style. His explicit lyrics hit the culture in 1983 and gained momentum through 1989 with every album released. Short opened the doors for many Bay area rappers and industry professionals alike. Because of his continuous contribution I give Too Short 5 mics for being one of the most influential legendary MC's of this decade.

The Sugar Hill Gang

If it wasn't for the fortitude and experience of Sylvia Robinson, the charisma of Wonder Mike, Big Bank Hank, and Master Gee, along with Chic's hit record "Good Times" where would Hip Hop be? The combination of the above brought us, "Rappers Delight," this track hit radio with a rocket, thanks to the "Good Times" instrumental. Mainstream America heard, for the first time, what we were jamming to in the underground for the past few years. Unbeknownst to the masses, this would be the birth of the incorporation of Hip Hop. Rappers Delight broke down barriers and opened new ears. For this reason alone, I give The Sugar Hill Gang 5 Mic's for being one of the most influential groups in Hip Hop.

Afrika Bambaata

Since the release of his 1981 album, Afrika Bambaata has contributed more to the culture than music alone. Credited as founder of the Zulu Nation, Bambaata headed a movement of consciousness all while introducing a new sound of Hip Hop called electro. The iconic track "Planet Rock" became a cult classic, and the soundtrack for many Break Dance crews. This Hip Hop legend is meshed into the fabric of the culture and for that he deserves 5 Crowns as one of the most influential Hip Hop legends.

Grand Master Flash and The Furious 5

In 1982, right when the masses started to listen, it was Grand Master Flash and the Furious 5 that delivered "The Message." When everyone else had you dancin', this crew had you thinking as they broadcasted the life of the Ghetto over national airwaves. Every Hip Hop head found themselves not only reciting the lyrics word-for-word, but many could identify with the track as they also lived it every day. Although the group's formation would be short-lived, I salute Grand Master Flash and The Furious 5 with 5 Crowns and 5 Mic's for being one of the most influential legendary Hip Hop groups.

Whodini

From 1983-1987 it was almost guaranteed that you would find one or more of Whodini's track's topping the charts. With hits like, "Friends," "Big Mouth," "Five Minutes of Funk," and "One Love," to name a few. The culture adopted many of Whodini's songs as soundtracks to their everyday lives. The trio's fluent and realistic lyrics over funky beats earned them 5 Mic's as one of Hip Hop's most influential rap groups.

RUN DMC

1984 ushered in a new rap style of deadly lyrics over hard hitting, rock and roll beats. The Kings of this style would be none other than RUN DMC. The trio released breakthrough records like "Walk This Way" and "Kings of Rock" which broke down both video and radio air play barriers. This created a new pathway for the rapidly growing culture, while grabbing the attention of a new fan base. Russell Simmons along with his Def Jam and Rush Management team took Hip Hop to a whole new level, and RUN DMC led the way. It goes without saying that the trio of RUN, JMJ, and DMC is one of the most influential rap groups in our culture and earned 5 Mic's.

Herbie Hancock & DJ Grand Mixer DXT

As the masses were beginning to become acquainted with Hip Hop, it would be the bold move of musician and producer, Herbie Hancock along with DJ Grand Mixer DXT, to take the Hip Hop DJ styles and technique that we were jamming to daily to an entirely new level. The duo released "Rock It," a genius music track that included mixing, scratching, and a cutting-edge video that earned the track a Grammy. While the masses were obviously intrigued by "Rock It," I have to give credit to Herbie Hancock and DJ Grand Mixer DXT for taking a chance on Hip Hop; for this I give them 4 Crowns.

Egyptian Lover

Known mostly for his electro sound and cult classic, "Egypt," Egyptian Lover won over the break dance crews with energetic beats and bass drops. At a time win electro Hip Hop was popular, Egyptian Lover was one of the top producers in the game and represented the sunny state of California. Although he only released a few records, I have to give this legendary producer 3 Crowns for his early influence in the culture.

Fat Boys

In the midst of the braggadocios era, three MC's carved their own niches with a comedic storyline, a human beat box, and funky beats that resonated with the nation. The Fat Boys made fun of their own weight, but were also very lyrical MC's. This combination raked in millions from record and movie sales. The trio sparked a flame that would ignite an entirely different lane for Hip Hop. Also known as the Disco 3, this iconic rap group definitely earned 5 Mic's for their influential contribution to the 80's.

Beastie Boys

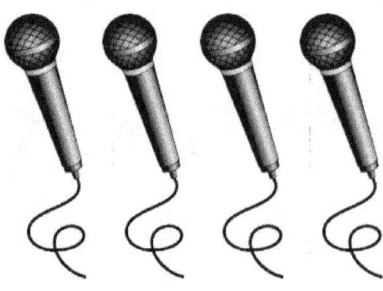

The Beastie Boys being the first white boy rap group to hit the scene, brought a new fan base to Hip Hop while opening doors to like MC's. Behind the production of Rick Rubin and Russell Simmons, the trio followed the RUN DMC blueprint for success. Although their album catalogue is quite short, the group did manage to release a few classics while on the Def Jam label. "Paul Revere," "Fight for Your Right," "Brass Monkey," and "No Sleep Till Brooklyn," earned the group 4 Mic's as one of the most influential groups of the 80's.

Newcleus

With a combination of bass, electro funk and synthesizers, Newcleus turned the culture on its ear when they released "Jam On it" and "Jam On Revenge (The Wikki Wikki Song)." Break-dancers, B-Boys and B-Girls, went crazy and bum rushed the dance floors every time the beat dropped, and it rocked for years and years. Newcleus introduced a new sound that struck a chord with anyone listening. The groups career was short lived, but their music will forever bring flashbacks to those who grew up on it and bob the heads of anyone listening for the first time.

U.T.F.O

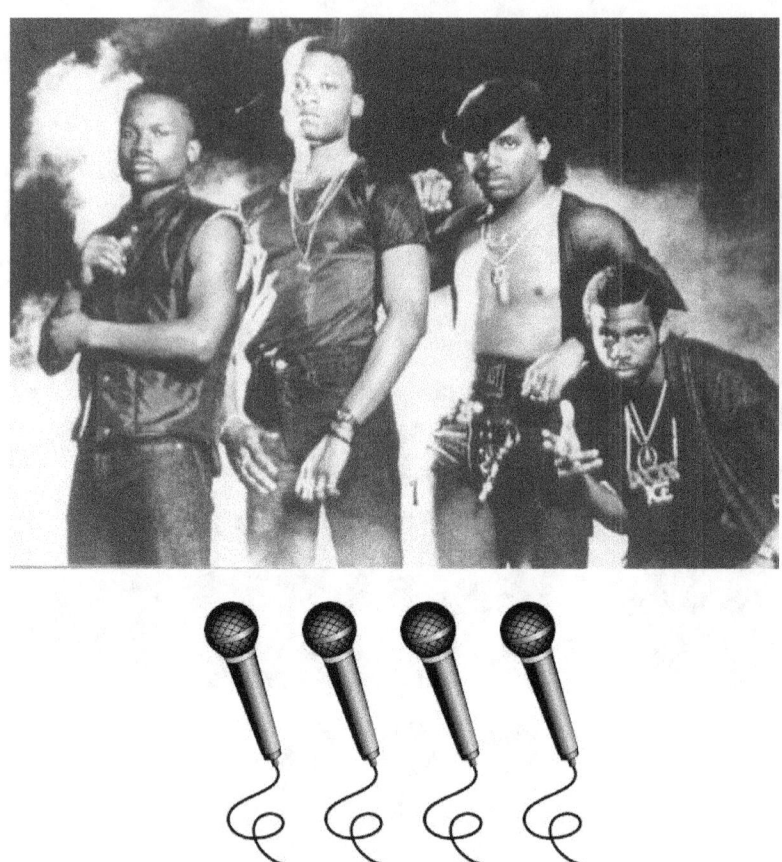

The group gained most of their recognition from their cult classic "Roxxanne Roxxanne" which sparked one of the longest rap battles ever and launched the careers of several female MC's who would carry the Roxxanne moniker. Behind the production of Full Force, this four-man crew built a brand that would be responsible for one of the most iconic rap competitions in Hip Hop known as the Roxxanne Wars. U.T.F.O and this one song opened so many doors on so many levels, it launched the careers of Roxxanne Shante', The Real Roxxanne, and even involved legendary DJ's and producer's Marley Marl and Mr. Magic.

LL Cool J

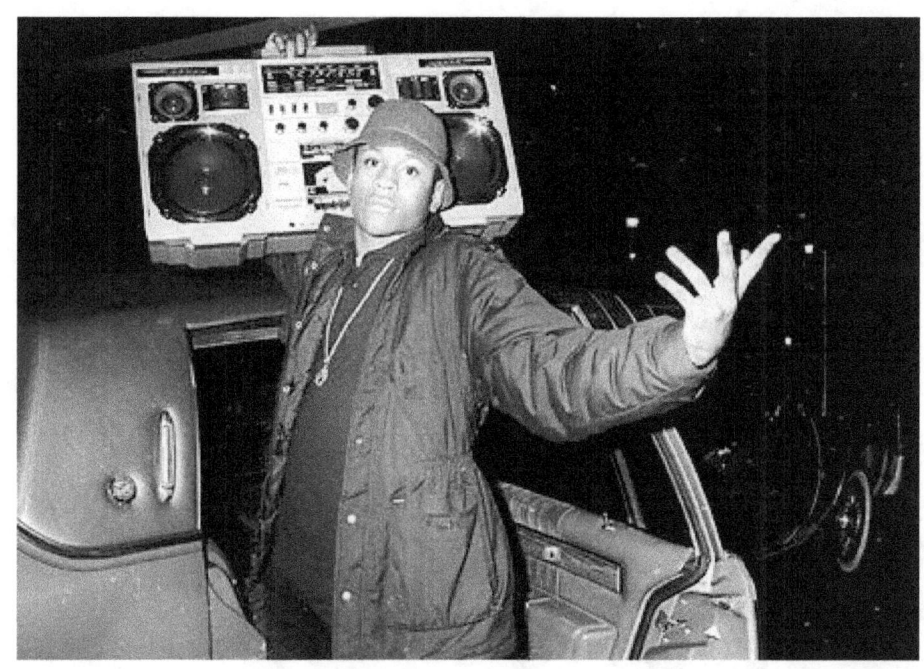

It would be the lyric's, style, and charisma that would bring LL Cool J and Def Jam together to form a perfect union. On the back of LL Cool J, the Flagship Hip Hop label raked in millions and continued to build its empire as LL led the way and set records for the culture. Even though Def Jam acquired several other Artist along the way, LL continued to sell out arenas and make platinum hits. With cult classics like, "My Radio," "Rock the Bells," and B-side hits like "Dear Yvette" and "Kanday," the 80's were just the beginning for this influential legendary MC.

Roxanne Shante'

Roxanne emerged on the scene when she released a response record to U.T.F.O's "Roxanne Roxanne" produced by the camp of Marly Marl and Mr. Magic aka the Juice Crew. The single caught fire and led to the Roxanne Wars, several other female MC's would emerge from the fall out with the moniker Roxanne but Shante' held down the originator title with her tight lyrics and bold dis statements towards U.T.F.O and its members. If it wasn't for U.T.F.O there wouldn't even be a Roxanne Shante' and the culture would've missed-out on all the great contributions she gave to Hip Hop, this legendary MC influenced the 80's tremendously and will forever be one of the best whoever did it.

MC Shan

MC Shan an official member of the Juice Crew represented Queens, N.Y to the fullest, his most noted track "The Bridge" is a cult classic. It was also the track that sparked the BDP battle track "The Bridge is Over" This led to one of the first rap battles and launched the careers of KRS-1 and Scott La Rock, aka BDP. Produced by Marley Marl, MC Shan would drop several other iconic tracks that influenced the 80's culture.

Kool Moe Dee

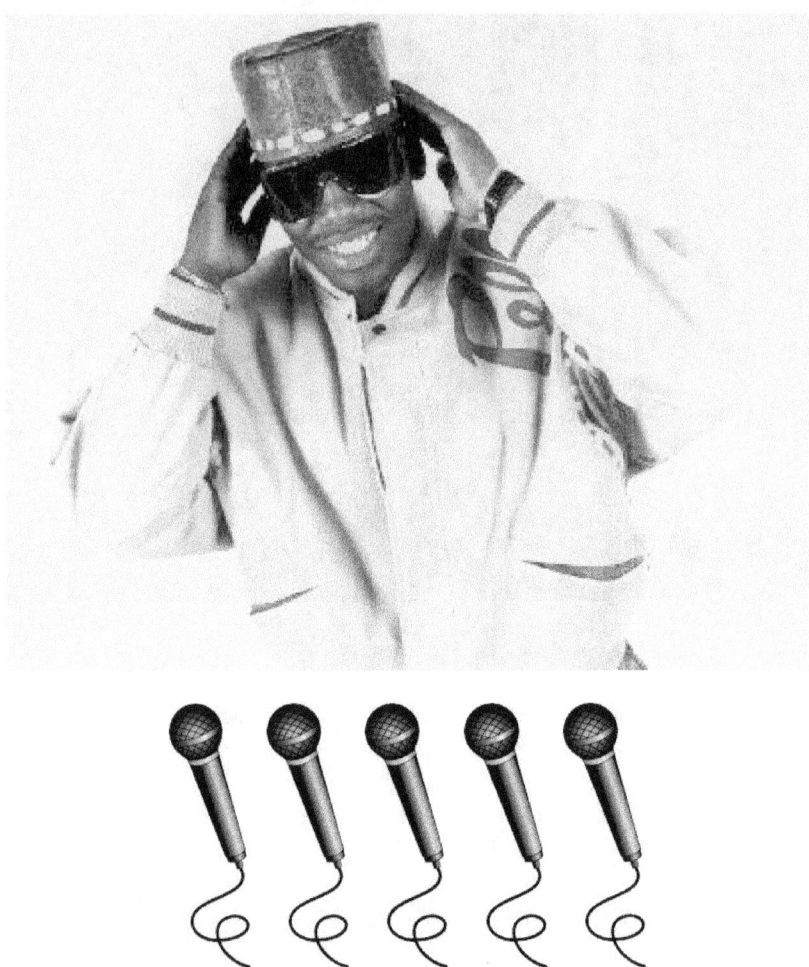

If there was a MC who paid his dues, it was Kool Moe Dee. Moe hit the scene during the late 70's as a member of the Treacherous Three who released pioneering classics, like "Feel the Heartbeat" and "Body Rock". Both records borrowed instrumentals from R&B and Rock & Roll music respectfully. Moe would embark on a solo career after the 3 disbanded in 84. As a solo artist he dropped classics, "Go See the Doctor," "How You Like Me Now," and the "Wild Wild West." It is well noted that Kool Moe Dee accused LL Cool J of stealing his rap style which led to several battle records between the two iconic MC's; from the early "Santa Rap" to the classics that followed, this legendary MC definitely left his mark on the 80's.

Schoolly D

Credited as one of the first Philadelphia MC's, Schoolly D was the total package, he was a pioneer of gangsta rap, a producer, and owned his record label. Schoolly branded his own style of rap and gained a pretty decent following. His most noted track "P.S.K. What Does It Mean'?" became a cult classic and inspired several other gangster rappers' content and rap styles.

MC Hammer

When it came to Hip Hop, Hammer broke all the rules as we knew it. While largely accepted by the main stream, he was branded by the culture as our first pop rap artist. His rap style was subpar by our standards as well as his attire. MC Hammer, however, was a perfect fit for the machine we called the industry. He was bankable! His impeccable choreography, funky beats, flashy clothes, and signature pants was entertaining and that's what sold records. While we were busy saying, "Hammer aint Hip Hop!" Mainstream America, and overseas for that matter, purchased his records by the millions and Hammer laughed all the way to the bank. Many labels followed this new pop rap pattern and found success while some weren't so lucky.

Steady B

The Philadelphia native made his mark in the 80's with classic hits and several collaborations with fellow Phila emcees. Although his time in the game was short lived, Steady B clearly left his mark on the culture.

2 Live Crew

When most of Hip Hop generated from the North, it was the Miami Bass sound that rocked the South. 2 Live Crew led by Luke and their mix of Miami Bass with explicit content introduced an entirely new feel to the culture. Their fast-paced music and sexually laced stage shows built a brand that resonated with the freaky conscious of Hip Hop.

Salt N Pepa

Salt N Pepa along with Dj Spindarella began their journey as the first successful female rap group towards the end of the decade. Salt N Pepa released hits that would sell out arenas, pack dance floors, and quickly built a fan base who would support their iconic careers under the production of Herby "Luv Bug."

Joe Ski Love

Joe Ski Love's chart topping single "Pee Wee's Dance" took the industry by storm. The track was based on a popular kid's TV show at the time "Pee Wee's Playhouse" and the Pee Wee Herman dance that was performed by the show's star character. Everyone was doing the Pee Wee Herman dance, young and old across the nation. The combination of Hip Hop and a popular TV show made for a historic and influential moment in the culture.

ICE – T

ICE – T introduced the playa, hustler, gangsta life style from the streets of California to the culture. His cult classic "Six in the Morning" heavily influenced the game and was an originator of gangsta rap music.

NWA

N***** With Attitudes, aka NWA struck a chord with the nation when they hit the scene. Their content boasted the life from the streets of Compton, California. At the time, the world really had no idea about the murder rate of the city, police brutality, and how gang banging ruled the Compton streets. Their controversial hit "F*** the Police" broke down barriers, ruffled a lot of feathers and said what many were too scared to say. This brand became the roots of gangsta rap and it sold millions without radio play all produced by Dre and Yella.

BDP

After the release of "Criminal Minded" a cult classic, BDP would undergo a significant image change due to the untimely and violent death of DJ Scott La Rock. KRS-1 dedicated himself to educating and uplifting the culture which sparked the "Stop the Violence Movement" and H.E.A.L. (Human Education Against Lies). BDP also produced tracks for other acts such as Steady B and Just Ice to name a few. From this moment on BDP front man KRS-1 would take on the moniker "The Teacher" and is considered to be one of the Top lyricists in the game.

Doug E Fresh & The Get Fresh Crew

Trendsetting sounds and lyrics best describes Doug E Fresh & The Get Fresh Crew. Classic hits like "The Show" & "Ladi Dadi" separated Doug E Fresh and the Crew from the rest, also known as "the Human Beat Box" or "The Entertainer;" it would be his collabo with then MC Ricky D now known as Slick Rick that left large impression on our Hip Hop Culture.

Public Enemy

One would only need to listen to "Shut Em Down", "Yo Bum Rush the Show" or "Don't Believe the Hype" to see that PE was serious about the message in their music. Some emcees produced tracks to make you bob your head, some released tracks to get lifted to, but PE, make no mistake about it, wanted to crack you in the dome with conscious messages. This Bomb Squad produced tracks laced with Chuck D lyrics and Flava Flav's energy against the backdrop of the S1W's and Professor Griff kept your mind influenced and body moving as Terminator X ripped the vinyl.

Jazzy Jeff & The Fresh Prince

Representing Phila, this duo quickly gained commercial recognition with the success of their 1989 hit, "Parent's Just Don't Understand" that also won them a Grammy. Jazzy Jeff's DJ skills rocked crowds and jammed dance floors, as the Fresh Prince's story telling painted vivid pictures that the culture related to on different levels, comedic or serious. This however was only be the beginning of the duo's success.

Eric B & Rakim

Before the emergence of Eric B & Rakim, Hip Hop was already a growing phenomenon, but this iconic group took us to an entirely different level. In 1987, Eric B's mastered art of sampling mixed with the deadly lyrics of Rakim brought us, "Paid in Full," "Move the Crowd," "My Melody," "I Ain't No Joke," and "I Know You Got Soul." It was these combinations of hits that heavily influenced the already innovative culture to take Hip Hop to the next level.

Heavy D & The Boyz

In 1987, This Money Earnin Mt. Vernon crew climbed to the top of the charts with their debut album, led by emcee Heavy D, coined as the "Overweight Lover" brought a conscious funk along with energetic dance moves to the culture. Heavy D made big guys look sexy and agile, while he blessed us with good music and entertaining dance moves.

Sweet Tee

In 1986 emcee Sweet T released "It's My Beat" which became an instant classic and influenced many aspiring female artists of that era. Sweet T gained the respect of the culture as she opened doors for the next generation and displayed her talents as an iconic legend of Hip Hop.

Big Daddy Kane

1988 ushered in several prolific emcee's, one of the most dominant being Big Daddy Kane. Kane proclaimed greatness from the start and his catalog proved it, coined as one of the top lyricists in the game, the end of the 80's would only be the beginning for this Hip Hop legend.

EPMD

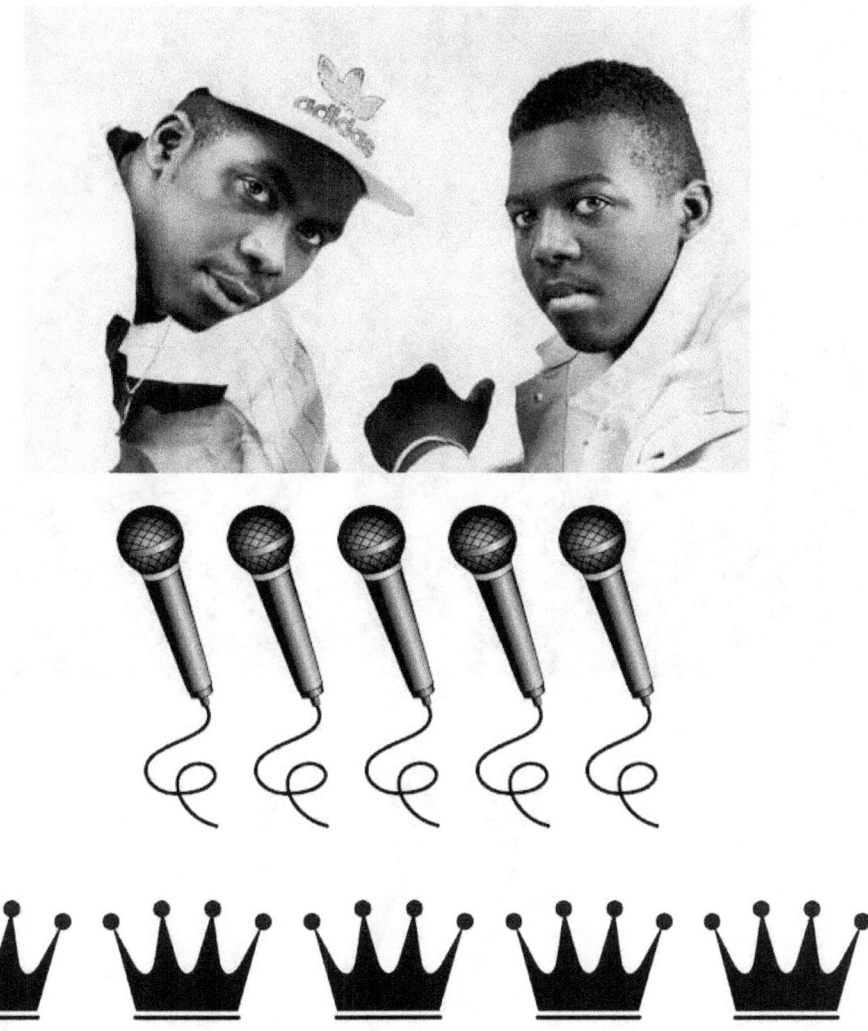

The class of '88 proved to be one of the best for the Hip Hop culture to date. EPMD delivered with classic hits, on point production, and a swagger that laid the foundation for a successful future. Eric Sermon alone would be responsible for producing several hit records for EPMD and several other artists.

Sir Mix-A-Lot

This Seattle Washington emcee, broke into the game with his iconic hit "Posse' On Broadway." He would be one of the few rappers to gain Hip Hop recognition from outside of New York or California.

Biz Markie

Another '88 classmen, Biz Markie came onto the scene when the beat box was a big part of the culture. Biz introduced his own style of rap to the culture and ran with it and released legendary tracks, "Vapors'," "Albee Square Mall," "Biz is Goin Off," "Make the Music with Your Mouth Biz," and the comedic classic, "Pickin' Boogers."

MC Lyte

The class of '88, just keeps getting better and better. MC Lyte hit the scene and quickly rose to the top of the lyricist chain. She dropped two albums at the end of the 80's; "Lyte as a Rock" in '88 and "Eyes on This" in '89, both albums included legendary hit records like "Paper Thin," "I Am the Lyte," and "10% Dis," which is considered to be one of the culture's hottest dis records.

Kid 'n Play

1988 classmen, Kid 'n Play created their own space within the culture. Their image became a commercial brand and dance moves were woven into our culture. Kid n' Play would bank on their commercial success and take it to the big screen creating a blue print for those to come.

Slick Rick

In 1988, MC Ricky debuted his first solo album as Slick Rick after departing with Doug E Fresh and the Get Fresh Crew. We, the fans, were already accustomed to the profound story telling of Slick Rick, but this album took it to the next level with legendary tracks, "Children's Story," "The Rulers Back," "Teenage Love," "Hey Young World," and "Treat Her Like a Prostitute."

Tone Loc

Tone Loc with his raspy voice and commercial rap appeal crushed the airwaves, TV and main stream America with his chart toppers, "Wild Thing" & "Funky Cold Madena." 1989 was a year of diversity and Tone Loc held his place at the top of the charts with a style that included a mixture of Hip Hop over Rock & Roll beats.

De La Soul

In 1989 the year of diversity, De la Soul painted broad bright strokes over the culture with their debut album "3 Feet High and Rising." It would the signature single, "Potholes in My Lawn" that made us take notice as we Hip Hop heads tried to break the cipher. It was totally different, the music, the lyrics, their clothes, but we were all in, especially when we heard "Buddy" and 'Me Myself and I"; De La Soul was the new Sh**t.

The D.O.C.

In 1989 the year of diversity, The D.O.C. made his mark on the culture in many ways. His debut album "No One Can Do It Better" topped the charts with several hit singles, but it would be his writing contribution to Ruthless and Death Row records that would influence the gangsta rap culture.

Queen Latifah

In 1989 the year of diversity, Queen Latifah stamped her mark on the culture with a conscious female empowerment message. Her debut album's, "All Hail the Queen," iconic track "Ladies First" laid the foundation for the Queen to begin her reign.

Kwame

Kwame emerged as the total opposite of what was to be expected in the Hip Hop culture. We had our sneakers, chains, hats, belts, and so did Kwame, but his brand was polka dots, signature died high top fades and a live band. Needless to say, polka dot ties and shirts experienced a rise in sales as some Hip Hop heads embraced Kwame's style and joined the band wagon.

Dj Magic Mike

DJ Magic Mike was very influential in the Miami Bass scene and covered significant ground as a DJ and producer. This would only be the beginning for this Dj/Producer as we all began to witness the evolution of Miami Bass and its effects on the South.

Marley Marl

1980's Production Credits

MC Shan

Roxanne Shante'

Biz Markie

Big Daddy Kane

Kool G Rap & Polo

Craig G

Steady B

Spoonie G

Hurby "Luv Bug" Azor

Pictured center

1980's Production Credits

Sweet Tee

Salt N Pepa

Dana Dane

Kid N' Play

Kwame

Teddy Riley

1980's Production Credits

Kool Moe Dee

Big Daddy Kane

Heavy D & The Boys

Spoonie G

Doug E Fresh

Creator of New Jack Swing

Bomb Squad

1980's Production Credits

Public Enemy

Ice Cube

Slick Rick

3rd Bass

Dust Brothers

1980's Production Credits

Tone Loc

Mellow Man Ace

Young MC

Def Jef

The 45 King

1980's Production Credits

Queen Latifah

Chill Rob G

Gang Starr

Lawrence Goodman

1980's Production Credits

Steady B

Jazzy Jeff & The Fresh Prince

Cool C

3X Dope

Rick Rubin

1980's Production Credits

RUN D.M.C.

LL Cool J

Beastie Boys

Dr. Dre

1980's Production Credits

World Class Wrecking Crew

NWA

Eazy E

The D.O.C.

JJ Fad

Larry Smith

1980's Production Credits

Kurtis Blow

Whodini

RUN DMC

Fat Boys

L.A. Posse

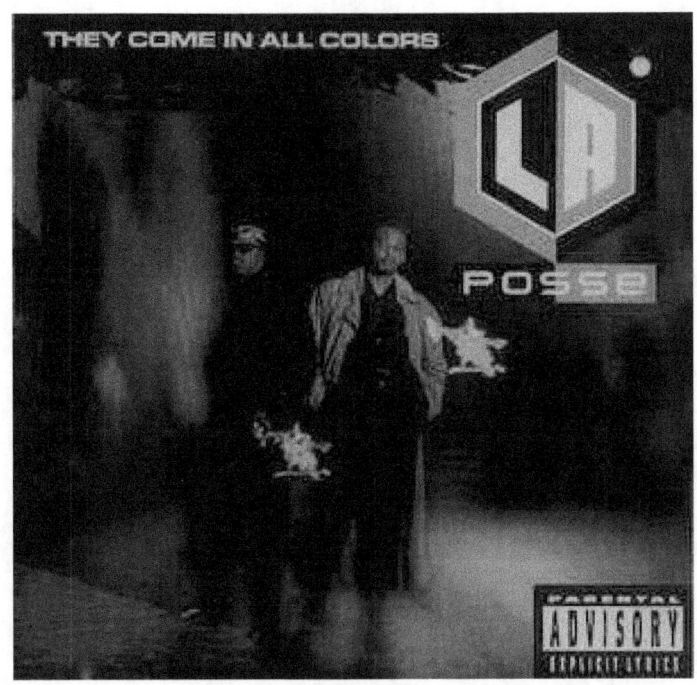

1980's Production Credits

Whodini

The Real Roxanne

Breeze

King T

LL Cool J

Thank you for reading "Hip-Hop History: Book 1 of 3" by PRINTHOUSE BOOKS; Author; Antwan 'Ant' Bank$. Please leave a review; we would love to know what you think.

Contact:

Banks4020@gmail.com

IG: Antwan_Ant_Banks

www.AntwanBanks.com

www.PrintHouseBooks.com

More titles are available from this Author.

MADE is Book 1 of an Epic, Crime Thriller; Trilogy. It's about Andy Cooper; a military vet, turned hustler, turned Gangster, turned Crime Boss. His marriage is on the rocks; fresh out of the military, AC finds himself broke and lost with a Wife and three kids to feed. Trapped in Sin City and working any job he can get from day to day, to make ends meet. Hating the state of mind he's in right now, a really f****d up way to be! Gone are the days when Uncle Sam paid for housing, day care and groceries. Now, all own his own again, with no idea of where life is going to take him. One thing for sure, Andy "AC" Cooper no longer wanted to wear that Army uniform another day. Coop loved every minute of it and would not trade it for the world but the next chapter of his life was about to start. It just so happen that he landed in Las Vegas, one of the hardest cities to make it in, it is truly the land of the Hustler. What the outsiders don't know is that beneath the bright neon lights, the delicious buffets and luxurious casino's, lays a whole different world that would eventually suck him in.

Inspired by True Events...

In book two of the Epic MADE Trilogy; AC, Manny and Duck come face to face with Sabrina's kidnappers. Nina, Denna, Loon and Big Will have bigger shoes to fill in their new roles, while Chief Espinoza suspicions escalates as Sin City crime rise's along with Hector's body count. Monica's back and has plans on picking up from where she left off. Cash flow is at an all-time high with Coop at the helms as Crime continues to pay big for the new Sin City Boss. The recipe of Sex, Drugs and Murder prove to be the perfect mix, as one family falls and the next Boss is donned; King of the Devils playground.

Three years ago, I lost my wife and family to this messed up economy. After that nothing was there to hold me back, with no more support from Uncle Sam; I decided to pave my own way. Never one to break the law, I traveled down the straight and narrow but to no avail, thanks to this B*** a** Cop; name Espinoza. So again I found myself in a corner. But as I gathered my thoughts and tried to come up with a plan; it was by fate that I met who would later become the love of my life. Sabrina in her own fortuitous way introduced me to the life I have today. Still no wife nor kids in the picture, even though they constantly held a place next to my soon to be cold heart. I witnessed my life change in a split second. Now that I think back on it; mine did that very day I dropped Pharoah's punk ass in that back parking lot. I should have known things would never be the same after that day. I still get a thrill when I think about the look he had in his eyes when I took his life away and the smile that remained on Sabrina's all that day. As I sit here smoking on this Cohiba, in this Mansion, with all this power, all this money and all the blood on my hands from those fools that stood in my way.

My heart still beats fast at the sight of the cars, money, houses, women and the sound of hot bullets piercing warm flesh. See I live for this shit because there's nothing else out there for me; but this. Don't blame my mother, don't blame my pops. Blame Uncle Sam for placing that M16 in my hands and brain washing me to kill without feeling a damn thing. Blame this messed up economy; that has so many people struggling. Yeah I made a choice and I am happy with it. Because of that; me and my crew will protect what's ours until the day we die. See we don't plan on going to no prison, jail or nothing like that. Yes we plan to go out with a fight, last man standing! Death before Dishonor; that's how we roll! Gangsters make the world go round and Sin City is its axes. It's time for me to stop talking now; you have a story to read; see you on the inside. MADE III; Death before Dishonor; Beware Thine Enemies Deceit. The Final Chapter.....

-Andy 'AC' Cooper; Don of Sin City. -777

Dear Reader, The word Adoration can be defined as fervent and devoted love or simply put; to worship. During our time on Earth we will all experience this powerful thing called Love. This novel will take you on a journey seen through the eyes of four couples and their relationships. For Love we endure amazing things and some of us will go to the limit to keep it. Love can fill your heart with joy or leave it filled with hate. Adoration explores love at several levels; some of them good; some bad. In Book One of this Series; hearts will break, tears will fall, blood will shed and bells will chime; all in the name of love.

Every School, City and County Library should have F.I.T.H (Fear Influences Thine Heart) on their shelves. It is a must read for any Parent, Teacher or Kid. F.I.T.H. is a Social Drama about a High School Freshman and a Bully. The situation becomes very intense when the bully does not let up. Although the victim tries his best to have tolerance and handle him accordingly, no matter what he tries, nothing seems to work. After several run ins and close calls, the victim is forced to become the Bully's favorite mark, influenced by an ever presence of fear, his life as he knew it; changed.

This book contains 179 Cocktail Recipe's; that Antwan'ANT' Bank$ had the pleasure of serving and creating during his days as a Bartender in Las Vegas during the late 90's. It's the perfect book for the at home bartender, constant party goer, novice bartender, party planner or for anyone that likes to experiment new spirits. The party life also has a dictionary, glossary and technique section for those of you that wish to gain more knowledge on the trade.

Gate Key: Turning your High School Education Into Millions attacks the glue that holds the very fabric of the higher learning institutions together. It gives hope to teens that find themselves in despair. It creates opportunity for those in lower class society who seem to be destined for a life of poverty and unemployment. It turns that one-way street to becoming a criminal into an 8-lane highway of self-preservation. Gate Key will not only spark the flame to ignite the inner fire that we call a dream. It reveals over 30 lucrative professions that can be started while in high school or immediately after which will place our youth on a road to success without the need for a college education. The awful truth is that only 4 out of every 7 teenagers will go on to attend college after graduating high school and for many reasons some will not complete this journey.

Everyone wants the American dream for their kids; they want them to get a degree, find a great job, get married and have children, buy a house with a white picket fence then live happily ever after. Here's a shocker! The American dream will be just that for many of our youth, a dream! Too often teens can't afford college, have no interest in going, did not prepare for it, have kids early or are undecided any one of which causes them not to attend college and to head straight into the sub-par job market. Minimum wage can barely pay utility bills let alone take care of a family; this, more times than not, places our kids in the lowest class of society (in reference to a three-tier society of Lower Class, Middle Class or the Upper Class). This book gives our youth a choice as to what class they want to end up in, how much income they want to earn and how to begin that journey while still in high school without getting any student loans or attending any college. It will put our youth on track to become prosperous entrepreneurs and professionals by making them aware of career choices that they probably didn't even know existed for them as teens. Gate Key doesn't only make our youth aware of these opportunities, but will show when, where and how to start one of these featured career paths while still a teen.

This book is designed to open doors for those that cannot or will not be attending college after high school for some reason or another. Even now you have the power in you to be whoever you want to be! My purpose is to open your eyes to some of the many options that the world has to offer. After all, it was said best by our forefathers in The Declaration of Independence: "We hold these truths to be self-evident, that all men are created equal, that they are endowed by their Creator with certain unalienable Rights, that among these are Life, Liberty and the pursuit of Happiness".

Growing up as an African-American, Hispanic or even a poor Caucasian in America is a challenge. The system is built to keep you in the lower class and it has its reasons. Billions of tax dollars are shelled out every year on food stamps, welfare, housing and many other Government assistant programs. Even if the beneficiaries of the above wanted to become productive citizens in their own neighborhoods and make it on their own, they would be hard pressed. The local education system as well as the local economy just simply can-not or will not support its people, so other measures need to be put in place! Some will find the fortitude to get into college and or leave their destitute neighborhoods to become productive citizens, employee's, business owners, etc. But that dream is few and in between. This environment almost always leads to the same impoverished cycle or for many, a life of crime. With no role models, local businesses or community programs around or Father figures in many of the homes; the streets usually find a way to take over. These circumstances are more common than we would like to admit. Many people will turn to the drug trade; some will become thieves, prostitutes, pimps, killers and drug attics.

The harsh reality of your family starving with-out lights or water will make any sane person do what they need to in order to survive. Compounded with the stress of everyday poverty-stricken life, hardcore criminals will emerge with a burning desire to succeed. Whether they take the legitimate route or illegal is the question. In the culmination of it all, I can assure you that no matter what the decision; someone will be profiting from these inequalities and in that majority will be the private prisons of America. A collective of legal Corporations who soul survival is to put warm bodies in cold cells to meet a Government contracted quota. Because of this need, Government has no incentive to help these low-income communities but to watch them falter instead; it's actually cheaper for them to pay Private Prisons than to invest in these communities. Giving way to an abundant prison population that serves as the modern-day slave trade.

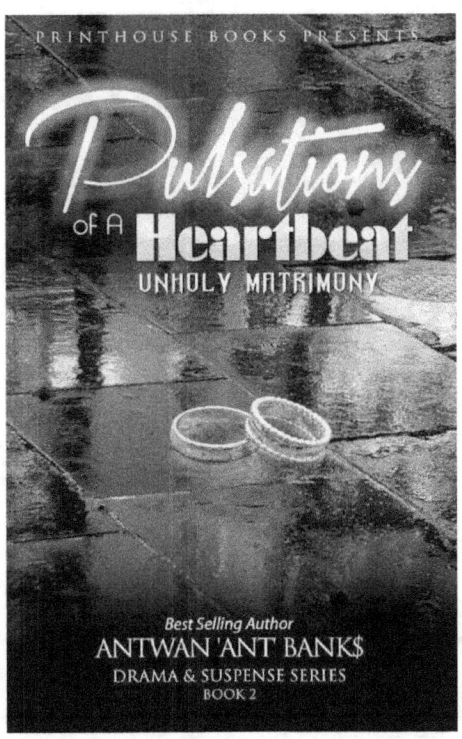

The one problem with love is that it has no boundaries. Once we as humans decide to go for it all and put our hearts on the line for L-O-V-E, we really are taking one of the biggest chances ever in life. Deep down inside we all know that there's always a chance that this journey we choose to share with another soul could all go south! In fact that's the very thing that hinders some of us from finding love even now. We're just damn scared of it all going wrong! I can't even tell you how many relationships I've gone into half-ass just because of that fear. This new series Pulsations of A Heartbeat tells the story from our point of view and by our, I mean the man's. My good friend, Lorenzo and I have both experienced the wrath of good for nothing women in our life times and we've decided to write a series focusing on what happens to us as men when we do. It truly changes us and most of the time it's not for the better and the next women in our lives often suffer because of this hurt.

Millions travel to the City of Angel's every year in search of that one shot at stardom. But most fail and find themselves caught in the underbelly with the homeless, the drug attics, prostitutes, thieves and murders. Candy and Joe unfortunately are no different than most and end up living in a different hotel every other night; doing whatever needs to be done just to survive.

In the City of Atlanta; the Gentlemen's Club Industry reign Supreme. Along-side the fledging music industry that contributes platinum hits every other month, together they both pull in Billions of dollars each year. You would actually have to live here or frequent the ATL to see the marriage these two have committed to each other. The biggest misconception is for someone to assume that it's all illegal. What many don't know, is that the city of Atlanta benefits off of every Stripper, Bouncer, Waitress, Dj and Bartender that works in the Gentlemen Club Industry. The truth of the matter is, for any girl wanting to strip here in the ATL clubs, such as Onyx, Majic, Strokers, Pin Ups, Shooter, Follies, Blue Fame, Blaze, Oasis, Cheetah, Pleasers, Diamonds, Babes to name a few, and trust me there many more! You must first have a permit, from the County that club is in, before you can even think about dancing on any stage in this city. Yep that's right! These permits can only be obtained from the County Sheriff Department where they perform a thorough background check for felonies and any open warrants. If you have a conflicting felony you will not get a permit! If you have a warrant, you will not be leaving through the front door but going to the back in handcuffs instead. Permits range from $250-$475 per year depending on which club you are getting a permit for (That's every-year!). How do I know, you ask! Well, let's just say when I first got to the A, I took a doorman position at one of the most notorious clubs in Atlanta where I met thousands of dancers whom led me to write this story.

The club shall remain anonymous because they fired my butt for hustling too hard; Hell I was just trying to show them how to get paper. After all, I did just close a club back in South Khak that I ran for 12 years. Anyway that's another story. Regardless of what you may have seen or heard, the competition in these clubs are fierce and that makes for some slow nights when it come to the cash flow for some girls. So some of them, more times than none; take it to the next level and do what they like to call private parties. For you squares out there, that means escorting, or tricking if you want to keep it street. I found myself in an interesting position while working at this ATL Gentlemen's club. The dancers confided in me and asked me to be their driver to some of these so called private parties. The stories from those nights and from other private discussions we had while riding in my car, was unreal! My true passion and God given talent is a writer, so I had to ask these girls if I could tell some of their stories; while keeping them anonymous of course. I was happy as a kid in a candy store when they agreed. So here it is; several accounts of the ATL night life through the eyes of many dancers that I rolled into one character, whom I named Tahiry. Laced with Cocaine, Molly, Weed, Lean and Z-Bars, this life is in no way, full of glitz and glamour, true crime rides along at every turn, from the streets of ATL this is our story, cold hearted and street official. R.I.P to the dancers we lost to the strip hustle. We got love for you.

I consider myself lucky to be born on the 29th of December in the year of 1970. On the other side of my Mother's womb awaited Afro's, bell bottoms, black power and soul music. However amidst the black love lay a dark cloud mixed with despair, poverty, racism, violent protest and civil unjust. Soul music was the one constant that seem to make it all go away if only for a few minutes. I can remember my parents spinning the 12 inch vinyl's and 45's of Stevie Wonder, The Temptations, Teddy Pendergrass, Lou Rawls, James Brown and so many more in our living room. There was a dark blue couch that looked like it was made of fur with two white leather straps across the arms. Crystal vases held fresh Crown and black musk incents filled the air. Often my Aunts, Uncles and their friends would gather at our place on the weekends to dance, play spades, drink and party. That feeling of family, joy and togetherness still warms my heart every time I hear one of the soul classics from back then.

It wasn't until I started elementary school that I realized how messed up the world really was. I wasn't in my little box anymore, protected by my parents, the music and family love. Racism was evident and still strong in the public schools back during the early 70's. I fought in school every day because of racial remarks toward me from white kids and sometimes even my own kind. As African American's we were so confused in school that we even hated ourselves. All we had really was the lyrics of Marvin Gaye, Diana Ross, Stevie Wonder, Michael and the like. Soul music thrived on making people feel good; it took our minds away from the negativity of the world. But it always knew when it had to focus on the bad just as well. As the decade moved along, the bad economy, racism, dirty politics and poverty had begun to take its toll and the soul music couldn't mask our feelings anymore.

A new generation had found a way to speak out through music but this time it would change the world and destroy anything or anyone in its path. Its content would be raw, bold and transcending. One might compare the wrath of Hip-Hop to a tsunami because nothing was going to stop this freight train. Fueled by desperation, police corruption, poverty, self-expression, crime, violence and soul, this new genre of music would stand on the shoulders of giants while trailblazing its way to unthinkable heights. This is the history of Hip-Hop; circa 1970-2010 in a two-book series; it is through this time travel that you will see how it became a multi-billion-dollar corporation and innovative industry. It is said to actually see something for what it is, you need to step away from it and look at it from a distance to see all the moving parts.

PrintHouseBooks.com

Read It! Enjoy It! Tell A Friend!

Atlanta, Georgia

For interviews, seminars or speaking engagements please use contact below:

Banks4020@gmail.com

www.AntwanBanks.com

IG: Antwan_Ant_Banks

www.ingramcontent.com/pod-product-compliance
Lightning Source LLC
Chambersburg PA
CBHW080932300426
44115CB00017B/2791